GOOGLE MAPS
HACKS™

Other resources from O'Reilly

Related titles

Mapping Hacks™	Google Advertising Tools
Web Mapping Illustrated	Google: The Missing Manual
Ambient Findability	Google Pocket Guide
Google Hacks™	Greasemonkey Hacks™

Hacks Series Home

hacks.oreilly.com is a community site for developers and power users of all stripes. Readers learn from each other as they share their favorite tips and tools for Mac OS X, Linux, Google, Windows XP, and more.

oreilly.com

oreilly.com is more than a complete catalog of O'Reilly books. You'll also find links to news, events, articles, weblogs, sample chapters, and code examples.

oreillynet.com is the essential portal for developers interested in open and emerging technologies, including new platforms, programming languages, and operating systems.

Conferences

O'Reilly brings diverse innovators together to nurture the ideas that spark revolutionary industries. We specialize in documenting the latest tools and systems, translating the innovator's knowledge into useful skills for those in the trenches. Visit conferences.oreilly.com for our upcoming events.

Safari Bookshelf (safari.oreilly.com) is the premier online reference library for programmers and IT professionals. Conduct searches across more than 1,000 books. Subscribers can zero in on answers to time-critical questions in a matter of seconds. Read the books on your Bookshelf from cover to cover or simply flip to the page you need. Try it today with a free trial.

GOOGLE MAPS HACKS™

Rich Gibson and Schuyler Erle

O'REILLY®

Beijing · Cambridge · Farnham · Köln · Paris · Sebastopol · Taipei · Tokyo

Google Maps Hacks™

by Rich Gibson and Schuyler Erle

Copyright © 2006 O'Reilly Media, Inc. All rights reserved.
Printed in the United States of America.

Published by O'Reilly Media, Inc., 1005 Gravenstein Highway North, Sebastopol, CA 95472.

O'Reilly books may be purchased for educational, business, or sales promotional use. Online editions are also available for most titles (*safari.oreilly.com*). For more information, contact our corporate/institutional sales department: (800) 998-9938 or *corporate@oreilly.com*.

Editor: Simon St.Laurent
Production Editor: Jamie Peppard
Copyeditor: Derek Di Matteo
Indexer: Nancy Crumpton

Cover Designer: Marcia Friedman
Interior Designer: David Futato
Cover Illustrator: Karen Montgomery
Illustrators: Robert Romano, Jessamyn Read, and Lesley Borash

Printing History:

January 2006: First Edition.

 This book uses RepKover,™ a durable and flexible lay-flat binding.

ISBN: 0-596-10161-9
[M]

For Heather, Molly, Maddy, and
Spencer, for everything.

—Rich

For Jo, who knows.

—Schuyler

Contents

Foreword

When we first entered the exciting world of geography, we brought with us an idea that there could be more to online maps than, well, maps. We hoped to build a Web site not limited to providing maps and driving directions, but one that could serve as a platform for all manners of location-based information and services. Or to put it in Google terms: a starting point for organizing the world's information geographically.

For this and other reasons we were thrilled to see "hackers" have a go at Google Maps almost immediately after we launched the site back in early February. Literally within days, their blogs described the inner workings of our maps more accurately than our own design documents did, and soon the most amazing "hacks" started to appear: Philip Lindsay's Google Maps "standalone" mode, Paul Rademacher's Housing Maps, and Chris Smoak's Busmonster, to mention a few.

It was an exciting day for our small team when we learned that premier publishing house O'Reilly was considering writing an entire book about Google Maps Hacks, and we were pleased to be able to announce our official maps API program at O'Reilly's Where 2.0 conference in June. It is both humbling and flattering to witness the astounding creativity surrounding our maps as chronicled in this wonderful book—already a few short months after Where 2.0, thousands of programmers from around the world feature Google Maps in their increasingly impressive and successful creations.

Mapping and geography is a wonderful field, and clearly the Web has made it possible to explore and advance the millennia-old field in new and exciting ways. There's so much more to do, and this marvelous book will serve as a great resource for mapping enthusiasts. We hope you will enjoy it as much as we did!

—Jens Rasmussen and Lars Rasmussen
Google Maps team

Credits

About the Authors

Rich Gibson believes that the world is made of stories, and has unlimited curiosity in the world. He indulges his brilliant, semi-manic children in super-long storytimes, weird science projects, and adventures of many varieties. It is only the steady support of his loving wife that permits him to organize his eccentricity into occasional coherent bursts of creative productivity. Life is very, very good.

Schuyler Erle is a linguist by training and a Free Software developer by vocation. He got into GIS and digital cartography with Rich several years ago, while trying to analyze the best lines-of-sight for a rural wireless community network. He actually believes that maps and GIS, properly applied, can tell compelling stories, and help improve people's lives. As of this writing, he lives with his wife near 42.375 N, 71.106 W.

Contributors

The following people contributed their writing, code, and inspiration to *Google Maps Hacks*:

- Tom Carden (*tom@tom-carden.co.uk*) writes passenger flow simulations for YRM Architects, London, and is studying for an EngD in Virtual Environments Imaging and Visualization at University College London's Bartlett School of Graduate Studies. He also gives occasional lectures for the Bartlett's MSc Adaptive Architecture and Computation. Online, he is a contributor to the OpenStreetMap project (openstreetmap.org), an active member of the community formed around the Processing development environment (processing.org) and posts sporadically to his weblog, Random Etc (*www.tom-carden.co.uk/weblog*). Offline, he can often be found at

Islington's Tinderbox coffee shop, staring thoughtfully into a latte and contemplating a world empowered by massively distributed collaborative mapping software.

- Reverend Daniel Catt resides in Stoke-on-Trent, U.K. (53.013, -2.1756) with his wife, Charlie Catt, and daughter, Modesty B Catt. A long-time keen walker, he first became involved with mapping in 1998, producing 3D views of national parks from map scans and Ordnance Survey data. His interest was foiled for a long time by the lack of open and free mapping data in the U.K. and not living in London. In 2005, pre–Google Maps API, when Google Maps hacking was really scary, this interest was rekindled in the form of *www.geobloggers.com* an ongoing project to consume, aggregate, visualize and push geoRSS-formatted data. He has a B.A. from Staffordshire University and publishes his thoughts at *http://geobloggers.blogspot.com* and *http://360.yahoo.com/revdancatt*. He can be contacted at *revdancatt@yahoo.com* or Yahoo! Instant Messenger at *revdancatt@yahoo.com*.

- Drew Celley is a giant fire-breathing monster, standing 300 feet tall. He can sometimes be found toppling buildings and knocking over elevated railways, but spends most of his time as a UNIX Systems Administrator in Pittsburgh, Pennsylvania. When he isn't rampaging through the city, Drew likes to tinker with technology and help forge snippets of The Future into existence by writing hacks, software, and letters to certain political officials. He is the cocreator of WiFiMaps.com and has a slew of other experiments and projects he's been working on, which you can read more about at *http://www.zhrodague.net/~drew*. In his spare time, he can be found gardening, brewing, printing, or searching for his next contract.

- Steve Coast (*steve@asklater.com*) started and runs Openstreetmap.org from London (the one in Europe), a project to collaboratively generate free geodata. He consults with two friends through Somethingmodern.com, doing a wide range of heavy-lifting computer work.

- Jared Cosulich created the CommunityWalk site *http://communitywalk.com* to let you share your community with the world, after work and on weekends while sitting in his apartment at 37.802565, -122.416051, watching the tourists wander by on their way to the curvy part of Lombard Street.

- Andru Edwards is a geek entrepreneur whose duties include acting as CEO of Gear Live Media, a technology blog network, and being the primary organizer and planner of the Seattle Mind Camp overnight geek confab event. Andru's goal is to use technology and new media to create community both online and off.

- Chris Goad is a computer scientist by training (PhD Stanford, 1980). He worked as a research associate at Stanford from 1980 to 1983 and cofounded two companies: Silma in 1983 and Map Bureau in 1993. His areas of work have included applications of mathematical logic to computation, computer vision, simulation software for 3D mechanical systems, programming language design, and the semantic web. During the last four years, he has concentrated on applications of semantic web technology to cartography, and on the design and implementation of Fabl, a programming language that represents programs as semantic web objects. Chris lives in Astoria, Oregon and works at Map Bureau. See *http://fabl.net/chrisgoad*.

- Michal Guerquin and Zach Frazier calculated the size of the Google Maps cache of the map of the world. Michal's web site is *http://michal.guerquin.com*.

- John T. Guthrie experiments with code and mathematical counterexamples at *http://counterexample.org*.

- Chris Heathcote is an interaction designer, with a focus on mobile and wireless experiences. He lives in Helsinki, Finland and works on Nokia's Insight and Innovation team. He writes about buildings and food at *http://anti-mega.com*, and can be emailed at *c@deaddodo.com*.

- Adrian Holovaty is a web developer/journalist in Chicago. He spends evenings hacking on open source code and side projects that make information accessible to the public. His Chicagocrime.org was one of the original Google Maps hacks. He's also lead developer of Django, an open source Python web framework (Djangoproject.com). By day, Adrian works as editor of editorial innovations for Washingtonpost.com.

- Anselm Hook is a reformed games developer and social cartographer. He's currently leading the *http://platial.com* engineering team.

- Will James is a designer and photographer living in New York City. He created the NYC subway map hack as a cheap stunt to promote his pet project *http://onNYTurf.com*. It's working.

- Richard Kagerer is a small business owner in Ottawa, Ontario. His company, Leapbeyond Solutions, provides Outlook-based software and cutting-edge consulting services to small and mid-size companies. In his spare time, he likes to water ski and stargaze.

- Tom Limoncelli has over 15 years of system administration experience and has been teaching workshops on time management at conferences since 2003. Tom has authored *Time Management for System Administrators* (O'Reilly) and *The Practice of System and Network Administration* (Addison Wesley). Outside of work, Tom has won awards for his activism in gay/bi/lesbian rights and now helps progressive causes use technology to further their goals.

- Robert Lipe, tired of being lost most of the time, bought his first GPS in 2001. Though it was originally justified for his business travels as a software engineer, geocaching quickly consumed it—and him. Frustrated with the available tools to talk to the GPS and the difficulty of moving data between programs, he wrote GPSBabel and made it available to the public at *http://www.gpsbabel.org*. GPSBabel is now used behind the curtains in programs such as Google Earth and GSAK, the Geocaching Swiss Army Knife. He also wrote and maintains a collection of technical GPS articles on the web at *http://www.mtgc.org/robertlipe*. Robert and his family live outside Nashville, Tennessee. He continues to develop software for GPS-related technologies for fun and for hire.

- Tom Longson is a web developer with an interest in cartography and wearable computing, which he often writes about on igargoyle (*http://igargoyle.com*). He gained an interest in software engineering from his father, who was a pioneer in digital arts and used programming to produce unique 3D constructions and CGI. Tom ultimately wants to develop software that will change the way people think and interact with each other, for better or worse, and mucking with maps seems like one of those things that will do so.

- Mikel Maron is an independent software developer and ecologist. He has built several geographic-oriented projects around the worldKit mapping package, including World as a Blog. Previously, he led development of My Yahoo! in the pre-RSS days. Mikel was awarded a Masters degree from the University of Sussex for building a simulation of the evolution of complexity in food webs. Originally from California, Mikel is presently based mostly in Brighton, U.K., where he lives with his wife Anna. Links to various things can be found at *http://brainoff.com*.

- Tom Mangan is a newspaper copy editor and page designer who blogs at *http://tommangan.net*. He is an avid hiker and photographer. He also maintains the "Banned for Life" of expressions "so hackneyed and insufferable that they should be forever banned from the nation's news reports."

- Ron Parker is a software engineer from Fort Wayne, Indiana who spends his days writing software for the blind and visually impaired and his evenings hacking on GPSBabel and other free software. He has two dogs, three cats, and four computers.

- Anthony Petito created the *http://www.stormreportmap.com* site to support his interest in weather. He is available for Google Maps consulting.

- Dave Schorr is a weather fan who runs *http://www.weatherbonk.com*.

- Chris Smoak runs the *http://busmonster.com* site that tracks buses on Google Maps.
- Edwin Soto is an entertainment columnist with *http://www.gearlive.com*.
- Mark Torrance is Chief Executive Officer and Principal Consultant at Vinq. He founded Vinq in 2003 to offer services including design, implementation, and support of sophisticated database-backed web applications. In this role, Torrance has grown an effective team of consultants and managers, grown the business in excess of 100% each year, and won new project work for the firm. Torrance was also the lead designer and implementor of KnowledgePlex 2.0, the first version of this web platform developed for Fannie Mae Foundation. KnowledgePlex serves as both a content management framework for its own affordable housing content and as a platform for cobranding and reuse on partner sites. Mark brings consulting expertise in the areas of open source software, rapid application development, design for usability, graphic design and aesthetics of web design, and taxonomy/ontology development.
- Hans van der Maarel is a self-employed GIS/cartographic engineer from The Netherlands. Maps have been a great passion of his since a young age, and he's very glad he got the opportunity to do cool things with them because he considers it a great field of work that he enjoys every day. Apart from maps, he likes travelling and listening to rock music.

Preface

A few years ago, using maps on the Web was hard. The maps were ugly, slow to load, and burdened with a clunky user interface—and if you think using maps on the Web was hard, imagine trying to *make* useful and interesting maps on the Web! Today, however, all that has changed. A good measure of the credit for this quantum leap in digital cartography on the Internet is due to Google and their Google Maps service. How did this come about?

Putting the World in the World Wide Web

It has been said that "the network is the computer," and, for most of us, the "network" means the World Wide Web. From its humble origins as a repository of hypertext documents, the Web has become a sort of distributed operating system, one that allows clever programmers (and more than a few random dilettantes) from far-flung places to build new applications by mixing and matching data and services in ways that the original designers of those services never considered.

In recent years, "traditional" commercial web sites, such as Amazon, eBay, and Google, have increasingly become platforms that support complex user ecosystems. Using openly published APIs, you can look up an item on Amazon, get a price history from eBay, and find reviews on Google—all at once, and all without Amazon, eBay, or Google ever talking with each other.

Until now, a crucial component has been lacking—location. What's important about location, you may ask? Well, for starters, it's everywhere! Everything has a location, and until now there were few reasonable options for mixing in location. There were expensive and complicated proprietary systems, as well as free and powerful—but still complicated—open source options, but they all required you to be part of the cartographer's elite. You had to pay with time, attention, aggravation, and even money! But today, Google Maps has opened mapping to everyone. Ah! Location!

Open APIs + Open Data Formats = Web 2.0 Heaven

Let's take Paul Rademacher's HousingMaps site at *http://housingmaps.com/* as one example. HousingMaps takes housing rental and for-sale listings from Craigslist and plots them on a Google Map, making it easier to find housing in the area that you're interested in. HousingMaps demonstrates what can happen when you give developers a toolset—and, mind you, developers don't even need a clean, well-documented toolset. The site was originally developed by hacking on Google's (initially) somewhat-obfuscated maps interface. The key is that neither Craigslist nor Google were involved in this endeavor, and that the result was something greater than the parts. In music this is called a *mashup*, and the term has crossed over and is now used in the world of Web 2.0.

Nowhere has this trend been more necessary than digital cartography, of course, for all the aforementioned reasons. Three things set Google Maps apart from what came before: a clean and responsive user interface; fast-loading, pre-generated map images; and a client-side API that makes it possible to put a Google Map on any web page. Of these three things, it might not be exaggerating to say that the openly published API behind Google Maps is far and away the most revolutionary of them all.

Who Will Aggregate the Aggregators?

A new approach to building web applications using *Asynchronous JavaScript + XML* (AJAX) has made this much easier. The AJAX approach employed by Google Maps and many other sites means that the web page is running code that dynamically fetches data as needed from a server, and that this data is usually in XML. "Yeah? So what?" you might say. Well, the "so what" is that these data sources are probably open and available for you to scrape. Sometimes they are published, and other times they are hidden in a page, but they are there.

A lot of new tech is established when developers have something that they can hack on. The Web has shown that the definition of *developer* is pretty wide! The original Web took off in large part because of the menu item View Source. Suddenly the barrier to entry was nearly microscopic. It was a shock when my own mother asked me for advice on web-authoring software, but that is what happens when you give people access to the tools that they can use to tell compelling stories. Google Maps, AJAX-based apps, and Web 2.0 remixing in general are similarly benefiting from the "View Source" mentality: others can look at your page, learn from your code, figure out where your data lives, and then remix it to make something greater.

The consequence is that Paul Rademacher can scrape data published in an open format by Craigslist and then put it on a map using an API openly published by Google. But what's to keep you from scraping Paul's site and a dozen others and putting that data on a map? To paraphrase Juvenal, who can live in our modern age and not write aggregators?

Not Just Where 2.0, But Also Why 2.0

Some people say "why should we give all our hard work to our competitors?" And you know, I'm not sure I have an answer for them. But I've noticed that most of the people and companies that ask that question are, well, boring or lame, while the coolest people and companies—and you probably know who I'm talking about—tend to be those that don't ask that question. Though sometimes good people and good ideas are stuck in environments where secrecy is key, more often it's as Rob Flickenger once said about the then-new copy-protected CD from Celine Dion that would not play on a computer: "Good! They are most of the way there. Now if they can only make a CD of Celine Dion that can't play in any CD player...."

Let's look a little bit deeper into this, though: maybe what makes the "open" camp seem interesting is that openness creates a space for interaction, and many interactions allow complex ecologies to form. Just as one example, we should point out that, thanks to Google's approach of offering open access to their mapping service, there is already at least one software development outfit on the Web that advertises Google Maps integration as its primary offering.

So why share your code? Why share your data? Ultimately, if there's one lesson that's emerging from the wild world of Web 2.0, it's that sharing and openness make the world a richer and more interesting place to live. Doing so might not make you as much money—but it might make you more—and the world will be more fun if you share. Our friend Marc Powell says that companies are a lot like kindergartners, and sometimes you just have to smile and say "That is nice, Billy, and would you like to share the crayons now?"

Why Google Maps Hacks?

The term *hacking* has a bad reputation in the press, where it is used to refer to someone who breaks into systems or wreaks havoc with computers as their weapon. Among people who write code, though, the term *hack* refers to a "quick-and-dirty" solution to a problem, or a clever way to get something done. And the term *hacker* is taken very much as a compliment, referring to someone as being *creative*, having the technical chops to get things done. The Hacks series is an attempt to reclaim the word, document the good ways people are hacking, and pass the hacker ethic of creative participation on to the uninitiated. Seeing how others approach systems and problems is often the quickest way to learn about a new technology.

Maps are a strange combination of the extremely simple and the extremely complex. Most people are familiar with paper maps, but are only starting to explore the possibilities of electronic maps. With the advent of Google Maps, incredible opportunities have opened up that go well beyond the usual expectations of paper maps. *Google Maps Hacks* will show you these opportunities and how to take advantage of them.

How to Use This Book

You can read this book from cover to cover if you like, but for the most part, each hack stands on its own, so feel free to browse and jump to the different sections that interest you most. If there's a prerequisite you need to know about, a cross-reference will guide you to the right hack. So, feel free to browse, flipping around to whatever sections interest you most.

How This Book Is Organized

The book is divided into seven chapters, organized by subject:

Chapter 1, *You Are Here: Introducing Google Maps*
> An introduction to *http://maps.google.com*, how to look up locations, get driving directions, look at satellite pictures, share links to maps in emails and on web pages, generate links to maps from a spreadsheet, and use del.icio.us (*http://del.icio.us*) to keep up with developments.

Chapter 2, *Introducing the Google Maps API*
> Google Maps makes it easy to put a map on your own web page. Learn how to put a map on your page, capture user clicks, create a slideshow connected with a map, create custom icons, and measure distances.

Chapter 3, *Mashing Up Google Maps*
> Are you interested in something? Chances are that someone has put some aspect of it on a Google Map. Learn about a variety of mashups, from mapping the news, to seeing where criminals "work," to weather maps, to answering the question: where is the International Space Station right now? You can also examine the blast radius of a nuclear explosion, find a place to live, or see what is roughly the size of Texas.

Chapter 4, *On the Road with Google Maps*
> Maps and travel go together like gruel and chipped teeth. Find the cheapest gas near to you, load driving directions into your GPS to take with you, look at your GPS tracklogs, explore hiking trails, figure out why your cell phone doesn't work at home, and even beat a traffic ticket.

Chapter 5, *Google Maps in Words and Pictures*

Pictures and maps are a natural fit. One of the great things about photos is that they are always taken *somewhere*. Learn how to geocode your photos on Flickr, set up a blog that knows about place, geocode literature, and examine the choices that go into which satellite images are included.

Chapter 6, *API Tips and Tricks*

You now know how to put a map on your own page; in the chapter, learn how to tweak and extend that map. Include a map within your map, overlay photographs and labels where you want them, and create a georeferencer to pin your own scanned or digital maps onto a Google Map.

Chapter 7, *Extreme Google Maps Hacks*

Push the boundaries! Use a clustering algorithm so that your own points fit properly on a map, create your own map tiles, connect to a database, use web standards to display other data (such as Landsat imagery) on your maps, and even figure out if your kids are likely to barf.

Conventions Used in This Book

The following is a list of the typographical conventions used in this book:

Italics

Used to indicate URLs, filenames, filename extensions, and directory/folder names. For example, a path in the filesystem appears as *Developer/Applications*.

Constant width

Used to show code examples, the contents of files, console output, as well as the names of variables, commands, and other code excerpts.

Constant width bold

Used to highlight portions of code, typically new additions to old code.

Constant width italic

Used in code examples and tables to show sample text to be replaced with your own values.

Gray type

Used to indicate a cross-reference within the text.

You should pay special attention to notes set apart from the text with the following icons:

 This is a tip, suggestion, or general note. It contains useful supplementary information about the topic at hand.

This is a warning or note of caution, often indicating that something might break if you're not careful, possibly quite badly.

The thermometer icons, found next to each hack, indicate the relative complexity of the hack:

beginner   moderate   expert

Whenever possible, the hacks in this book are not *platform-specific*, which means you can use them on Linux, Macintosh, and Windows machines. However, some things are possible only on a particular platform.

Using Code Examples

This book is here to help you get your job done. In general, you may use the code in this book in your programs and documentation. You do not need to contact us for permission unless you're reproducing a significant portion of the code. For example, writing a program that uses several chunks of code from this book does not require permission. Selling or distributing a CD-ROM of examples from O'Reilly books *does* require permission. Answering a question by citing this book and quoting example code does not require permission. Incorporating a significant amount of example code from this book into your product's documentation *does* require permission.

We appreciate, but do not require, attribution. An attribution usually includes the title, author, publisher, and ISBN. For example: "*Google Maps Hacks* by Rich Gibson and Schuyler Erle. Copyright © 2006 O'Reilly Media, Inc., 0-596-10161-9."

If you feel your use of code examples falls outside fair use or the permission given above, feel free to contact us at *permissions@oreilly.com*.

How to Contact Us

We have tested and verified the information in this book to the best of our ability, but you may find that features have changed (or even that we have made mistakes!). As a reader of this book, you can help us to improve future editions by sending us your feedback. Please let us know about any errors, inaccuracies, bugs, misleading or confusing statements, and typos that you find anywhere in this book.

Please also let us know what we can do to make this book more useful to you. We take your comments seriously and will try to incorporate reasonable suggestions into future editions. You can write to us at:

O'Reilly Media, Inc.
1005 Gravenstein Highway North
Sebastopol, CA 95472
(800) 998-9938 (in the U.S. or Canada)
(707) 829-0515 (international/local)
(707) 829-0104 (fax)

To ask technical questions or to comment on the book, send email to:

bookquestions@oreilly.com

The web site for *Google Maps Hacks* lists examples, errata, and plans for future editions. You can find this page at:

http://www.oreilly.com/catalog/googlemapshks/

The authors maintain the Mapping Hacks web site, which is related to the latest in digital cartography on the Web. On their site, you can find more information about the topics explored in this book. The Mapping Hacks site can be found at:

http://www.mappinghacks.com/

For more information about this book and others, see the O'Reilly web site:

http://www.oreilly.com

Got a Hack?

To explore Hacks books online or to contribute a hack for future titles, visit:

http://hacks.oreilly.com

Safari Enabled

When you see a Safari® Enabled icon on the cover of your favorite technology book, that means the book is available online through the O'Reilly Network Safari Bookshelf.

Safari offers a solution that's better than e-Books. It's a virtual library that lets you easily search thousands of top tech books, cut and paste code samples, download chapters, and find quick answers when you need the most accurate, current information. Try it for free at *http://safari.oreilly.com*.

## CHAPTER ONE

You Are Here:
Introducing Google Maps
Hacks 1–9

In February of 2005, Google quietly announced the debut of a new service, Google Maps, that changed the face of mapping and cartography on the Web for an overwhelming number of people. Gone were the tiny, slow-loading, and sometimes ugly digital maps that people were pretty much accustomed to using on the Web, maps that fell below the "fold" of a web page, and were often impossible to navigate. Instead, using the latest in web browser scripting technology, Google Maps offers a fast-loading, tiled map display, a simple yet deep user interface, asynchronous display updates in place of the tiresome click-and-reload routine, and, ultimately, even a rich scripting API. Although many of these features had been seen before in one place or another, no one had seen them all integrated with the attention to detail that we've come to expect from Google. Let's take our first look at how Google Maps changed how people use maps on the Web forever.

HACK #1 Get Around http://maps.google.com
Sometimes you need a map to the map.

Google applied its trademark, carefully designed simplicity, to provide us with its (first) view of place. Go to *http://maps.google.com/*, and you'll get the view shown in Figure 1-1. If you want maps of the United Kingdom, try *http://maps.google.co.uk/*, and you'll get the view in Figure 1-2. A similar map exists for Japan at *http://maps.google.co.jp/*.

This shows us what appears as a standard Google search box (called the Location Search box), an overview or orientation map of the country in question, and a results area with instructions and sample searches.

Figure 1-1. http://maps.google.com/

Figure 1-2. http://maps.google.co.uk/

Please remember that this book was written using beta software, and the Google engineers are continually tinkering with the site in order to provide the most compelling possible system. This means that things will change!

What's Different About Google Maps?

Google Maps is a web mapping service that solves the same old problem of online mapping. So why, ten years or more into the web revolution, is Google Maps such a big deal? Some of the excitement comes from the Google name and its philosophy. Google states on its corporate philosophy page at *http://www.google.com/corporate/tenthings.html* that "you can make money without doing evil." However, more of the interest in Google Maps may stem from other ideas stated on the philosophy page—for example, "The interface is clear and simple" and "Pages load instantly."

Clean pages and fast performance? A commitment to avoid doing evil? Which drives traffic and mind share? Maybe at this moment on the Web you can have it all. In addition to these features, Google Maps also offers a number of innovations in web user interfaces.

Single search box
> The first thing that draws attention is that Google uses a single search box for location searches. Do you want to look up an address? Just type it in the box. No more tabbing between different fields for street address, city, state, and ZIP Code! (In Internet Explorer, you can even paste multi-line addresses into this box, believe it or not.)

Draggable maps
> The standard in web mapping is the usual web interface, in which you click on a button to pan the map and see more terrain. What if you wanted to just click and drag to navigate the map? Well, now you can!

Integrated local search
> You can use that single search box to look for the things you want, such as "hotels near Sebastopol," or, for more choices, "hotels near SFO" (SFO is the code for San Francisco International Airport). If you just want to find all the hotels in a given area, zoom into that area, then search for "hotels," and Google Maps will constrain its search to the area shown on the map.

Satellite imagery
> With a single click you can flip between viewing a map and viewing satellite or aerial photography [Hack #4]. How cool is that?

Keyboard short cuts
> You don't need to click and drag your mouse, or strive to hit the little Zoom In and Zoom Out icons: you can use the arrow keys to move around in your map [Hack #3].

Getting Around

Google Maps starts with the overview map shown in Figure 1-1. You can move around that map by clicking and dragging your mouse on the map, by double-clicking your mouse on the map, or by using the arrow keys. Holding the mouse button down and dragging will cause the whole map to move, as if the web browser is providing a small window onto a much larger map. If you double-click on a spot, the map will smoothly pan until the point you clicked on is centered. Using the arrow keys has the same effect as clicking and dragging with the mouse. We explore the user interface in more detail in "Navigate the World in Your Web Browser" [Hack #3].

Entering a Location

There are many ways to enter locations [Hack #2], but let's start off easy. The conventional way of entering a location is a street address. We've come to accept address lookups in online mapping services as commonplace, but there is a great deal of behind-the-scenes work. In order to display a map of a street address, the system must first find a latitude and longitude that corresponds to this address. The process of linking something (e.g., a street address) with a latitude and longitude is called *geocoding*.

When you enter a query into the search box, Google takes your input and does its best to turn it into a location that can be mapped. So let's start close to home and enter the street address of O'Reilly Media headquarters into the search box:

    1005 Gravenstein Highway North, Sebastopol, CA 95472

You could also enter the company name and get the same result:

    O'Reilly Media, Sebastopol, CA 95472

Click Search and you'll get the map shown in Figure 1-3, which shows the address (as best as Google can determine) and hyperlinks to get directions to or from this spot.

The satellite view in Figure 1-4 (zoomed in from the area shown in Figure 1-3) clearly shows that the O'Reilly Empire is centered in a parking lot median strip....

You can also enter a street intersection; for example:

    Hollywood & Vine St, Hollywood, CA 90068

The act of looking up a location has set your search area, or the *extents* of your search area, and you can now use the search box to get more information. For example, if you first zoom in to San Francisco, you can then search for "great sushi" and return results limited to the San Francisco area.

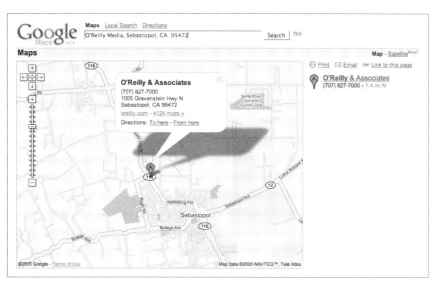

Figure 1-3. A Google map of O'Reilly Media's headquarters

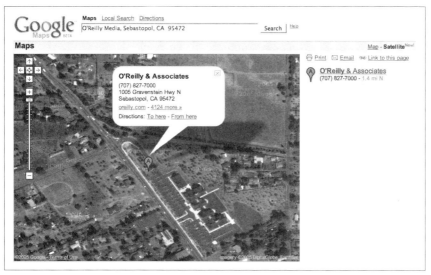

Figure 1-4. O'Reilly Media, apparently located in a median strip of a parking lot

The Google Maps tour suggests that a search on "Great Sushi in New York" is useful. It turns out that "great sushi in San Francisco" also brings up a list of restaurants, but for some reason, "great sushi in Sebastopol" just doesn't work. To be fair, "great sushi in Sebastopol, CA" does bring up our two sushi places. But it also brings up the Larkspur Elementary School District, 37 miles from Sebastopol.

Varying the adjective used—say from "great" to "mediocre"—brings up a new grouping of restaurants. These are not the same places that show up when you do a Google search on "mediocre sushi in San Francisco," so I'm not sure what the qualifications are. "Cheap but filling sushi in San Francisco" might be a more palatable search!

Finding meaningful results for local search is still an unsolved problem. Fortunately, Google is good at search—and getting better all the time.

HACK #2   Find Yourself (and Others) on Google Maps

Google Maps supports many ways to specify location.

Using addresses to find a place makes a lot of sense for places that have an address, but what do you do when you don't have an address? Fortunately for you, the Google Maps team has supplied a number of additional ways to find yourself.

I suspect that the goal is to create a system in which, if you can imagine a somewhat standard way of representing a location, then Google Maps will support it. The functionality is not quite there yet, but it does support a lot of ways of finding places. As with all of the hacks in this book, and as a general philosophy of life, experimentation is your friend!

The number one rule for finding places using Google Maps is that if there is a way of specifying location that makes sense to you, go ahead and try it! As we saw in "Get Around http://maps.google.com" [Hack #1], standard addresses work, but so does entering a city and state, or a ZIP Code alone. Street intersections also work, as long as you add a city and state.

You can also enter coordinates as latitude and longitude, like 38, -122, or 38 N, 122 W. Most modern people don't relate to latitude and longitude directly, but it is a compact and precise way to mark a location.

Google Maps is good at searching by business name. You can search by business name, city, and state—for example, "O'Reilly Media, Sebastopol, CA"—with good results. Entering a business name and a city, or a business name and a state, brings up a list of possible matches.

The best Google Maps feature ever is the proximity search, at least for one of my friends, who is a vegetarian and travels a lot. Before Google Maps, he spent a lot of time on other map services planning for trips. A common query was for the closest Whole Foods Market in whatever city he was visiting. Now he can just type his query into the single search box: "whole foods market near Boston, MA." As long as he remembers to change *Boston, MA* to his current city, he is set. Table 1-1 shows examples of searches that do and don't work.

Table 1-1. The limits of Google Maps' understanding

Example	Works?	Description
1005 Gravenstein Highway N, Sebastopol, CA 95472	Yes	Full street address works great.
79th St and Broadway, NY 79th St and Broadway, 10024	Yes	Intersection and city, or intersection and ZIP Code.
Santa Rosa, CA Santa Rosa, NM	Yes	City and state works.
San Francisco Moscow	Yes	The bare city name works absurdly often. If the same city appears in more than one state it appears to pick the largest. International cities were added recently, but data quality varies.
CA or California	No	State or state abbreviation alone doesn't work.
94305	Yes	ZIP Code works. Postal codes for other supported countries, such as Canada and the U.K. work as well.
LAX SFO	Yes	Airport codes work.
Paddington	Yes	In the UK and Japan, subway stations work as locations.
37, -122	Yes	Latitude and longitude expressed as decimal degrees with - to express West longitude or South latitude.
37 N, 122 W	Yes	The same, but use N and S and E and W.
N 38 24' 08.8" W 122 49' 44.2"	No	Latitude and longitude as degrees-minutes-seconds doesn't seem to work, but perhaps after partaking of the magic syntax elixir….
Range and township	No	Google Maps doesn't seem to do range and township. This would be a great feature for genealogy buffs that get records of their forbears' property transactions.
[location] to [location]	Yes	Any of the above locations that work can be mixed and matched with the word *to* in between them to get driving directions.
[thing] near [location]	Yes	You can use any of the above locations to search for nearby businesses and points of interest.

Odd and Surprising Ways to Find Things

Not everything is documented! Like Google's search, there are a lot of things that just work that are not documented (or at least they are not documented where you are likely to see them). For example, as of April 30th, 2005, I could find no mention that entering a latitude and longitude in the search box would have any effect, and yet it works!

The moral is that when you have a wild idea about a way to search for something, try it first, and then if it doesn't work, enjoy that temporary feeling of satisfaction that comes from being ahead of the curve (well, either ahead of the curve, or plumb crazy, but since there is no reliable way to determine which is which, you might as well enjoy it).

When Locations Fail: The Importance of Context

Unless you specify a location in your search—e.g., "edible food near King's Cross"—Google Maps assumes that the place that you are searching for falls within the area, or *extent*, that is currently shown in the map. As a result, a search that works on the full extent will sometimes fail if you have a local context set. You can reset that context by adding "near [some location]" to your search, or by clicking on the Google Maps logo in the upper left of the page.

Navigate the World in Your Web Browser

There is no doubt about it: Google has significantly raised the bar for user interfaces to maps on the Web. Here's why.

When Google Maps was launched in February 2005, the public response was instant and almost overwhelmingly positive. Although the remarkable speed with which any map appeared, tile by tile, had a great deal to do with people's appreciation of Google Maps, most of the praise and recognition was saved for the browser interface itself. The Google Maps user interface is clean, simple, straightforward, quick loading, and easy to use. In other words, it offers yet another classic Google user experience.

Just a Click Away...

The main thing about the Google Maps user interface that really wows everyone the first time they see it is the *drag panning*. Go to any location in Google Maps, position the mouse pointer anywhere on the map, click and hold your left mouse button, and then move the mouse itself. Lo and behold—the map moves with it, and the page in your browser doesn't even reload! Releasing the mouse button, of course, causes the map to stop panning.

You'll notice that, in the background, your browser has already loaded many of the tiles outside your original view, so that you don't have to wait for them to load as you're panning around—that is, unless you're on a slow Internet connection, or you try to pan very quickly from one edge of the map to the other.

If dragging the map feels a bit wild or difficult to control, the Google Maps interface also allows you to double-click your left mouse button anywhere on the map to recenter it at that location. Double-clicking to recenter gives you a more precise, but somewhat less dynamic way to pan around the map.

The ability to click and drag the map around in the browser window, while not, strictly speaking, new, has never been seen before in a major mapping service on the Web. Gone are the days when browsing a map on the Web involved a tedious wait for the entire web page to reload every time you tried to recenter or zoom the map! Hooray!

You Control the Horizontal and the Vertical

Over on the left side of the map, you should see a number of controls in gray and black, as shown in Figure 1-5. If panning by dragging or double-clicking doesn't suit you, you can use the four arrow buttons to scroll the map north, south, east, and west. The somewhat less obviously labeled button in the center of the other four, which depicts four arrows pointing inwards, returns you to the original view of the last thing you searched for. This button lets you pan around the map, zoom in and out to your heart's content, and then click the return button to go right back to the place you were originally looking at.

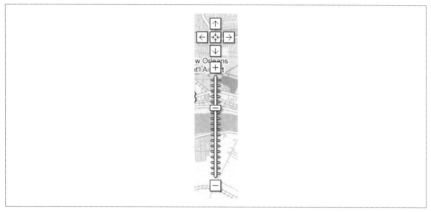

Figure 1-5. The Google Maps navigation controls

Below the pan controls lie the zoom controls. Google Maps features 18 zoom levels, from a view that shows multiple copies of the Earth's surface right down to the individual city block. The button marked with the plus sign (+) zooms in one level, while the button at the bottom marked with the minus sign (–) zooms out. Between them runs a long vertical ruler, marked with a tick for each zoom level, with a "handle" indicating the current zoom. You can click anywhere along this ruler to zoom directly to a given map scale, or click and drag the zoom handle up and down the ruler to zoom in and out dynamically. As you zoom in and out, the scale bar at the bottom left changes accordingly. In the smaller versions of the Google Map interface, the vertical zoom control ruler is omitted, leaving the zoom-in and zoom-out buttons stacked immediately below the pan controls.

Last but not least, in the upper right-hand corner of the map, you'll find the map display controls, as shown in Figure 1-6. As of this writing, Google Maps has three modes: *Map*, *Satellite*, and a new *Hybrid* mode that displays streets and labels semi-transparently over a satellite or aerial image. For New Orleans, there is also a "Katrina" view, which is aerial imagery of New Orleans taken August 31, 2005. The user interface features a button for each mode, with the button for the current mode highlighted in bold. Clicking any one of these three buttons changes modes, allowing you to identify features or intersections in one view, and then immediately switch to another to get more information about what's there.

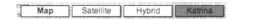

Figure 1-6. The Google Maps modes for New Orleans

You'll notice that clicking on the map itself with the left mouse button doesn't actually do anything in the plain vanilla Google Maps interface. Instead, the left-click is reserved in order to allow you to perform custom actions at any point on the map. We'll see a number of these custom uses for left-clicking on the map later in the book.

Economies of Scale

On the lower left side of the standard Google Maps view, you'll see a scale bar, which indicates distances horizontally across the center of the map in both miles and kilometers, as shown in Figure 1-7. Not only can this be useful for estimating distances "as the crow flies," but it also gives a sense of how the *cartographic projection* used in Google Maps distorts and exaggerates the Earth's surface as you head towards the north and south poles. (This is why Greenland looks bigger than Australia on Google Maps, when in fact it is much smaller.)

2 mi
2 km

Figure 1-7. The Google Maps scale bar

One cute way to see this in action is to pan up to the islands in northern Canada, zoom in a bit, and then click the map and slowly drag it upwards, thereby panning south. As you move the map, you can watch see the scale bar get smaller and smaller, and then flip over to a larger increment, before continuing to shrink.

Not only is this a good example of the dynamic nature of the Google Maps interface, but it also illustrates one of the downsides of using the familiar *Mercator projection*, as Google Maps does. The reason Google Maps uses the Mercator projection instead of one that might provide less visual distortion is that, as with other rectangular projections, it treats all lines of latitude as being perpendicular to all lines of longitude. This property makes doing any kind of calculation to place things on the map so much easier that it outweighs the aesthetic detriments of having distorted northern and southern extremes on the map. Additionally, over smaller areas, the Mercator projection preserves angles across local areas on the map, making it suitable for guiding navigation. (Indeed, this is one major reason the Mercator projection continues to be used after 500 years, in spite of its tendency to distort the areas around the poles.)

Take the Shortcut

But, wait, there's more! With Google's typical thoroughness, the Google Maps user interface makes good use of *keyboard shortcuts* in the web browser as well. Keyboard shortcuts allow you to accomplish the same tasks that most people use their mouse for without ever taking your hands off your keyboard's home row. (And if you're a command-line jockey like me, you gotta love 'em.)

The most immediately useful keyboard shortcuts in Google Maps are, of course, the arrow keys, which allow you to pan the map in much the same way as the aforementioned pan buttons in the upper-left corner of the map, with one difference: if you hold down any arrow key, the map continues to pan—and fairly smoothly at that, if your computer and 'Net connection are fast enough—until you let up on the key. With a little practice, you can scoot around a neighborhood in Google Maps like a pro, without ever touching your mouse.

If you want to pan around faster at one go, you can use the diagonal arrow keys: PgUp and PgDn pan three-quarters of the way across the map north and south respectively, and Home and End quickly pan west and east by the same amount. Finally, the plus (+) and minus (−) keys zoom in and out by one level, respectively. On some Apple keyboards, such as the one supplied with iBooks, Fn-/ generates a plus sign, Fn-; is minus, and Fn-arrow keys provides the PgUp, PgDn, Home, and End functions.

In Mozilla Firefox, you may find that if you just typed something into the search box above the map, your browser's
focus is still be on the text box, which means that key
presses will show up there, rather than going directly to the
map. If this happens, just hit the Tab key (or left-click once
anywhere on the map itself) to move the browser's focus
away from the search box. Then the keyboard shortcuts
should work as advertised.

Taste the Secret Sauce

It is a curious fact that, as of this writing, although all the pan and zoom
controls have associated keyboard shortcuts, there do not seem to be keyboard shortcuts for switching modes. One almost wonders if this isn't an
inadvertent oversight on Google's part. Fortunately, as the patient and
attentive reader will discover, since Google's code is running on your web
browser, you the hacker can fix any such oversights yourself by dipping into
Google's secret sauce.

The secret sauce by which Google offers so much rich functionality with
such a seemingly simple interface is referred to by some people as AJAX,
which (sometimes) stands for "Asynchronous JavaScript And XML." By
using client-side JavaScript to detect user actions and act on them in the
background, Google Maps offers a very pleasingly usable interface to a map
of the world, all without the interminable wait for the entire page to reload
any time something happens. As we'll see later in the book, the deep integration with the browser interface at the JavaScript level is also the source for
much of the extreme hackability of Google Maps!

Get the Bird's-Eye View

Maps are good, but a picture is worth...

Maps show what the mapmaker chooses to show. Google Maps, like most
of the online map services, shows maps that are designed primarily for getting around in a car. In America, we pretend we've (d)evolved into *homo
automobilious*, but despite our best efforts there is more to the world than
scenery and billboards flying past the bug-smeared windshield.

One neat feature of Google Maps is the ability to flip between viewing a map
and viewing satellite imagery. In Figure 1-8 we see a map of the Upper West
Side of Manhattan, with an odd little shape sticking into the Hudson River
on the left side. By clicking on the Satellite link on the upper-right side of the
window, you get satellite and aerial imagery.

Figure 1-8. Upper West Side Manhattan

The aerial view in Figure 1-9 provides a lot more context! You can see the buildings and Riverside Drive. You can even make out individual boats at the 79th Street Boat Basin. You can use the same navigation tricks to pan around in satellite and aerial imagery as you can on the map layer [Hack #3].

Figure 1-9. Aerial view of the Upper West Side and the 79th Street Boat Basin

The satellite imagery's level of detail varies by where you're looking; some places have much more detail than others.

Is It Really There?

You can use the aerial imagery as a sanity check. For example, let's say you are in the North Bay area and are interested in dairy products. You could search for cheese near Petaluma, CA and get a map like Figure 1-10.

Figure 1-10. Looking for cheese in all the wrong places

To visit Rouge et Noir Cheese Factory (*http://www.marinfrenchcheese.com/*), you could click on the link on the right side in the list of results, zoom in a bit, and flip to satellite view to get the view in Figure 1-11.

Where's the cheese? It doesn't look like it is there. Could it be in that circular compound on the right-hand side? Maybe, except I happen to know that this isn't the case. It seems that there's a disconnect between databases at Google. The business listing for Rouge et Noir puts it at 7500 Red Hill Road, Petaluma, CA 94952, but the map pointer is 4.5 miles northeast. Of course, this *is* beta software!

Entering the address, rather than the business name, into the search box rewrites the address as 7500 Point Reyes-Petaluma Rd and comes closer to locating the Cheese Factory, as shown in Figure 1-12. The pointer is still a bit off, but that can be attributed to the difficulty in geocoding locations from street addresses on roads with long patches between intersections.

Figure 1-11. Cheeseless in Marin

 You may sometimes find that the satellite imagery is slightly out of date with respect to the roads and other things shown on the map.

Figure 1-12. Thar be cheese!

Hybrid Vigor

Now, as if that weren't enough, Google has added a *Hybrid* mode to Google Maps. The Hybrid mode takes a version of the original street map tiles with transparent backgrounds, and then lays them over the satellite tiles. The result is pretty fantastic, as you can see from Figure 1-13, making it much easier to identify what's being shown in the satellite image.

Figure 1-13. Manhattan's Upper West Side, in Hybrid mode

The ability to flip between maps and satellite imagery is amazingly cool, and is just a hint of what (I assume) is coming. There is plenty of room next to the Map, Satellite, and Hybrid hyperlinks for other views or, as we say in Geographic Information Systems, other *data layers*. One prominent example was the Katrina button that showed up in the map display of the Gulf Coast of the United States in the aftermath of Hurricane Katrina in August 2005. Clicking this button displayed up-to-date satellite imagery, allowing you to compare before-and-after views of the hurricane's tragically destructive wake.

What could Google add? How about a link to terrain or elevation data? Or a current weather overlay? Thanks, Google, may I have another?

HACK #5 Driven to a Better User Interface

Driving directions and the single search box.

How much work does it take to get driving directions? With MapQuest, you need to click on a link to the Directions page, enter your starting street address, hit Tab (or even worse, take your hands off the keyboard, put them on the mouse, and click on the next field), enter your city, hit Tab, enter your state, hit Tab, enter your ZIP Code, hit Tab, and then repeat that Enter-Tab ballet for your destination.

In Google Maps, you enter your starting street address, city, state, and (optional) ZIP Code, then **to**, and then the street address, city, state, and (optional) ZIP Code of your destination—into the single search box. Would you trade a click and seven tabs or clicks for a single **to**? I sure would! In addition, Google Maps provides lots of alternatives for asking directions. The usual way is to enter the beginning and ending destinations into the search box [Hack #2].

To get directions from O'Reilly Media to the San Francisco airport, you can enter the starting address and the airport code:

    1005 Gravenstein Hwy N, Sebastopol, CA 95472 to SFO

You can even get directions from one airport to another. For example, for directions from San Francisco International to Oakland International try SFO to OAK. This pulls up the driving directions shown in Figure 1-14.

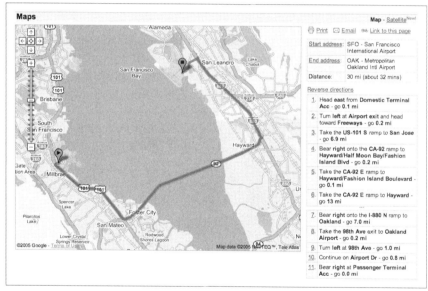

Figure 1-14. Driving directions from the San Francisco to the Oakland airports

When I get driving directions, I'm usually familiar with either the starting or ending location, but not both. Google provides a neat map-within-a-map effect to help navigate that last little bit. If you click on the Start Address or End Address links in the top of the results area on the right of the screen, a mini-map appears in the info window of the starting or ending address (Figure 1-15).

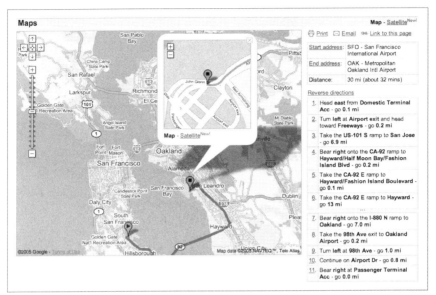

Figure 1-15. A detailed map of the destination

You can also click on the individual steps in the driving directions to get a mini-map for that navigational maneuver. The mini-map that appears is a complete map, with its own zoom (but not pan) controls, so you can position the map, zoom in, and print the map and directions. To add another level of cool, flip the mini-map to satellite view, as shown in Figure 1-16.

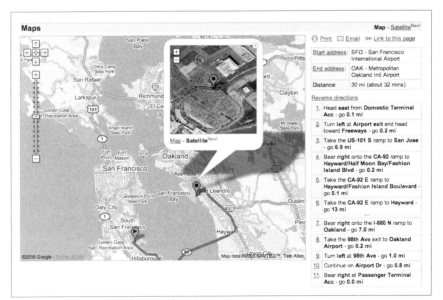

Figure 1-16. The detailed satellite view of the destination

We have a friend who lives *donde el Diablo se perdido su poncho* ("where the devil lost his poncho"), and having this imagery makes it a lot easier to understand what is happening as you traverse miles of single-lane former stage coach roads to pay a visit.

Using the Info Windows

When you search for an address or click on a local link, Google Maps produces the (hopefully) now-familiar info window, as shown in Figure 1-17.

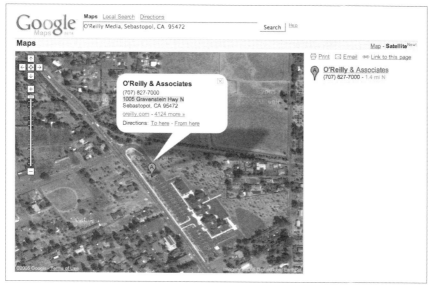

Figure 1-17. You can search in the info window

You can click on the info window links to get directions to or from that address. When you click on one of those links, you get a mini search box into which you can type a location, as shown in Figure 1-18.

Other Ways to Search

As mentioned above, you can use any of the methods of entering a location mentioned in "Find Yourself (and Others) on Google Maps" [Hack #2] and probably several more that we haven't found! So you can get the direction from an airport to a city (LAX to Hollywood, CA) or between two ZIP Codes (94305 to 95472), or any combination of the two.

You can even get directions to a latitude and longitude. This can be fun if you are interested in the Degree Confluence Project (*http://www.confluence.org/*), which is attempting to collect pictures and stories from each of the latitude

Figure 1-18. The search box in the info window

and longitude integer degree intersections in the world. So you could search for LAX to 34, -118 and get Figure 1-19, showing the closest degree confluence to Los Angeles.

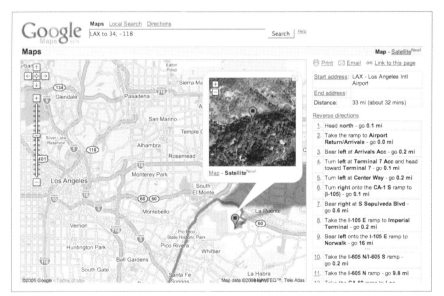

Figure 1-19. LAX to the nearest Degree Confluence—34 N, 118 W

Share Google Maps

Found something good? Email a link, bookmark it, or post it on your web site.

Are you having a party and needing to let people know where it will be held? Did you find a cool spot that you want to show your friends? Google Maps can create an email with a link that will show your friends (mostly) the same view you see—or generate a link to post on your own web site.

Without maps, many of us are reduced to near-incomprehensible grunts if forced to provide directions to our homes. Even if we've lived in the same place for years, our direction-giving process too often includes putting a hand over the phone handset and asking whoever is around, "What is the name of that street?"

The problem doesn't end there. Even if we are good at providing directions, our would-be visitor must keep track of fragments of data such as "the red mailbox" and "right after the hill—and if you hit the corner, you've gone too far." With online map services, though, most of the time it is enough just to have a street address, and with most, emailing or posting a link to a map helps a visitor find the location quickly.

Figure 1-20 shows driving directions from W 88th St and Broadway, NY, NY to W 92nd St and Central Park West, NY, NY. It also includes a destination mini-map.

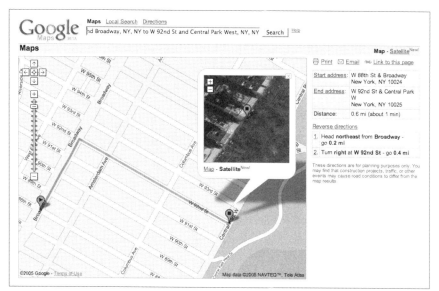

Figure 1-20. Getting around New York in Google Maps

Click the Email link just under the line that includes the Map and Satellite links, and Google opens your email client and inserts this link to this map, along with a set of driving directions, in the body of the email:

```
http://maps.google.com/maps?q=W+88th+St+and+Broadway,+ny,+ny+
    to+W+92nd+St+and+Central+Park+West,+ny,+ny&ll=40.789110,-73.966550&spn
    =0.007782,0.013467&hl=en
```

All you need to do is fill in the email address of your friend and send it off.

Bookmark a Google Map or Post It on Your Web Page

Google Maps makes deep use of JavaScript to dynamically redraw the map without (apparent) requests to the server. This means that the location bar in your browser does not get updated. This only becomes an issue when you decide to bookmark a map to use later.

When you bookmark Google Maps, you find that you've bookmarked the overview map of the whole United States—almost certainly not what you intended! Fortunately Google has provided a way out. Next to the Email link, under the Map and Satellite links, is a link to "Link to this page," as shown in Figure 1-21.

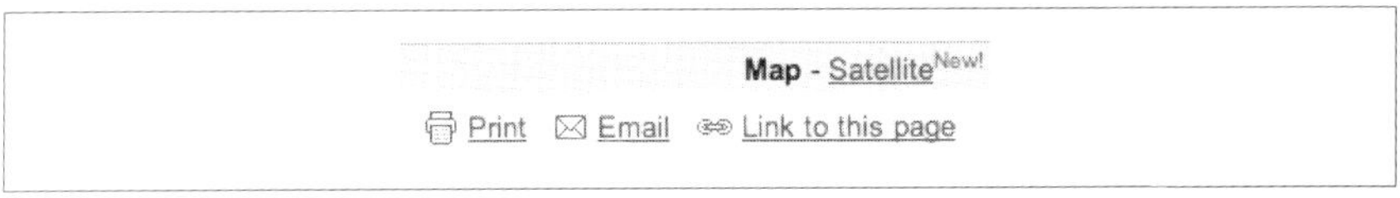

Map - Satellite^{New!}

🖨 Print   ✉ Email   ⊕ Link to this page

Figure 1-21. Print, email, or link to this map

Clicking "Link to this page" updates the address bar in your browser. Now you can bookmark the page in your browser or share the link on del.icio.us [Hack #9]—or copy the link from the address bar and paste it into your own web page. alternatively, you can right-click on "Link to this page" and select Copy Link Location (in Firefox) or Copy Shortcut (in Internet Explorer) to copy the link directly to the clipboard.

To post a link on your web page:

1. Find a map that you like.
2. Right-click on "Link to this page" and select the Copy option.
3. Paste the link into your web page within an appropriate anchor tag.

For example, here is a link to a map of Salina, Kansas: *http://maps.google.com/maps?q=Salina,+KS&spn=0.124512,0.215467&hl=en.*

You could include it in your web page with this HTML:

```
<a href="http://maps.google.com/maps?q=Salina,+KS&spn
    =0.124512,0.215467&hl=en">Salina, Kansas</a>
```

Shorten That Link!

Sometimes, if you just want to paste a URL of a Google Map into an email, you may find that the URLs are just long enough to break in the middle and wrap to the next line in your email client, which may make it more difficult for the recipients of your email to use. Metamark offers a solution to this problem at *http://xrl.us/*. There you'll find—no kidding—a link-shortening service, which takes unwieldy URLs like those produced by Google Maps and generates a permanent redirect from a much shorter URL to the much longer one you're having trouble with. Here, for example, is Metamark's shortened version of the Central Park driving directions that were shown in Figure 1-20:

```
http://xrl.us/hu9c
```

When others visit the shortened URL, their browsers will immediately be redirected to the longer URL you started with. You can also choose to use a mnemonic "nickname" in place of the string of random letters after *xrl.us* in the shortened URL, as well as apply a password to keep your URL under wraps.

Limits on Email and Links

The link generated by Email and "Link to this page" produces *almost* the same view when clicked as you have when you create the links. Sometimes the map is not centered in the same place as when you clicked on the link, as browser window sizes vary, and Google Maps does its best to show the area requested. Occasionally, this may even result in a different zoom level being displayed, in order to make the requested area fit in the available browser window space.

Also, it is quite possible, since Google Local searches appear to be regenerated on demand, that someone using your link could see a slightly different list of businesses than you did when you created the link.

Currently, the link does not save embedded mini-maps, so if you've created driving directions and opened up a mini-map at the start or end address, it will not be included in the email or link that you generate.

Maps help us gather together, and being able to communicate with more precision than "drive past the third gate, then turn right" means more people will show up where they want to be, rather than lost by a frog pond (though searching for "lost by a frog pond" brings up an absurd number of links).

HACK #7 Inside Google Maps URLs

Gain control of your links to Google Maps by understanding the URLs.

"Share Google Maps" [Hack #6] showed how to have Google Maps generate a link (i.e., Uniform Resource Locator or URL) that creates a view of the current map. A little exploration of Google Maps URLs can provide a lot of power!

We have no particular inside information, so much of what follows—especially what I think the abbreviated names stand for—is just semi-knowledgeable guesses. Let's start with a basic URL. This is what you get if you search for Key West, Fl and then click on "Link to this page."

```
http://maps.google.com/maps?q=Key+West,+Fl&hl=en
```

The *http://maps.google.com* part should be familiar. This is the basic Google Maps address. Next, /maps is a program running on Google's servers that generates maps. Web programs can accept parameters. The syntax for parameters is to start with a question mark and then put the name of a parameter, an equal sign, and the value of the parameter. If you need a second (or third, or more) parameter, you put an ampersand between the first value and the second parameter's name. So ?q=Key+West,+Fl&hl=en means there is a parameter named q with the value Key+West,+Fl and a parameter named hl with the value en.

Note that the spaces in "Key West, Fl" have been replaced with plus signs. This is because spaces aren't allowed in URLs and must be escaped.

The parameter hl is the language for the results, and q is the query, or location that you are searching for. If you speak French, replace the en with fr, and so on. If you leave off the hl parameter, Google Maps will try to display things in whatever language the user's web browser prefers.

The q or query parameter can be any of the things that are discussed in "Find Yourself (and Others) on Google Maps" **[Hack #2]**. For example, here is the URL to a map for latitude 38 degrees north, longitude 122 degrees west:

```
http://maps.google.com/maps?q=38,-122&hl=en
```

Google Maps follows the convention observed by most web mapping software and Geographic Information Systems, and uses negative values to denote latitude south of the Equator and longitude west of the Prime Meridian.

Here, for example, is ZIP Code 94305:

```
http://maps.google.com/maps?q=94305&hl=en
```

The query string for driving directions matches what you would enter into the search box, which is just as you'd expect. Here is San Francisco International (SFO) to Los Angeles International (LAX):

```
http://maps.google.com/maps?q=SFO+to+LAX&spn=3.984375,6.894949&hl=en
```

The spn parameter shows how much territory the map spans. It appears to be the number of degrees of longitude and latitude (in that order) that are shown on the map. The first value appears to be the number of degrees of longitude that are shown to the left and right of the center of the map. The second value is the same for the number of degrees of latitude that are shown above and below the center point.

For example, if the values are 1,1, then about 2 degrees of longitude (about 90 miles from east to west), and about 2 degrees of latitude (around 138 miles from north to south) are shown on the map.

When you search for driving directions, the span of the map is automatically set so that both the starting and ending points are shown. The span sets the zoom level. The fully zoomed-out map has a span of 63.750000, 110.319191, while the fully zoomed-in map is 0.003891, 0.006733 (at least for one sample map—it is likely that this varies with latitude). At this point it doesn't appear that you can manually enter an even smaller span. The system seems to have a minimum, beyond which it will not go.

At the equator, one degree of latitude or longitude is equal to about 69 miles, or 111 kilometers. As you go north or south of the equator, the degrees of latitude remain the same, but one degree of longitude shortens to approximately the cosine of the latitude multiplied by 69 miles. So, at 40 degrees north latitude, a degree of longitude is about 46 miles.

More Parameters!

Table 1-2 lists the parameters we've been able to figure out. Here, for one example, is a search for "pizza" when the span of the map has already been limited to a local area:

```
http://maps.google.com/maps?q=pizza&sll=38.402193,-122.829009&sspn
   =0.031128,0.053867&hl=en
```

The parameter sspn appears to be the search span, and sll is the search's latitude, longitude center point—so this query is looking for pizza within .031128 degrees of longitude and .053867 degrees of latitude from latitude and longitude 38.402193, -122.829009.

For linguistic reasons, we tend to think latitude and then longitude (i.e., lat/long), but when we draw graphs we think x,y. Latitude maps to the y axis, so to be consistent we'd talk about either y,x graphs or latitude, longitude coordinates. Google appears to have adopted both conventions in expressing geographic coordinates in this URL. People are not consistent, and Google can happily have a URL that specifies the center point as latitude, longitude but the span in x,y.

To see the satellite view, add the parameter and value t=k. Maybe that means *type* is k? What could *k* mean? (*keyhole*, perhaps?) As of August 2005, the letter *k* and the number *1* both cause a satellite map to appear, and the letter *h* causes hybrid maps to appear. From experimentation (i.e., trying all the other letters), no other special tricks live in the t parameter. Perhaps the other letters and digits will be used for coming features.

This URL represents a satellite view and driving directions from SFO to LAX:

    http://maps.google.com/maps?q=SFO+to+LAX&spn=5.603027,7.481689&t=k&hl=en

Or, to get just the driving directions:

    http://maps.google.com/maps?q=SFO+to+LAX&spn=3.984375,6.894949&hl=en

Table 1-2. Google Maps URL parameters

Parameter	Example	Description
q	94305 38,-122	Query string. This is what goes into the single search box.
hl	en fr	Language.
t	h k 1	Imagery type. Show satellite imagery if set to *k* or *1* and hybrid maps if set to *h*.
ll	-122.7 38.4	Longitude and latitude of the center point of a generated map.
z	3	Zoom level. Ranges from 3 to 18.
spn	5.603027 7.481689	Number of degrees of longitude and latitude across the entire map.
sspn	0.031128 0.053867	Search span. Define area to search for local search. Same format as the spn parameter.
sll	38.403193 -122.82709	Search latitude and longitude. The center point for a local search.

Finding More Parameters?

Another cute thing you can do with Google Maps queries is to add a custom title to the location by putting the title in parentheses after the search location. For example, the following URL shows the location of Google's headquarters, titled with the word "Google":

    http://maps.google.com/maps?q=
        1600+Amphitheatre+Parkway,+Mountain+View,+CA+94043+(Google)

Google Maps is filled with hidden (to us) options. The way to find out what it can do is to experiment! Try different things and to see what it all means, click on "Link to this page" often! You never know what might work—that is the essence of hacking!

See Also

*   "Generate Links to Google Maps in a Spreadsheet" [Hack #8].

Generate Links to Google Maps in a Spreadsheet

HACK #8

Get a handle on your own data with Google Maps.

What if you could create a private (or public) web page with links to Google Maps for each of the people in your company? Or all the members of your social club or church? You would be able to click on the names of people in your group and pop up a map of their location. Well, you can!

In "Inside Google Maps URLs" [Hack #7], we examined the structure of Google Maps URLs. Now we will use that information to create links to Google Maps that show your own contacts. We'll assume that you've got your contacts in a spreadsheet program, such as Microsoft Excel, Gnumeric, or OpenOffice Calc.

Figure 1-22 shows a sample data set with a name, street address, city, state, and ZIP Code set up in columns. This spreadsheet is available as *http://mappinghacks.com/google/sample_data.xls*.

	A	B	C	D	E
					sample_links.xls
1	Some Sample Addresses				
2					
3	Name	Street Address	City	State	Zip
4	O'Reilly & Associates	1005 Gravenstein Hwy N.	Sebastopol	CA	95472
5	Sonoma Coast Bamboo Reef	5702 Commerce Blvd	Rohnert Park	CA	94928
6	Sushi Tozai	7531 Healdsburg Ave	Sebastopol	CA	95472
7					

Figure 1-22. Name, address, city, state, and ZIP Code in spreadsheet columns

We can go from this format to a full HTML link in Excel. The HTML link for each element will look like this:

```
<li><a href="http://maps.google.com/maps?q=1005+Gravenstein+Hwy
    +N.,Sebastopol,CA,95472+(O'Reilly)&hl=en">
O'Reilly & Associates</a></li>
```

The li tag will put each line in an HTML bulleted list. You will be able to click on the name and pop up a map centered on the address that goes with that person or company.

The first step is to use the concatenation function to put the name, address, city, state, and ZIP Code together in a new column. You can do this by using either the concatenation function or the shortcut *&* that does the same thing:

```
=CONCATENATE(B4,",",C4,",",D4,",",E4,"(",A4,")")
```

or:

```
=B4 & "," & C4 & "," & D4 & "," & E4 & "(" & A4 & ")"
```

This creates an address that looks like this:

```
1005 Gravenstein Hwy N.,Sebastopol,CA,95472 (O'Reilly)
```

You'll note that we use the custom location title trick [Hack #7] to associate the locations on the map with the names from our spreadsheet.

Next, we'll replace the spaces with plus signs and ampersands with %26 (so they don't mess up the format of the URL), and then add the q= part of the query. Excel provides the Substitute( ) function. You give it a string, then the value you want to get rid of, and a new value to replace the old value. In this command I concatenate the q= part of the parameter with the result of replacing the spaces in the combined address with plus signs.

```
=CONCATENATE("q=", SUBSTITUTE(SUBSTITUTE(F4," ","+"), "&", "%26"))
```

The result looks like this:

```
q=1005+Gravenstein+Hwy+N.,Sebastopol,CA,95472+(O'Reilly)
```

Next concatenate the other parts of the Google URL:

```
=$G$1 & G4
```

G1 is an absolute reference to a cell containing http://maps.google.com/maps?hl=en& and G4 is the cell with our cleaned up query parameters. Note how the order of the parameters doesn't matter. We can list the q= part first or hl=en first. This gives us the full Google Maps URL of:

```
http://maps.google.com/maps?hl=en&q=
    1005+Gravenstein+Hwy+N.,Sebastopol,CA,95472+(O'Reilly)
```

We have to make just one little addition in order to get the full HTML that we want:

```
="<li><A href="""&H4&""">" & ">" & A4 & "</a></li>"
```

This is sort of ugly because we need to include double quotes (") in the result, but the double quotes are used as the string delimiter. In Excel you can insert a double quote into a string by entering *three* double quotes. The result is:

```
<li><a href="http://maps.google.com/maps?hl=en&q=
    1005+Gravenstein+Hwy+N.,Sebastopol,CA,95472+(O'Reilly)">
O'Reilly & Associates</a></li>
```

Now we want to get those links into our own HTML page. Most spreadsheet programs provide other tools to manage hyperlinks, but the simplest way is to just copy the column by selecting the whole thing with Edit → Copy (or Ctrl-C) and then pasting it into your HTML file.

Open that local file in your browser. You can use the power of the browser without exposing this page onto the Internet. If you are extremely paranoid, you need to aware that you are of course exposing your addresses to Google, which could in theory track address searches by your IP address and do something nasty with that information. Given Google's written commitment to avoid being evil, that shouldn't be a real risk.

You can open a local HTML file by selecting File → Open in Internet Explorer, or File → Open File in Firefox. The result is a page of links like those in Figure 1-23.

Link
- O'Reilly & Associates
- Sonoma Coast Bamboo Reef
- Sushi Tozai

Figure 1-23. A page of links to Google Maps created in Excel

See Also

- "Inside Google Maps URLs" [Hack #7].

Use del.icio.us to Keep Up with Google Maps
Other people want to help you keep up with Google Maps (and anything else)!

What would you say to a world-wide community of people who spend a great deal of effort to maintain a chaotic but powerful set of links to most of the most interesting material that is available on the Web? How about "thank you" and welcome to *http://del.icio.us/?*

Quoting from *http://del.icio.us/doc/about*, Joshua Schacter created del.icio.us as a:

> …social bookmarks manager. It allows you to easily add sites you like to your personal collection of links, to categorize those sites with keywords, and to share your collection not only between your own browsers and machines, but also with others.

One key to the service is that your collection of links is intrinsically shared with others. So you can use del.icio.us to manage your own bookmarks, or you can just browse other people's links. Once you create an account by going to *http://del.icio.us/register* and picking a username and password, you can use the service to bookmark your own links.

A major part of the power of del.icio.us comes from the ability to tag your links. A tag is just a bit of text that *you* feel categorizes the link. Figure 1-24 shows a page of links that I tagged with the *gmaps* tag.

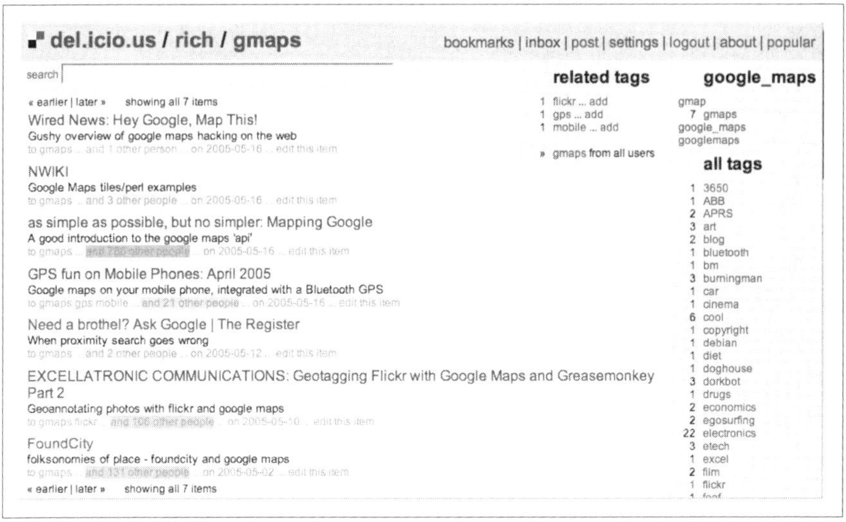

Figure 1-24. del.icio.us posts about Google Maps

Since all bookmarks on del.ico.us are shared, you can look at other sites that people have tagged with the same tags. So if you wanted to see all of the sites tagged with *gmaps*, you can click on "gmaps from all users" or go directly to this url: *http://del.icio.us/tag/gmaps*. Or to see the sites tagged with *gmap*, try *http://del.icio.us/tag/gmap*. Other people use *googlemaps* and *google_maps*, so you can get to those with *http://del.icio.us/tag/googlemaps* and *http://del.icio.us/tag/google_maps*.

Once you've looked at other people's links, you will want to create your own. Joshua provided some nifty little bookmarklets that you can drag onto your bookmark toolbar. When you find a page you want to remember, you just click on this bookmarklet in your own toolbar. This will bring up a form like that shown in Figure 1-25. (There are a few different bookmarklets, so yours might look slightly different.)

Figure 1-25. Bookmarking a page in del.icio.us

When you click on the "post to del.icio.us" bookmarklet, it copies the URL and title from the current page and then pre-fills the "post to del.icio.us" form. You then can add an extended description and tags.

If you wish, you can totally ignore the rest of the world and use tags that are only meaningful to you. Or, you can strive to use a set of common and authoritative tags in all of your links.

Well, you could use that set of common and authoritative tags, except that no such thing exists, nor, really, is it capable of existing. The problem of classifying web pages is so difficult that it has driven otherwise brilliant people to near lunacy. And some of those folks were even Perl programmers!

So instead of a set of authoritative taxonomies, del.icio.us allows you to roll your own. In the case of the link shown in Figure 1-24, I decided that the tag *gmaps* (for Google Maps), fit, since the article is about connecting a GPS to a mobile phone and then loading maps from Google Maps onto the phone.

Of course, *gps* also fits, since there is a GPS in the system, and mobile phones are *mobile*, so I threw both of those in as well. Multiple tags are supported, and encouraged; they just need to be separated by spaces.

Why did I use *gmaps* instead of *gmap*? This brings up a weakness of these informal taxonomies; sometimes they are too informal, and redundancy creeps in. Did I say *creeps*? No, redundancy doesn't creep in, it is thrust in! Heaved in, piled in so that the resulting taxonomy creaks from the weight of repetition.

And it turns out that this overwhelming cruft of repetition just doesn't matter. The ability for everyone to create meaningful categories that work for them, while allowing everyone to share in this collective taxonomical work, has created a system of incredible power.

Tag-based classification systems are jumping into existence all over the Web. So much so, that they have fostered the term *folksonomy* to describe these "folk"-driven taxonomies. Folksonomies have thrilling emergent properties, such as automatically generating taxonomies, and providing the data to allow for automatic generation of link clusters. Folksonomies also have weaknesses, and few people are suggesting that professional taxonomy be eliminated!

del.icio.us has lots of cool features, and it is in a state of continual improvement. One of the neat features is that you can subscribe to tags and to users. So if you subscribe to the *gmaps*, *gmap*, *googlemaps*, and *google_maps* tags, interesting links will just magically appear in your del.icio.us inbox, and you will get continual updates on what is happening with Google Maps.

Our friend (and *Mapping Hacks* contributor) Mike Liebhold maintains an extensive set of links to geo-related topics: mapping, GIS, GPS, and so on. He created the del.icio.us account *starhill_blend* as a repository for his absurdly detailed subscriptions to geo-related web sites. Sometimes two-thirds of the posts will be about Google Maps, but he is looking at every-thing from *location-based-game* to *psychogeography*. You can follow this page at *http://del.icio.us/inbox/starhill_blend*.

As befits a modern data aggregating application, all the interesting pages are also available via RSS content syndication. If you spend a lot of time on the Web and you don't know about RSS, you can do yourself a favor and save a lot of time by learning about it.

See Also

- The Google Maps Mania blog at *http://googlemapsmania.blogspot.com/* maintains a good ongoing review of all things new and Google Maps.
- *Developing Feeds with RSS and Atom* by Ben Hammersley (O'Reilly).

Introducing the Google Maps API
Hacks 10–16

The Google Maps site at *http://maps.google.com* is awesome, with an easy user interface, one-box searching, and integrated satellite imagery. But it gets better! The Google Maps team has made it possible to include Google Maps with almost all of its great features onto your own web pages. They have done this by providing an open Application Program Interface, or API.

An API defines a standard way for one program to call code that lives within another application or library. The Google API defines a set of JavaScript objects and methods that you use to put maps on your own web pages.

Before Google Maps, it was much harder to put simple maps on your own pages. MapQuest had a program that let you create a link to a map. You could not embed the map on your own page, you could not put it into a frame, you couldn't even use Target=_new to open a new browser window.

There were—and are—open source solutions to generate maps. For example, the UMN Mapserver (*http://mapserver.gis.umn.edu*) is very powerful, allowing you to do things that Google Maps cannot yet equal, but there is a rather steep learning cliff. There are also industry standards for web mapping promulgated by the Open Geospatial Consortium (OGC) at *http://www.opengeospatial.org*.

The OGC-defined Web Mapping Service (WMS) and Web Feature Service (WFS) standards define a powerful web services interface to geospatial data. There are now free and easy-to-use open source clients for WMS and WFS data. For example, you can use the open source JavaScript library from *http://openlayers.org/* to access public data sources and put free maps on your page.

These are great options that either were not available or were not easy to use when the Google Maps API was released. Some folks argue that Google did nothing new. There was free data out there, and there were web-enabled GIS systems. But clearly Google did something.

Creating feature-complete interfaces to geographic data that are so complex as to be inpenetrable by all but the highest of high priests seems to be nearly inevitable. Programmers start with a simple model, and then the world, the data, and the weight of history intrude to "complexify" our models and break our metaphors. When Walt Kelly wrote "We have met the enemy and he is us," he could have been describing the creators of most geospatial apps.

Somehow Google avoided that trap. As GPSBabel author Robert Lipe says, "We've seen an explosion in applications using the API. It's easy enough that you don't really need to be either a geo-geek, a cartographer, or a progamming jock to produce some really usable results."

Google has provided a readable introduction to the API, available at *http://www.google.com/apis/maps/*. They have created a "Hello World" of Google Maps that embeds a Google Map on a web page:

```
<!DOCTYPE html PUBLIC "-//W3C//DTD XHTML 1.0 Strict//EN" "http://www.w3.org/
    TR/xhtml1/DTD/xhtml1-strict.dtd">
<html xmlns="http://www.w3.org/1999/xhtml">
  <head>
    <title>Google Maps JavaScript API Example - simple</title>
    <script src="http://maps.google.com/maps?file=api&v=1&key=abcdefg"
type="text/javascript"></script>
  </head>
  <body>
    <div id="map" style="width: 300px; height: 300px"></div>
    <script type="text/javascript">
    //<![CDATA[

    if (GBrowserIsCompatible()) {
      var map = new GMap(document.getElementById("map"));
      map.centerAndZoom(new GPoint(-122.141944, 37.441944), 4);
    }
    //]]>
    </script>
  </body>

</html>
```

You need a bit of glue in the form of the above div element and the script src= line, but there are only two important lines of code required to create and display a map centered on a specific point. The key code in this example creates a new GMap object and then centers the map on a specific point:

```
var map = new GMap(document.getElementById("map"));
map.centerAndZoom(new GPoint(-122.141944, 37.441944), 4);
```

In programming terms, the first line creates a new variable that contains a new GMap object. The GMap object will be linked with the section of the page marked with <div id="map">. The second line then calls the centerAndZoom method of the GMap class.

The GMap class represents a single map on your page (yes, you can have multiple maps on the same page, each displaying a unique view).

There are other classes that provide additional features, such as GPoint to define a point and GPolyLine to define a line (there is not yet true polygon support), as well as a built-in XML parser and XSLT processor. Take a look at the API documentation at *http://www.google.com/apis/maps/documentation.*

HACK #10 Add a Google Map to Your Web Site

Here's how to get started using the Google Maps API.

At O'Reilly's Where 2.0 converence on June 29, 2005, Google announced an official and documented API for Google Maps. The API makes it possible for anyone to add a Google Map to a web page by cutting and pasting a few lines of JavaScript from the Google Maps Developer's site.

People reacted to the new API in one or more ways. My first act was to scratch my own itch by writing a bit of code to display my GPS waypoints on a Google Map. Fortunately, better GPX-to-Google Maps solutions have been created, one of which is documented in "View Your GPS Tracklogs in Google Maps" [Hack #37]. After scratching that itch, I looked to our Geocoder. us site. Schuyler had spent a lot of time figuring out the Census Bureau's public TIGER/Line Map Server API, and how to display the resulting map with a neat little zoomable interface. The results were slow and clunky, but they worked.

The Google Maps API gets rid of the need for that level of head scratching! The march of progress in computers (possibly in society at large) works by first figuring out ways to do new things, and then progressively making those tasks easier, and leaving the old practitioners to eat cat food and write programs for their Osborne luggable computer.

I used Google Maps to bring the geocoder.us site into the protective embrace of the Google Maps API. Geocoder.us, online at *http://geocoder.us/*, is a free U.S. address geocoder. You can go to the web site and get the latitude and longitude for a U.S. street address. You can also use a web service interface to get the latitude and longitude automatically for a group of addresses [Hack #62]. You can geocode using Google Maps by scraping their search results, but it's not a part of the official API, and doing so violates Google's terms and conditions of service. By contrast, the Geocoder.us site is based on free data without limited terms of service for non-commercial use.

Figure 2-1 shows the results of geocoding the address of O'Reilly Media's headquarters with the original TIGER/Line map, with a pushpin showing the location of the address that we just looked up. We'd like to replace this somewhat

slow map generated by the Census Bureau with the much faster, more attractive, and more easily navigable maps offered by Google Maps. (The original
Geocoder.us map view can be seen at *http://geocoder.us/demo_tiger.cgi.*)

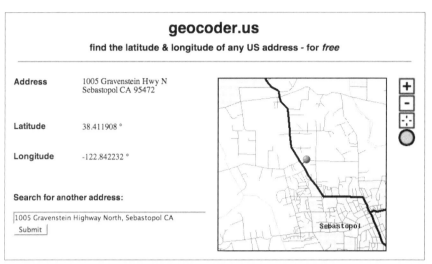

Figure 2-1. The Census Bureau map originally used by http://geocoder.us/

Get a Developer Key

The first step in putting a Google Map on your page is to generate a developer's key, which is an alphanumeric string that identifies your web site to
Google, and helps them track usage of Google Maps. Having to sign up for a
developer's key can be something of an annoyance, but it's a small price to
pay for being able to include free (as in beer) maps on your web site with
such relative ease.

You'll need a distinct developer's key for each directory on your site that
includes Google Maps. You don't need a key for each individual web page
or script. So if you have several pages that generate calls to Google Maps
from the same directory, you only need one key.

Fortunately Google has made getting developer's keys as easy as filling in a
web form. The Google Maps API page is at *http://www.google.com/apis/
maps/.* This includes links to documentation, examples, Terms of Use, and
the page to get your key. There is a human version of the Terms of Use, then
the full legalese version. Figure 2-2 shows the form with the URL we want to
use for our maps. You must agree to the Terms of Service, then click Generate API Key.

Google Maps API Terms of Use

Thank you for using the Google Maps API! By using the Google Maps API
(the "Service"), you ("You") accept and agree to be bound by the
following terms and conditions (the "Terms of Use").

   1. Service.

      1.1 Description of Service. The API consists of Javascript that
allows You to display Google map images on your website, subject to
the limitations and conditions described below. The API is limited to
allowing You to display map images only, and does not provide You with
the ability to access the underlying map data, any services provided
by Google in connection with its maps service (such as local search or
directions), or any other Google service.

☑ **I have read and agree with the API terms and conditions** (printable version)

My Web Site URL:

http://geocoder.us/

Generate API Key

Figure 2-2. Enter a server and path to generate a developer's key

In our case, we wanted to enable Google Maps for a single
script on our server. If you want to enable Google Maps for a
whole directory, you can leave off the script name and just
specify the host name and directory portion of the URL.
Unfortunately, the API key isn't good for directories inside the
one you specify, just the files and scripts in that directory.

Almost instantly, a key will be generated, along with an example web page
that Google refers to this as the "Hello World" of Google Maps. To put this
on your web site, copy the HTML/JavaScript section in Example 2-1 and
paste it into a new file on your own web site in the directory that you used
when you created the developer's key.

Example 2-1. Google Maps "Hello World"

```
<!DOCTYPE html PUBLIC "-//W3C//DTD XHTML 1.0 Strict//EN"
"http://www.w3.org/TR/xhtml1/DTD/xhtml1-strict.dtd">
<html xmlns="http://www.w3.org/1999/xhtml">
  <head>
    <script
        src="http://maps.google.com/maps?file=api&v=1&key=[your API key]"
        type="text/javascript"></script>
  </head>
  <body>
    <div id="map"
        style="width: 500px; height: 400px; border: 1px solid  #979797"></div>
      <script type="text/javascript">
      //<![CDATA[
```

Example 2-1. Google Maps "Hello World" (continued)

```
var map = new GMap(document.getElementById("map"));
map.addControl(new GSmallMapControl());
map.centerAndZoom(new GPoint(-122.1419, 37.4419), 4);

//]]>
    </script>
  </body>
</html>
```

Developer keys work only when they are used on a web page that lives in the server and directory that you specified when you created the key. So you can't copy this listing and have it work until you change the developer's key to match your own. In general, most of the code examples in this book will require you to substitute your own valid developer key in order for them to work.

Hello, World!

The "Hello World" page shown in Example 2-1 is a standard HTML page, with a bit of JavaScript. The first interesting part is the opening script element:

```
<script
src="http://maps.google.com/maps?file=api&v=1&key=[Your API Key]"
type="text/javascript"></script>
```

This imports the Google Maps JavaScript library into our page. A JavaScript-compliant browser will automatically fetch the contents of the provided URL. Google can then compare the developer's key and the server name and path that is included in the HTTP headers of your request with their records, to see if they match.

The v=1 parameter in the above URL is important, because it specifies the Google Maps API version that your script expects. If Google ever changes 'its API in such a way that backwards compatibility is broken, the v parameter will allow your script to continue to function with the original API and give you some breathing room to update your code to the newer version of the API.

The next three interesting lines are:

```
var map = new GMap(document.getElementById("map"));
map.addControl(new GSmallMapControl());
map.centerAndZoom(new GPoint(-122.1419, 37.4419), 4);
```

These lines are pretty much self explanatory (for an object-oriented JavaScript programmer). But you don't need to understand much to put powerful maps on your own pages!

By default the size of the map is determined by the size of the HTML element that contains the map. In this example, we are using the div element to define a division in the page, which provides an area that you can control and format independently from other parts of the page.

The first line creates a new GMap object and places it within the div named map. (There's nothing magic about the name of the div element, by the way—we could call it "Tim," and so long as the JavaScript mentioned the same name, it would still work.) The next line adds the small pan and zoom control to the map, and the third line centers and zooms the map to longitude -122.1419, latitude 37.4419 at zoom level 4.

In our example, the div element is 500×400 pixels high and has a 1-pixel-wide gray border around the edge. You can also specify the width and height in percentages, such as style="width: 50%; height: 40%". The border itself is totally optional, but it does set the map off nicely from the rest of the page.

```
<div id="map"
style="width: 500px; height: 400px; border: 1px solid  #979797"></div>
```

The *demo.cgi* page at *http://geocoder.us/* was already template driven, so to add Google Maps functionality I added the script= line to load the Google Maps library, and then included these lines in my template:

```
<div id="map" style="width: 500px; height: 300px; border: 1px solid
#979797"></div>
<script type="text/javascript">
//<![CDATA[

var map = new GMap(document.getElementById("map"));
map.addControl(new GSmallMapControl());
map.centerAndZoom(new GPoint([% long %], [% lat %]), 4);

var point =  new GPoint([% long %],[% lat %]);
var marker = new GMarker(point);
map.addOverlay(marker);

//]]>
</script>
```

The map will automatically size itself to fit within the <div id="map"...> tag. In our templating system (Perl's Template Toolkit, as it happens), [% long %] will be replaced with the contents of the variable long, or the longitude. The only differences from the sample code are that the sample constants for lat and long are replaced with variables that will be set in our program, and that a point marker is added for the location of the address the user looked up.

Getting Outside of Your Head

The "Hello World" example presumes that the HTML script element that imports the Google Maps API library into your web page is nestled safe within the HTML document's head element. Certainly, this is the right place for it to go, but web browsers are perfectly capable of handling script elements elsewhere in an HTML document. Furthermore, situations will occur where you might want to include the API library from elsewhere—say, for example, one where you have an HTML templating system that provides a boilerplate header and footer for each page on your site. In this circumstance, you don't want the API library to be imported into every page on the site, because every page outside the directory associated with your developer's key will load up with a developer key error message.

Fortunately, you can indeed import the API library almost anywhere in your document, so long as it appears before the JavaScript code that needs to use it. The only thing you really need to know is that some browsers—Internet Explorer, in particular—will wait for a script element to execute before rendering the rest of the page, to make sure that the JavaScript itself doesn't modify the page layout. For some reason, this behavior sometimes has a bad interaction with the Google Maps API when the script element is used outside the head—a JavaScript execution error is the most common result. The workaround is to add a defer="defer" attribute to the script element, which will tell the browser not to worry about it and get on with rendering the page. In that case, our earlier script element example looks like this:

```
<script src="http://maps.google.com/maps?file=api&v=1&key
    =[Your API Key]"type="text/javascript" defer="defer"></script>
```

Getting Right to the Point

Once you've got a Google Map on your page, adding points to it is easy. You'll first create a new GPoint object, then create a marker icon at that point, and finally add that marker to the map. We'll look more at adding points and lines to Google Maps in other hacks. For now, enjoy Figure 2-3, which shows a pretty Google Map replacing our TIGER map.

But is that (always) better? Are there reasons not to use Google Maps? Yes! Google Maps are great, and Google has a history and reputation of being the good guys, but it is a profit-making business and its goals might not be your goals. The Google Maps terms of service are extremely generous, but when you use Google Maps, you are relying on Google. There are restrictions on what you can do with Google Maps; for example, Google Maps cannot be

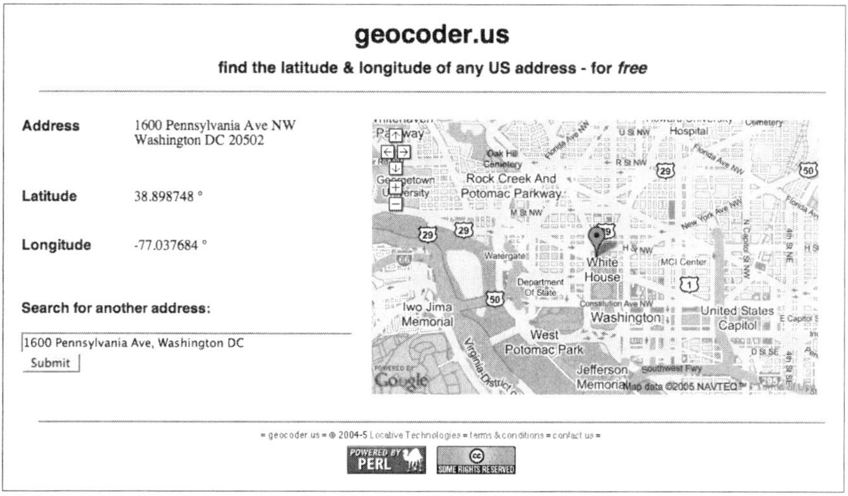

Figure 2-3. http://geocoder.us/ with a Google Map

used on a site that is inaccessible to the general public, such as a paid pre-mium content site or a corporate intranet. There are limitations on volume, as well: if you expect more than 50,000 hits in a day, Google expects to hear from you first. You can't do certain things, such as scrape Google's images or remove its imprint from its imagery, and it has explicitly reserved the right to put ads on the maps at any time. You can read more about the fine details at *http://www.google.com/apis/maps/faq.html*, but you should also review the terms of use at *http://www.google.com/apis/maps/terms.html* to be on the safe side.

There are (at least currently) limits on the data available from Google. There is far more aerial and satellite data and map imagery available on the Web [Hack #12] from public Web Mapping Service (WMS) servers than is available from Google.

See Also

- Google Maps are free-as-in-beer but not free-as-in-speech. So if the power, beauty, and ease of use of Google Maps don't meet your needs, projects such as Geoserver (*http://geoserver.sf.net/*), Mapserver (*http://mapserver.gis.umn.edu/*), and the Ka-Maps client interface to Mapserver (*http://ka-maps.sf.net/*) may fill the bill. The downside, as is often the case with open source software, is that you may have to do more of the work yourself! O'Reilly's *Mapping Hacks* and *Web Mapping Illustrated* have much more to say about free and open source mapping solutions.

Where Did the User Click?

#11   Find the location of a click on a map and display it on your web page.

Google Maps makes it easy to put an interactive map on your web page. At *http://www.naffis.com/maphacks/latandlon.html* you can click on a map and have the corresponding latitude and longitude displayed in a Google Maps info box.

In Figure 2-4 you can see the location of the Washington Monument.

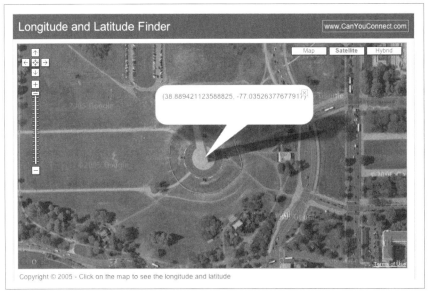

Figure 2-4. The Washington Monument at 38.88941 N, 77.03517 W

This site solves the common problem of figuring out the coordinates of a location from a map view and is an example of the sort of quick hack that Google Maps has made possible. This page illustrates one way to get the latitude and longitude from a click on a map and display results in an info box. So how can you do it? At *http://mappinghacks.com/projects/gmaps/click.html* there is a simplified example of updating a form from the coordinates of a click on a map.

This is the Hello World map with three changes. An HTML form has been added to receive the latitude and longitude from the click event:

```
<form>
Latitude:  <input type="text" value="38.4094"  id="click_lat"
onclick="this.blur()"> 
Longitude: <input type="text" value="-122.8290" id="click_long"
onclick="this.blur()"> 
</form>
```

In the script, the latitude and longitude used to set the initial map location with centerAndZoom( ) now comes from these form elements. This code defaults to starting at 38.4094 N, 122.8290 W. Change those values to change the initial focus of the map. The important change to the script is the addition of a GEvent.addListener. This code and the above form can be pasted into the body of your HTML page. Change the developer's key and you can capture clicks on a map:

```
<script src=
  "http://maps.google.com/maps?file=api&v=1&key=replacewithyourkey"
type="text/javascript">
</script>

<div id="map" style="width: 400px; height: 300px"></div>
<script type="text/javascript">
//<![CDATA[

    var map = new GMap(document.getElementById("map"));
    map.addControl(new GSmallMapControl());

    // center and zoom to the lat/long in the form
    map.centerAndZoom(new GPoint(
            document.getElementById('click_long').value,
            document.getElementById('click_lat').value), 3);

    GEvent.addListener(map, 'click',
        function(overlay, point) {
            if (point) {
                document.getElementById('click_lat').value = point.y;
                document.getElementById('click_long').value = point.x;
            }
        }
    );
    //]]>
</script>
```

This code adds a listener to the GMap object named map. If you click on the map, the code in the event handler will be run. The code is given both an overlay (a marker) and a point. If you click on a marker, the overlay will be set. If you don't click on a marker, then a GPoint object is given to the code.

These two lines are standard JavaScript. They ask the document for the value of the elements click_lat and click_long. The only elements with those names are the form elements. point.x and point.y are the longitude and latitude of the GPoint object that marks where you clicked.

```
document.getElementById('click_lat').value = point.y;
document.getElementById('click_long').value = point.x;
```

The end result is shown in Figure 2-5.

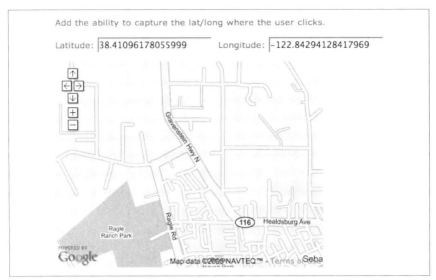

Figure 2-5. The click is back

The next steps are to add markers to the map from the click, populate a map from an external data source, and update an external data source based on the map.

HACK #12   How Far Is That? Go Beyond Driving Directions

Draw routes and calculate distances on your own Google Maps.

How far is it? That's a basic question we often ask of maps. Google Maps' driving directions answer that question, but driving directions are not (yet) accessible to the developer's API. More importantly, they simply give driving distances assuming the optimal route, where *optimal* is defined as getting there as quickly as possible in an automobile. They are not optimized for "scenic drive" or "safest bicycle route" or "quiet stroll" or "jog around the park."

There are at least two sites that allow you to create routes and calculate distances by clicking on maps. The Gmaps Pedometer at *http://www.sueandpaul.com/gmapPedometer/* shown in Figure 2-6 estimates cumulative distance—and even includes a calorie counter.

Use the standard map controls to zoom into your area of interest, and then click Start Recording. When you double-click a point on the map, it will re-center to that spot and add a marker there. The second time you click, the map will recenter to your new point, the marker will be moved, and a line will be drawn from the last point clicked to this one. Each time you do this, the Total Distance and Last Leg Distance fields will be updated.

How Far Is That? Go Beyond Driving Directions

HACK
#12

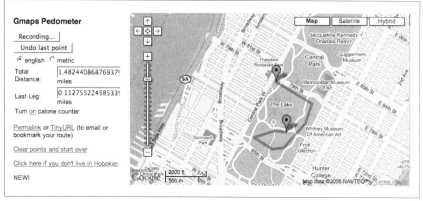

Figure 2-6. Sue and Paul's Gmaps Pedometer

Handling double clicks is a bit awkward and browser dependent. Sue and Paul are doing browser detection and then setting the appropriate event handler based on the browser:

```
if (navigator.appName == 'Microsoft Internet Explorer'){
    document.ondblclick = handleDblClick;
    bIsIE = true;

} else {
    window.ondblclick = handleDblClick;
    bIsIE = false;
}
```

Do you see the difference between the two ondblclick events? It is a difference in how they implement the Document Object Model. Internet Explorer handles double-clicks at the document level, hence document.ondblclick and everyone else (well, everyone else according to this code) uses the window object, so window.ondblclick. In both cases when there is a double-click the variable bDoubleClickHappened is set to true.

This will become important in a bit. You can't add a double-click listener with the Google Maps API, so the map does not directly capture the double-click event, but rather the moveend event, which according to the API documentation is "Triggered at the end of a discrete or continuous map movement. This event is triggered once at the end of a continuous pan."

This means that when there is a double-click event, Sue and Paul's handleDblClick function is called to set the bDoubleClickHappened variable. Next the Google Maps equivalent of handleDblClick is called.

Once Google Maps has finished the move or pan, the moveend event is triggered, the function set to listen for moveend events is called, and the anonymous function set in this code is called:

```
GEvent.addListener(map, "moveend", function( ) {
    if (bDoubleClickHappened){
        addLeg(map.getCenterLatLng( ).x, map.getCenterLatLng( ).y);
        drawPolyLine(gPointArray);
    }
    bDoubleClickHappened = false;
});
```

I love this code! It is an example of not always getting what you want, but finding a way to get what you need. We don't want to add a leg to our route on every move, just the ones that were initiated by a double-click. When the double-click handler was called, the bDoubleClickHappened variable was set. This code is called any time the map is moved, and if the map was double-clicked the addLeg and drawPolyLine functions are called.

Walk Jog Run, shown in Figure 2-7, works in similar ways, but it captures single clicks. If you click on the map it asks if you want to start a new route. If you say yes, it captures each click, adds a marker, and draws a line connecting all of the points you've clicked.

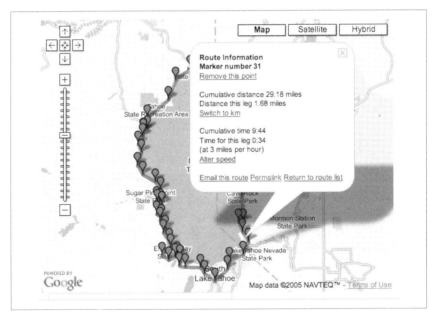

Figure 2-7. Walk Jog Run

If this is the first click, the route will be empty, so startRoute( ) is called; otherwise, this is the continuation of a route, so this point is added to the list.

```
GEvent.addListener(map, 'click', function(overlay, point) {
        if (overlay) {
            /* do nothing */
        } else if (point) {
                if (route.length == 0) {
                    startRoute(point);
                } else if (route[route.length-1].x != point.x ||
                        route[route.length-1].y != point.y) {
                    route.push(point);
                    currentRouteId = null;
                    drawRoute(route);
                }
        }
    });
```

The prototype for a click event handler accepts an overlay and point parameter. The overlay parameter is set when the user clicks on an overlay (that is, a line or marker). Most of the time we handle click events on markers by setting a listener when the marker is created. The drawRoute method is called when a new point is added and then goes through the list of points in the route, setting up the text for the marker overlays and calling this createMarker code to draw them, and then drawing the polyline of the route.

```
function createMarker(point, mtext, icon) {
  var marker = new GMarker(point,icon);
  var html = "<b>Route Information</b><br />" + mtext;
  GEvent.addListener(marker, "click", function() {
    currentPoint = marker.point;
    map.centerAndZoom(currentPoint, map.getZoomLevel());
    marker.openInfoWindowHtml(html);
  });
  return marker;
}
```

This illustrates the creation of a marker with embedded text. If you want your markers to open, add a listener for the click event of the marker. The standard choice when clicking a marker is the openInfoWindowHTML() method for the marker. This pops up the standard HTML-enabled info window, but you can do anything when a marker is called.

In the wouldn't-it-be-cool-if category, wouldn't it be cool if there were an Internet-enabled game of Risk using Google Maps as the interface? You would have a map of the world with markers that represent the Risk countries. Clicking on the marker would bring up an HTML form with your options in regards to that country—from just getting information, to launching an attack. Given the pace of development on Google Maps, I suspect that googling for "Google Maps Risk" will bring up three different implementations by some time Tuesday (depending on which Tuesday).

HACK

#12 How Far Is That? Go Beyond Driving Directions

Walk Jog Run aims to be the *http://del.icio.us* of maps for the running community. It lets you save your own routes as well as search and comment on the shared list of routes. You can look at the information relevant to any of the intermediate points on the route. Walk Jog Run shows you an estimated time for the total route and for each segment and allows you to delete any points from a route, unlike Sue and Paul's, which will only let you undo the last point.

Lines or Points? Both services let you add points by clicking. GMaps Pedometer shows a marker for your start and most recent position and hides the markers for the intermediate points. The result is a clean path overlaid on the map. Walk Jog Run leaves the markers on the map, which lets you view statistics for each segment of a completed route. They each have advantages.

Both GMaps Pedometer and Walk Jog Run aim to be full-featured sites. As a result, the code has a lot of detail that might make it hard to understand what is going on. Our page at *http://mappinghacks.com/projects/gmaps/lines.html* has another example of adding markers and lines, and then calculating distances in response to click events, as shown in Figure 2-8.

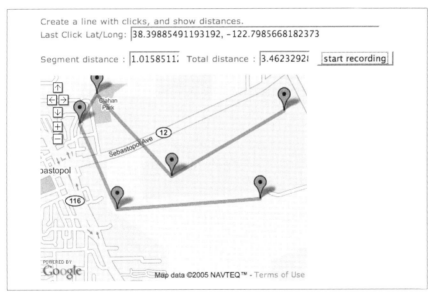

Figure 2-8. Adding markers and lines

When the user clicks on the Start Recording button, the code sets up a listener to process click events and the recording_flag is set in the JavaScript. If it is set the current position is added to the arrays that hold our x and y positions (where, you'll recall x equals longitude, and y equals latitude), and the drawRoute function is called. Finally, the current latitude and longitude

How Far Is That? Go Beyond Driving Directions

HACK
#12

are shown in the form elements click_lat and click_long. Capturing clicks is described in more detail in "Where Did the User Click?" [Hack #11].

```
GEvent.addListener(map, 'click',
        function(overlay, point) {
            if (point) {
                if (recording_flag > 0) {
                    addPoint(point.y, point.x, keepPoint);
                    x_array.push(point.x);
                    y_array.push(point.y);
                    drawRoute();

                    document.getElementById('click_lat').value = point.y;
                    document.getElementById('click_long').value = point.x;
                }
            }
        }
    );   // end of GEvent.addListener
```

The drawRoute( ) function is a bit longer, but hopefully straightforward. The first trick when updating markers is to clear all the existing markers by calling clearOverlays( ). Next the code walks the array of longitudes, x_array. Distances are calculated for the segment and the running distance of the route up to this point. The segment_distance and total_distance form elements are updated to show the distances.

The point is then created and a marker added. The created point is added to the array points. Once all of the elements in the x and y arrays have been processed, the array of points is added as a new GPolyLine.

```
function drawRoute( ) {
    map.clearOverlays();
    var points = [];
    for (i = 0; i < x_array.length; i++) {
        if (i>0) {
            segment_distance_array[i] = calcDist(x_array[i-1], y_array[i-1],
                x_array[i], y_array[1]);
            total_distance_array[i] = total_distance_array[i-1] +
                segment_distance_array[i];
            document.getElementById('segment_distance').value =
                segment_distance_array[i];
            document.getElementById('total_distance').value =
                total_distance_array[i];
        } else {
            // initialize the first element distances to 0
            document.getElementById('segment_distance').value = 0;
            document.getElementById('total_distance').value = 0;
            total_distance_array[0] = 0;
            segment_distance_array[0] = 0;
        }
        var point = new GPoint(x_array[i], y_array[i]);
        points.push(point);
        var marker = new GMarker(point);
```

HACK
#12

How Far Is That? Go Beyond Driving Directions

```
        // define the text that appears in the marker
        var html = "location <b>" + y_array[i] + ', ' + x_array[i] + "</b>";
        GEvent.addListener(marker, "click", function( ) {
            marker.openInfoWindowHtml(html);
        });
        map.addOverlay(marker);
    }
    map.addOverlay(new GPolyline(points));
}
```

This is not the only, or even best, way to do this! There is more than one way to do it!

Now, let's move on to calculating distances. Walk Jog Run and GMaps Pedometer use similar functions to calculate distance. I used the one from Walk Jog Run in my demo because it specifically had a Creative Commons Attribution-NonCommercial-ShareAlike license.

```
/* calcDist( ) function is from  Adam Howitt
    Copyright Adam Howitt 2005
    Email: adamhowitt@gmail.com
    This work is licensed under a Creative Commons
    Attribution-NonCommercial-ShareAlike 2.5 License.
    http://creativecommons.org/licenses/by-nc-sa/2.5/
*/
function calcDist(lon1,lat1,lon2,lat2) {
    var r = 3963.0;
    var multiplier = 1;
    // var multiplier = currentUnit == "miles" ? 1 : MILESASKM;
    return multiplier * r * Math.acos(Math.sin(lat1/57.2958) *
            Math.sin(lat2/57.2958) +  Math.cos(lat1/57.2958) *
            Math.cos(lat2/57.2958) * Math.cos(lon2/57.2958 -
            lon1/57.2958));
}:
```

Note that the variable multiplier has been commented out. In this code, I'm displaying the values only in miles. The multiplier represents the conversion factor from miles to whatever units you need. MILESASKM is *Miles as Kilometers*, the number of kilometers in one mile, or 1.609344. The multiplier is set using the ternary operator. If the current unit equals miles then the multiplier is 1 (as 1 mile equals 1 mile); otherwise, it is set to the number of kilometers in a mile. You don't need to understand this formula, but if you want to learn more, see "How to calculate distance in miles from latitude and longitude" at *http://www.meridianworlddata.com/Distance-Calculation.asp.*

The constant 3,963 is close enough to the radius of the earth in statute miles. 57.2958 is the number of statute miles (5,280 feet, as opposed to nautical miles) in one degree of latitude anywhere, or one degree of longitude at the equator. A nautical mile is defined as 1 minute of latitude (or 1 minute of longitude at the equator).

With the multiplier code commented out, you can copy this function into your own code and calculate distances between anything. Go distance crazy!

HACK #13 Create a Route with a Click (or Two)

You can even take Google Maps where the roads don't go.

Driving directions don't always take you where you want to go, or they may take you the wrong way. You can use a little Google Maps hack to build up your own list of points that can be saved in different formats that can be loaded into a GPS or other tool that supports the GPX standard.

The click-to-route tool is at *http://mappinghacks.com/projects/gmaps/ clicktoroute.html*. You click on the map to create a continuous track. An example is shown in Figure 2-9.

Figure 2-9. No roads—only walkers, horses, and bikes here!

Once you've created your route, click on one of the Export buttons. Clicking on CSV (Comma Separated Values) generates a pure-text file with the latitude and longitude separated with commas. GPX Track makes a GPX Tracklog file. GPX Route generates a set of points that can be loaded into a GPS. Here is a sample of the route as a CSV file:

```
38.4047068183193, -122.84743666648865
38.4041771393969, -122.84764051437378
38.403941725296505, -122.84796237945557
```

And here is an example of a GPX Tracklog:

```
<?xml version="1.0"?>
<gpx>
<trk><name>Google Maps Hacks is Good</name>
<trkseg>
<trkpt lat="38.41324840580697" lon="-122.84113883972168"></trkpt>
<trkpt lat="38.402688973080245" lon="-122.82877922058105"></trkpt>
<trkpt lat="38.4049085997449" lon="-122.84637451171875"></trkpt>
</trkseg>
</trk>
</gpx>
```

Many GPS units have a limit on the number of points that can be used in a route. This GPSBabel command will simplify your list of points to 30.

```
gpsbabel -r -i gpx -f route.gpx \
    -x simplify,count=30 -o gpx \
    -F shorter_route.gpx
```

See "Load Driving Directions into Your GPS" [Hack #35] for more on reducing the number of points and loading a route file into your GPS.

The Code

This hack is almost identical to "How Far Is That? Go Beyond Driving Directions" [Hack #12], with the addition of one function that generates the formatted list of points, and buttons to call this function. The buttons are inserted with this HTML code:

```
<input type="button" value="Export CSV" onClick="exportPoints('csv'); ">
<input type="button" value="Export GPX Track"
onClick="exportPoints('track'); ">
<input type="button" value="Export GPX Route"
onClick="exportPoints('route'); ">
```

The onClick event is set to call the exportPoints function with a parameter to set the format of the exported points. This example shows the exportPoints function with the code for the GPX exports removed. The GPX format is simple XML, and that clutters up the example.

```
function exportPoints(format) {
    var export_string;
    if (format=='csv') {
        //csv header
        export_string = export_string + "latitude, longitude\n";
    }

    for (i = 0; i < x_array.length; i++) {
        var lon = x_array[i];
        var lat = y_array[i];
        if (format=='csv') {
```

```
                    export_string = export_string +  lat + ", " + lon + "\n";
                }
            }

            // write into document
            document.getElementById("output").value=export_string;
        }
```

The results of your selected route will appear in a textarea below the map. You may need to scroll down to see the list. You can select the whole text area and paste it into your own document. Once you have a list of points to map back on Google Maps [Hack #37], export the points to your GPS [Hack #35], and even calculate driving directions between the points [Hack #36].

You can also use this technique to plan a trip or to explore more about a trip you took without a GPS (or a trip where the GPS didn't work because the darn satellite signals wouldn't penetrate the steel canyons of the city).

HACK #14 Create Custom Map Markers

Adding custom markers to your Google Map can enhance its readability and appeal.

Almost immediately after the Google Maps API announcement, Jeff Warren made a hack that used custom icons to do a map depicting Star Wars ATATs attacking Google's home town, Palo Alto, as shown in Figure 2-10. You can launch your own Imperial assault on Google's home base at *http://www.vestaldesign.com/maps/starwars.html*.

This hack immediately demonstrated the flexibility of Google's new API. If you wanted to use a house icon instead of the generic marker, you could. Likewise, if you wanted to make a multiplayer game using Google Maps, the API was flexible enough to allow you to let users submit their own icons.

To create an icon, you need two things: a foreground image for the icon and a shadow image in the PNG 24-bit file format. If you are only changing the color of the generic marker, you can reuse the generic shadow, but for this hack we're going to make something completely different.

Find the Right Foreground Image

Instead of doing something generic and boring, I decided to take a headshot of a friend of mine and turn it into a Google Maps marker icon! I grabbed a suitable shot from a digital photo, loaded it into Adobe Photoshop, and started erasing, as shown in Figure 2-11. About halfway through, I could tell this was going to make a great foreground image.

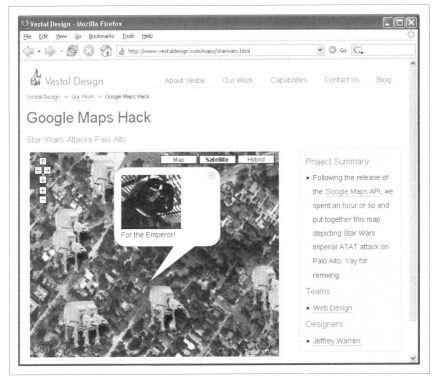

Figure 2-10. You too can send Imperial ATATs to attack Google's headquarters

If you're not into commercial software, the GNU Image Manipulation Program, or GIMP, offers an open source alternative with the same basic features. You can find the GIMP at *http://www.gimp.org/*.

Once I finished erasing around Karl's head, I scaled down the image, cropped it, and expanded the canvas to give Karl's head some breathing room. I wouldn't want him to get claustrophobic, and when we start working on the shadow, we're going to need a bit of extra room. You can see the finished result in Figure 2-12.

Finally, I went to the File → Save for Web option, and saved my file in the PNG-24 format with transparency. 24-bit PNG format is ideal for custom map icons, because it's lossless and the alpha layer support allows for some wonderful transparency effects.

Casting the Shadow

Now that you have the foreground image saved, you might want to show it on your map right away—but don't run ahead yet. We're going to want to reuse

Figure 2-11. Erasing around the head to create the foreground image

our work to create a shadow image. This is an image that gets placed behind the foreground image to give it that 3D effect, like it's sitting on top of the surface of your map. Using a shadow is optional, but it gives your custom markers more depth and character. This step is a little more complicated, but definitely worth your time.

Here's the rundown, again from Adobe Photoshop:

1. Image → Adjustments → Brightness/Contrast

   Set both the Brightness and Contrast to -100.

2. Edit → Free Transform

   Adjust the layer to exactly half its original height by grabbing the top line and dragging down.

3. Edit → Transform → Skew

   Grab the top line and drag to the right to skew the image 45 degrees.

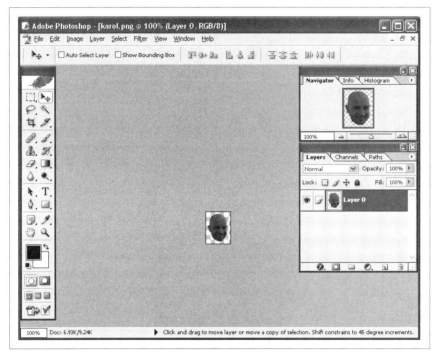

Figure 2-12. The final version of the foreground image

4. Image → Canvas Size

   Adjust the canvas so that it fits your new drop shadow. Give it a bit of extra room so nothing gets cut off.

5. Filters → Blur → Gaussian Blur

   This will give your shadow that fuzzy look. Try setting it to 0.9.

6. Layer → Layer Style → Blending Options → Fill Opacity

   Make the shadow transparent, so it doesn't look like a big black blob. Set the Fill Opacity to about 50%.

7. File → Save for Web

   Remember to keep it a 24-bit PNG file with Transparency.

Figure 2-13 shows the finished shadow layer for the icon.

Add Your New Icon to a Map

Now that the two source images have been created, let's add them to your map. If we were making a generic marker, we would create an instance of the GMarker class, using a GPoint object as an argument. To create a custom marker on the other hand, we need to add an additional argument to the

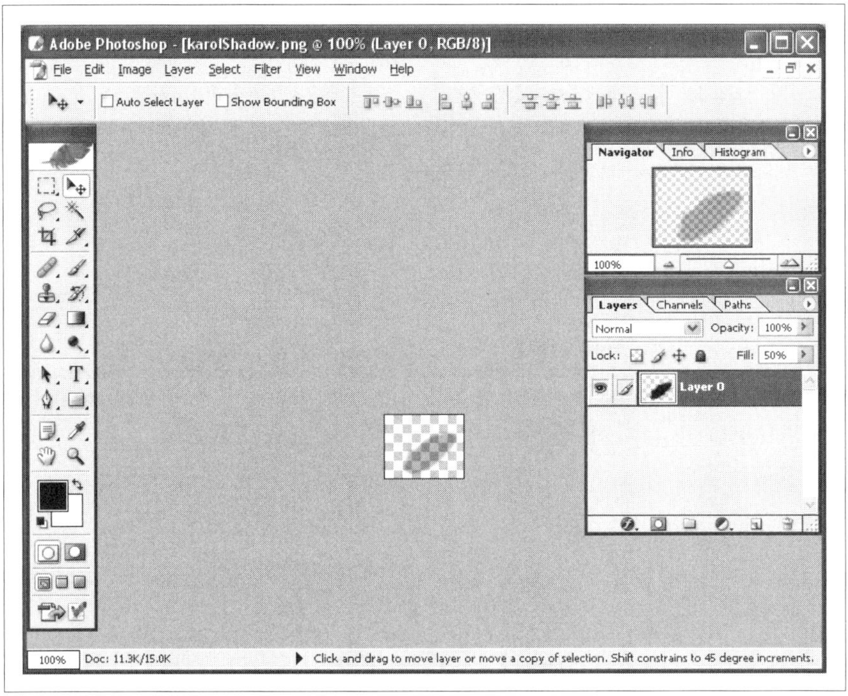

Figure 2-13. The head has a shadowy background

GMarker constructor, a GIcon object. Here is an example of how to use the GIcon constructor:

```
var icon = new GIcon( );
icon.image = "http://igargoyle.com/mapfiles/karol.png";
icon.shadow = "http://igargoyle.com/mapfiles/karolShadow.png";
icon.iconSize = new GSize(43, 55);
icon.shadowSize = new GSize(70, 55);
icon.iconAnchor = new GPoint(0, 0);
icon.infoWindowAnchor = new GPoint(9, 2);
icon.infoShadowAnchor = new GPoint(18, 25);
```

The GSize object holds the size of your image. In this case, icon.image has a width of 43 pixels and a height of 55 pixels. The corresponding icon.shadow has a width of 70 pixels and is 55 pixels high. Specifying these image dimensions are critical, because if you don't, your photo will end up being distorted.

The iconAnchor property stores the point on the icon, relative to the top left corner of our icon image, where it should be anchored to the map. The infoWindowAnchor property is similar, except it specifies the anchor point on the image of the information window. Finally, the infoShadowAnchor indicates where the drop shadow below the info window should be anchored under your marker. If your icon is shaped like the standard Ride Finder icons, you can leave it as it is; otherwise, you should use your image editor to figure out where these points lie on your custom icon.

Finally, to add this to a new marker, you need to use the GMarker constructor with the GIcon as an extra argument.

```
var marker = new GMarker(point, icon);
map.addOverlay(marker);
```

Figure 2-14 shows our custom map icon on a satellite map showing Burning Man.

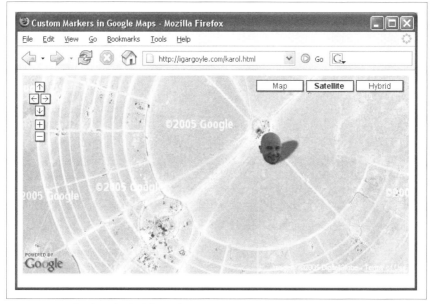

Figure 2-14. The disembodied flying heads all swarm to Burning Man

So now that you know how to create an icon with both a foreground image and a shadow, break out your artistic skills and make your map uniquely different. You can make it look professional, stylish, or even silly, like I did. The message *your* map communicates will be all the stronger for it.

See Also

- Find some good, free, generic icons at *http://brennan.offwhite.net/blog/archives/000211.html.*

—Tom Longson

Map a Slideshow of Your Travels

#15 Show your friends and family not just what you saw on your vacation, but where you saw it.

Wouldn't it be cool to be able to show your friends and family not only what you saw on your vacation, but also where each photo was taken? Thanks to Google Maps' simple API, you can very easily make a slideshow to put on your web site.

Travelogue slideshows are as old as the film slide projector itself. The Google Maps API and a dab of JavaScript can dust off the ancient tradition, and show off the places you've been with an amazing amount of detail. What's more, little touches like the API's animated map panning function lend a sense of motion to the story of your travels. Figure 2-15 shows a slideshow I put together of my vacation last year to the Burning Man Festival in Black Rock City, Nevada. This slideshow can also be seen online at *http:// igargoyle.com/slideshow.html*.

Figure 2-15. Make a slideshow that will captivate your friends and family

For my map, I took the photos from Black Rock City and added titles and descriptions for each image to better tell the story of my trip. Since my relatives live on the other side of the world, this makes it very easy for me to update them about what's going on in my life—and show off photos without having to lob off enormous emails, stuffed with unreadable attachments.

To get started, you're going to need photos, each with its own latitude and longitude coordinates. The easiest way to do this is by bringing along a GPS when you photograph, and mark each image with a waypoint or write the location on a notepad. If you're interested in doing large batches of photos, pick up a copy of O'Reilly's *Mapping Hacks* and learn more about cross-referencing GPX tracklogs with the EXIF timestamp of digital photographs. alternatively, you can adapt the technique described in "Where Did the User Click?" [Hack #11], and use your memory and a few map clicks to find the coordinates of where your photos were taken.

The Code

However you assemble the metadata for your photographs, you'll wind up with a JavaScript object that probably looks like this:

```
var myObj = {"photos": [
        {"img": "http://igargoyle.com/theman.jpg",
         "longitude": "-119.236402821", "latitude": "40.754786911",
         "title": "Black Rock City: 2005",
         "description": "A Playa Slideshow using Google Maps. Just email
this to your friends, and when it loads, it will start playing
automatically."},
        {"img": "http://igargoyle.com/hammockhangout.jpg",
         "longitude": "-119.233165", "latitude": "40.7590351",
         "title": "The Hammock Hangout",
         "description": "A GIANT tent that uses passive solar principles to
stay cool during the day. Housed 50 hammocks, and had room for people to set
up their own too."},
        {"img": "http://igargoyle.com/us.jpg",
         "longitude": "-119.246943567", "latitude": "40.752424806",
         "title": "Some of the gang in camp ROAMnet",
         "description": "Karl, Jay, Jana, and Nym."},
        ]
};
```

To set up the timers for these slides, we can access the data array like so:

```
for (i = 0; i < myObj.photos.length; i++) {
    img = myObj.photos[i].img;
    longitude = myObj.photos[i].longitude;
    latitude = myObj.photos[i].latitude;
    title = myObj.photos[i].title;
    description = myObj.photos[i].description;

    loadPhoto(img, longitude, latitude, i, title, description);
}
```

The loadPhoto function takes these arguments and creates an anonymous function that calls the browser's built-in window.setTimeout function. This is the most important part of the hack because it tells the function to run at a certain time, specified in milliseconds. In this function, 10000 * time calculates the time for each photo, so the first photo loads immediately, the second photo loads after 10 seconds, the third photo loads after 20 seconds, and so on.

```
function loadPhoto(photoURL, longitude, latitude, time, title, description)
{
    // A simple timer, which delays the creation of the new
    // marker, changes the photo, and recenters the map.
    window.setTimeout( function( ) {
        // Create and place a marker for the photograph's location
        var marker = new GMarker(new GPoint(longitude, latitude));
        map.addOverlay(marker);

        // Change the titleBox and descriptionBox to reflect the
        // new photo's title and description
        document.getElementById("titleBox").innerHTML = title;
        document.getElementById("descriptionBox").innerHTML = description;

        // Change the src location of the photo element to the new location.
        document.getElementById("photo").src = photoURL;

        // Have our Google Map recenter or pan to the new location
        map.recenterOrPanToLatLng(new GPoint(longitude, latitude));
    }, 10000 * time); // Change 10000 to speed up or slow down the
slideshow.
}
```

The function inside the setTimeout does all the real work, though. To begin with, it creates the marker for your photo using the GMarker constructor, and then a call to the map's addOverlay function. Secondly, this function displays the title and description on the page by calling each container and setting its respective innerHTML properties. Next, the function changes the source location of the only img element on our page to that of the current photo. Once all this is done, the map is re-centered on the new marker by using a call to the map's recenterOrPanToLatLong method. In my example, I made sure the points were close enough together to cause the map to pan instead of re-center, because it's great to see the map glide from one location to another.

A slideshow is a wonderful way to captivate your audience and tell a story. So get out there and make something truly wonderful that your family and friends will remember for years to come!

See Also

- This hack shows the relative ease in setting up a slideshow with Google Maps, but it also has the potential to offer an even richer experience. Try making the markers clickable or give each markers its own custom icon [Hack #64]. The slideshow concept can also be integrated with photos stored on Flickr [Hacks #47 and #48].

—*Tom Longson*

How Big Is the World?

If you wanted to make your own Google Maps server, how much hard drive space would you need?

Google Maps renders maps by stitching small images together. We seek to discover the storage capacity of such an image repository. By capturing and examining screenshots of Google Maps in action, we can estimate the map scale at each zoom level, which will give us an idea of how much space is necessary to store all the tiles for that zoom level. Finally, we can add the storage requirements for each zoom level and apply some simple rules of thumb to arrive at an idea of how much hard drive space is necessary to support a web mapping service such as Google Maps.

Economies of Scale

First, we need to discover the scaling factors used at each of the fifteen zoom steps. To accomplish this analysis, we use a tool called Art Director's Toolkit, which comes bundled with Mac OS X and which offers an overlay desktop ruler image for measuring pixel distances onscreen. In zoom levels 0 to 6, we measure the pixel length between the northeast corner of Colorado and the southeast corner of Wyoming. This distance is clearly marked on the map as a horizontal line, which makes measuring it easy. Figure 2-16 depicts zoom levels 0, 1, and 2, where the distances in question are 12, 24, and 48 pixels, respectively.

Figure 2-16. Zoom levels 0 through 2

In Figure 2-17, we see that, for zoom levels 3, 4, and 5, the same distances are 98, 196, and 394 pixels.

For zoom level 6, the distance between the northeast corner of Colorado and the southeast corner of Wyoming measures out at 790 pixels. Zoom level 7 was skipped because there was nothing to measure for it—smaller things were too small, and bigger things were too big. (Skipping it did not negatively impact the analysis.)

Figure 2-17. Zoom levels 3 through 5

In zoom levels 8 through 14, we measure the pixel length of the path from the intersection of Trenton Street and East 16th Avenue to the intersection of Verbena Street and East 16th Avenue in Denver, Colorado, which is within the metropolitan area closest to our previous locations. For zoom level 8, the distance is 9 pixels. For zoom levels 9, 10, and 11, the distances are 19, 37, and 74 pixels. The results are shown in Figure 2-18.

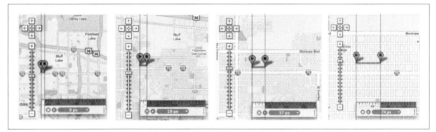

Figure 2-18. Zoom levels 8 through 11

For zoom levels 12, 13, and 14, the distances are 147, 295, and 590 pixels. Figure 2-19 depicts this measurement.

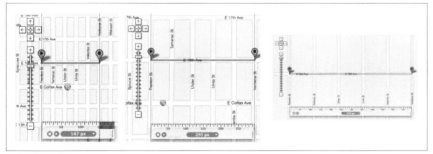

Figure 2-19. Zoom levels 12 through 14

Now we can take the information from these measurements, and attempt to establish the numeric scale ratio between one zoom level and the previous one. Figure 2-20 presents the same relationships in three nicely formatted line graphs and Table 2-1 summarizes the data we collected.

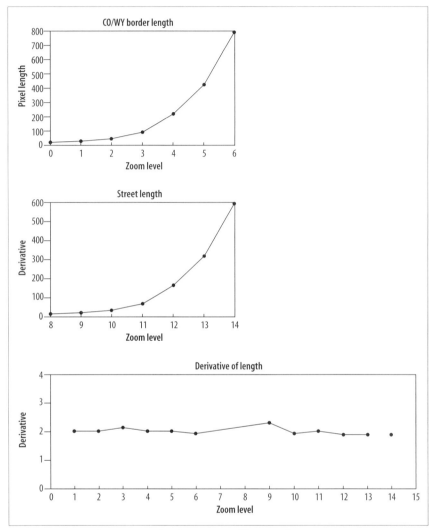

Figure 2-20. Length ratios visualized in a series of line graphs

The conclusion we draw is that we can be fairly certain that the scale doubles with every increment of the zoom bar.

Table 2-1. Length ratios from one zoom level to the previous zoom level

Zoom	State border length	Ratio	Zoom	Street length	Ratio
0	12	n/a	8	8	n/a
1	24	2	9	19	2.38

Table 2-1. Length ratios from one zoom level to the previous zoom level (continued)

Zoom	State border length	Ratio	Zoom	Street length	Ratio
2	48	2	10	37	1.95
3	98	2.04	11	74	2
4	196	2	12	147	1.99
5	394	2	13	295	2.01
6	790	2.01	14	590	2

So, How Much?

By zooming almost all the way out in Google Maps, we see that North America fits nicely in a 600×800–pixel rectangular region, amounting to 480,000 pixels. Armed with this approximation, we proceed to estimate the pixel-area of this body at each zoom level. Table 2-2 depicts these relationships.

Table 2-2. Approximate area in pixels of North America for each zoom level

Zoom	Scale	Width	Height	Area in pixels
0	1	800	600	480,000
1	2	1,600	1,200	1,920,000
2	4	3,200	2,400	7,680,000
3	8	6,400	4,800	30,720,000
4	16	12,800	9,600	122,880,000
5	32	25,600	19,200	491,520,000
6	64	51,200	38,400	1,966,080,000
7	128	102,400	76,800	7,864,320,000
8	256	204,800	153,600	31,457,280,000
9	512	409,600	307,200	125,829,120,000
10	1,024	819,200	614,400	503,316,480,000
11	2,048	1,638,400	1,228,800	2,013,265,920,000
12	4,096	3,276,800	2,457,600	8,053,063,680,000
13	8,192	6,553,600	4,915,200	32,212,254,720,000
14	16,384	13,107,200	9,830,400	128,849,018,880,000

If we add up the areas, we find that 171,798,691,680,000 (171 trillion) pixels are needed to store all the bitmap information. Since all maps are made up of 256×256 tiles, one can venture to guess that there are 171,798,691,680,000 ÷ (256 × 256) = 2,621,439,997 (2.6 billion) potential tile files.

The color histogram of the maps in Figure 2-19 shows that about 60 percent of it is water. Assuming that Google observes such statistics, we guess that a single tile is used for all water regions. There are also lots of regions (such as tundra, deserts, and forests) where uniformly colored tiles can be used. Computing this accurately is difficult, but we will say it amounts to 10 percent of the data. So, only 30 to 40 percent of the tiles have unique data on them. This reduces the amount of data to 50 to 70 trillion raw data pixels stored in 750 million to 1 billion image files. Assuming a modest 1 byte per 6 pixels compression ratio (for LZW-encoded GIF format images), the storage required might be 50 to 70 trillion pixels * (1 byte/6 pixels) = 8 to 11 terabytes. If we consider that Google supports three map types at present (Map, Satellite, and Hybrid), this suggests that 24 to 33 terabytes are needed to store all the image data.

What About the Rest of the World?

Since we did our original analysis, Google Maps UK, Google Maps Japan, and Google Earth were introduced, providing further evidence of a lofty goal to create a world atlas. So this puny analysis (as compared to the world's topology and architectural landmark data necessary for Google Earth), makes an attempt at covering the whole earth with tiles. To do this, we must learn more about the world. The *CIA World Factbook* provides just what we need.

To wrap the world requires 510 million km² of surface. Of this, only 29.2%, or 147 million square kilometers, is land. North America's surface area is about 21.4 million square kilometers (9.9 for Canada, 9.6 for the United States, and 1.9 for Mexico) or 13.6% of the world's total land surface area.

We concluded from our analysis that covering North America requires somewhere between 750,000 and 1 billion distinct tiles to be fully described. Now we know that this is only 13.6% of the tiles necessary to describe the world's land tiles. So, anywhere from 5.5 to 7 billion distinct tiles ought to cover the world's surface area. Assuming the compression ratio described above, the world's tiles amount to 61 to 81 terabytes just for the rendered vector maps, and *182 to 243 terabytes* for all three map types. That's a lot of data—but then storing and retrieving huge amounts of data *is* Google's stock in trade!

 Since this was written, Google has added three more zoom levels to Google Maps, for a total of 18! The extra math is left as an exercise for the interested reader.

In some ways, it seems a bit comical to attempt such a calculation where every step of the way requires an approximation. That's why in the end we have such a wide chasm of error. And, of course, this rough analysis does not cover area distortion introduced by mapping the globe's points onto a two dimensional surface. However, even with this rough estimate, we think we've managed to get a decent sense of just what it takes to map the entire world in the style that Google Maps has pioneered.

—*Michal Guerquin and Zach Frazier*

## CHAPTER THREE

Mashing Up Google Maps
Hacks 17–28

In music, when you create a new song by taking the melody from one song and the lyrics from another, it is called a *mashup*. A lot of times things go poorly, but now and then the results are stunning. What happens when you take pieces from two web sites and mix them together? You get a Web 2.0 mashup.

The Web is moving from a collection of disconnected web sites to a ubiquitous computing platform. This new reality is often referred to as *Web 2.0*. In the beginning, we had static web sites with a few links between them. This evolved into dynamic content and data-driven sites. The next step has been using the web as a platform.

eBay is a useful site for buying and selling trinkets, trash, or treasure. In that role, it is what might be called "Web 1.5." But eBay is also a platform. There is a whole ecology that has built up around eBay that uses the platform in ways that were not initially intended by the programmers.

Amazon and Google Search have also become platforms. Amazon, eBay, and Google (not to mention Flickr, del.icio.us, and many more) have created public Application Programming Interfaces (APIs) that allow anyone to mix and match information from one site with information from another.

The missing piece in the ecology of open web APIs has been location. Nearly everything we do, on the Web or off, has a location. Everything we touch, write about, read, think, or work on has to happen somewhere. Everything has a geospatial component. Perhaps the geospatial component of some things is irrelevant. Do you really care where you were when you remembered to add dish soap to your shopping list?

Yes! We are the species that looks for patterns, and where we are, and where we have been, is one of the strongest sources of pattern in our lives! We are able to learn huge amounts from rooting through other people's trash, er, treasure—and we can learn similar amounts by analyzing the debris of our passing as recorded in position.

At the Where 2.0 conference in San Francisco in June of 2005, Tim O'Reilly explained his fascination with Paul Rademacher's Housing Maps site (*http:// www.housingmaps.com*), described in "Find a Place to Live" [Hack #23]: "Google Maps with Craigslist is the first true Web 2.0 application, as neither of the sites was involved....A developer put it together. Hackers are teaching the industry what to do."

Google Maps brought location into the world of open APIs, and the results have been stunning! The result brilliantly demonstrates the elegance of the Web 2.0 concept—a brave new world in which hackers can combine open standards and open APIs in novel ways to create new sites and services that fill a need or are sometimes just plain cool.

Mixing it up with data or code from multiple sites is the heart of the Web 2.0 experience. These mashups are leading the way to a Web that allows each of us to author our unique experiences of the Web, and to share those experiences with others.

In this chapter we explore just a few of the nearly countless Google Maps mashups that have come into existence in just a few months.

HACK #17   Map the News
See where it happened with BBC News and Google Maps.

Human beings have spent most of their time in small groups of 100-odd individuals, and our information-processing abilities came from those experiences, not from our current world. If we want to keep track of disturbances in Denmark, fog in Finland, elections in Istanbul, and war all over, we need tools to help us: assisted cognition.

At *http://boneill.ninjagrapefruit.com/wp-content/bbc/newmaps/* you can see the locations associated with the last 12 hours of BBC news, as shown in Figure 3-1. As with most cartographic efforts, there is the nearly inevitable, but still regrettable, focus on just one place—so the last 12 hours of BBC news will generally be more interesting if you prefer news of the British Isles.

Clicking on the markers brings up an information window like that shown in Figure 3-2. This includes the lead from the story, as well as date and time information and a link to the full story. As we can see, human interest and soft news can make an appearance!

This hack is possible because, well, the BBC rocks. They have decided that their responsibility to the public trust means they need to open their content to the public. See *http://backstage.bbc.co.uk/* for data and ideas so that

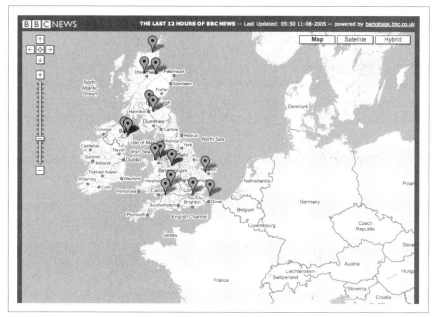

Figure 3-1. Geolocations for the last 12 hours of BBC News

Figure 3-2. Not all geolocated news is created equal

you can "build what *you* want using BBC content." This is the heart of the Web 2.0 concept—the idea that open APIs and open formats allow us to make more use of and draw richer connections between the vast amounts of information that are already out there on the Internet.

In 2003, the BBC announced plans to open their archives of radio and television programs for non-commercial use. Its intent is good, but sadly there are issues that must be worked out. Ben Hammersley wrote a stirring call to action for the Guardian at *http://www.guardian.co.uk/online/story/0,,1522351,00.html.*

The archive, Ben writes, "is a vault of the most important public culture of the past three generations. It is a gift for the future that is so far-sighted, and so much a good thing, that it is the duty of the BBC and, especially, the government to follow through."

What's more, "[d]igital technology not only makes the Creative Archive possible, but by doing so makes it a moral imperative." Mapping the news is an example of something we can do now, with just the textual content. Imagine the possibilities of geocoded audio and video!

As Ben's article concludes, "Now that we can, we must."

HACK #18 Examine Patterns of Criminal Activity

Augment your local government's crime reports with Google Maps.

Chicagocrime.org (*http://www.chicagocrime.org/*), one of the original Google Maps hacks, is a freely browsable database of crimes reported in Chicago. It combines data that was screen scraped from the Chicago Police Department's Web site (*http://12.17.79.6/*) with Google Maps, enabling many new ways for Chicago residents to keep tabs on their neighborhoods and explore crimes reported throughout their city. The site lets you browse crime reports in many ways: crime type, street name, date, police district/ beat, ZIP Code, city ward, and generic "location" (e.g., bowling alley, bar, gas station). Figure 3-3 shows a rash of peeping toms around residential Chicago, while Figure 3-4 shows the locations for bogus check reports. There's also a City map page at *http://www.chicagocrime.org/map/* that lets you combine search criteria.

Figure 3-3. The most recent reports of illegal surveillance activity in Chicago

Figure 3-4. The most likely places to find bogus checks in Chicago

I developed Chicagocrime.org over a month's worth of nights and weekends in April 2005. Having gotten excited by the recently launched (at that time) Google Maps site, I spent a few evenings digging around Google's JavaScript and trying to embed custom maps into my own pages. After some hacking, I was able to display a custom map successfully. With my hacked-together map framework in place, it was just a matter of screen scraping the CPD's web site, geocoding each crime, and displaying the data. After Google released its official API at the end of June 2005, I updated Chicagocrime.org to make use of it.

Adding Ward and ZIP Code Boundaries

Aside from displaying a custom Google Map with relevant crime data on almost every page, Chicagocrime.org uses the Google Maps API in a couple of innovative ways. One way of navigating crime data is by police district. Because some residents of Chicago may not know their assigned districts, I created a "Find your beat and district" feature—*http://www.chicagocrime. org/districts/*—that helps people figure out which police beat and district they live in. It's simple to use: just pan and zoom the map to center it on a location, then click "Guess district."

It's simple under the hood, too. When a user clicks "Guess district," a bit of JavaScript calculates the center longitude and latitude of the current map view and sends that through a JavaScript XMLHttpRequest to a server-side script. The server code, written in Python and Django (*http://www.djangoproject.com*), uses a spatial query against PostGIS, a set of spatial extensions to PostgreSQL, to determine which district contains the given point. Finally, it passes the answer back to the site's JavaScript in your browser.

 You can find out more about PostGIS at *http://postgis. refractions.net/*. O'Reilly's *Web Mapping Illustrated* offers a good tutorial on PostGIS, as well.

Similarly, Chicagocrime.org lets you navigate crimes by city ward, and there's a "Find your ward" feature on the ward page: *http://www. chicagocrime.org/wards/*. For ward and ZIP Code pages, chicagocrime.org uses the Google Maps polyline-drawing API to draw the border for the given ward or ZIP Code on the map. I did this by obtaining the ward and ZIP Code boundaries in ESRI Shapefile format from the City of Chicago's GIS department at *http://www.cityofchicago.org/gis/*. I loaded the shapefiles into a PostgreSQL database and converted the data into longitude-latitude coordinates using the conversion functions in PostGIS. Finally, it was just a matter of feeding the points into the Google Maps polyline-drawing API, and *voila*: we have ward and ZIP Code borders.

See Also

- Rendering arbitrary GIS vector data on Google Maps is an interesting and still evolving subject. "How Big Is That, Exactly?" **[Hack #28]** involves rendering vector data from GIS sources on top of Google Maps.

—Adrian Holovaty

HACK #19 Map Local Weather Conditions
Find out whether there's weather where you are.

It's a well-known fact that everyone likes to talk about the weather, yet no one ever seems to do anything about it. Seriously, though, whenever two strangers meet and make small talk, it's inevitable that the recent meteorological conditions will make an appearance in the conversation. The state of the weather outside today, whatever it turns out to be, is something we all have in common—we're all obliged to endure it or enjoy it—at least, those of us that go out of doors.

The Situation Outside Is...

Naturally, it didn't take long for someone to set up a Google Maps site devoted to tracking the weather—and we don't just mean any old weather, we mean detailed weather data, including temperature, wind speed and direction, relative humidity, and daily rainfall. Dave Schorr's Google Weather Maps site, at *http://www.weatherbonk.com/*, collects meteorological data aggregated by Weather Underground and Weatherbug from thousands of personal weather stations across the world, and then plots that information in a rich Google Maps interface on the Web.

Figure 3-5 shows the default view of *weatherbonk.com*, centered on San Francisco, California. If, as chance would most likely have it, you're not in San Francisco, you can start by entering your location in the search box at the top of the page. Valid location styles take the form **city, state**, or **city, country**. U.S. ZIP Codes also work. In addition, you can overlay points from multiple locations by separating each query with a semicolon (;). For example, entering 33010;33446 will give you points along the southeast coast of Florida.

> While a good number of international cities come up with results, you may need to be careful about what you type in here; for example, typing in "London, UK" returns nothing, while "London, England" returns what you would expect.
>
> Also, at the time of this writing, Google only has detailed street maps for the U.S., U.K., Canada, and Japan. If you see broken image links in the background of the map, Google has not yet created street maps for your area. In this case, keep zooming out until the map appears, and/or click the Satellite button on the map to switch to the satellite view.

As you can see from Figure 3-6, the Weatherbonk.com site uses dynamically generated marker icons to convey a great deal of information at once. Each one of the weather station markers plotted on the map is color-coded according to the local temperature, ranging from blue (coldest) to red (hottest). Also, the temperature reading is displayed on the markers themselves, in either degrees Fahrenheit or Celsius, at your option.

If present, a spike extending from a marker points into the prevailing wind direction—i.e., toward the wind, not away from it—while the number of ticks shown on the spike indicates the observed wind speed, ranging from no ticks, representing a wind speed of under 4 mph, up to four ticks, indicating winds of 16 mph or more. Additionally, a marker may contain an icon illustrating other current conditions, such as sunshine, overcast, or rain. A key to these markers is shown at the bottom right corner of the page.

Clicking on any of the markers opens an info window with the details for that weather station, as shown in Figure 3-6. If the station is affiliated with Weather Underground, temperature, wind speed and direction, and relative humidity are shown. Below these readings, you'll see a graph illustrating the 24-hour history for both temperature and dew point. The title at the top of the info window is linked to the homepage of the maintainer of that particular station.

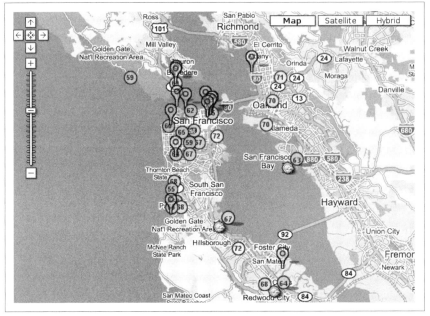

Figure 3-5. The default view, showing the current conditions in San Francisco

The *dew point*, in case you're wondering, is the temperature at which the water vapor in the air begins to condense into liquid water. Relative humidity, which is what's shown in the info windows, is calculated from a combination of ambient temperature and dew point. Frosty drinks on a hot day often lower the temperature of the air immediately around them to a level below the dew point, which is why a layer of condensation forms on the outside of the glass.

By contrast, a Weatherbug-affiliated station shows an info window with a daily rainfall figure, in place of the historical graph. Some Weatherbug stations also have webcams, which are shown in the info window, if present. Weatherbug stations aren't shown on the map by default—you need to select the Weatherbug checkbox at the top of the page and then click the Update Map button at the top right of the map.

Other, not necessarily weather related, webcams can be shown on the map as well. Select the Webcams checkbox at the top of the page, if it isn't already selected, and then click Update Map. These locations, which are often educational institutions, are identified on the map by transparent markers. As you'd expect, clicking on a webcam icon opens an info window showing the current image from that location.

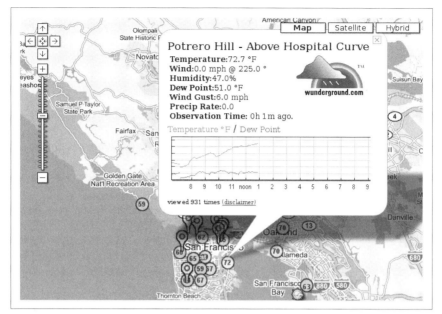

Figure 3-6. Weather station details are shown in an info window

> The info windows shown on the map can often be quite large, what with all the weather information and webcam images they include. One result of this is that the X button used to close the info window can occasionally wind up obscured by other things on the map. Fear not—you can always close an open info window by clicking on the associated marker a second time.

More Than Just the Weather

The Weatherbonk.com site supports some other interesting features. On the right side of the map, you can select various sources of radar data, to depict cloud cover on the map. Additionally, under the Google Earth section of the page, you can access different sources of cloud radar imagery in KML format, for use with Google Earth.

From the standpoint of Google Maps, however, the most interesting additional features are the three map control buttons at the top right corner of the map, immediately below the map type control. These buttons are labeled Zoom Box, Clear Points, and Update Map. The Clear Points button wipes all the markers off the map, while the Update Map button loads new data from the server, which can be handy if you zoom or pan the map to view a different area.

The Zoom Box feature is particularly nifty and bears a bit of explanation. If you hold down Shift-Z, and then left-click and drag your mouse across the map, a red box appears and follows your mouse drag. Releasing the left mouse button causes the map to zoom into the area within the red box, which can be quite handy for drilling down to a particular local region. Clicking Update Map after you've used the zoom box feature can sometimes reveal weather stations that weren't shown on the larger area map, as the site tries to avoid crowding the map with too many points at any given zoom level. Also, you don't actually need to click the Zoom Box button before using this feature—the button itself doesn't do anything useful, beyond displaying helpful instructions in an alert window.

Microclimates and Distributed Weather Reporting

Like so many other things, the Internet has made it possible for weather reporting to be distributed among many people on a ground-up basis, rather than centralized in a top-down fashion, as it traditionally has been. One thing that this decentralization makes possible is witnessing for yourself the striking variety of weather conditions in an area with lots of microclimates, like the San Francisco Bay Area. Try it mid- to late-afternoon Pacific Time (GMT -7 during the Daylight Savings Time, GMT -8 otherwise), when the fog usually starts to creep in off the ocean, thus cooling some areas, while other places are still clear and warm. To augment this view, try adding the Bay Area fog overlay from the Overlays drop-down on the right side of the page. The differences across an area even as small as San Francisco can sometimes really be quite striking.

See Also

- The Weather Underground site at *http://wunderground.com/* has RSS feeds for weather reports in various metropolitan areas.
- *http://api.weatherbug.com/* is the home for Weatherbug's data access API.
- METAR is a very terse text format used around the world for reporting weather data. You can find out more about METAR, and get live METAR feeds from the U.S. National Weather Service at *http://weather.noaa.gov/weather/metar.shtml.*
- *http://anti-mega.com/weather/* offers a series of (non-georeferenced) RSS-based weather feeds, using data scraped from *worldweather.org.*

—written with assistance from Dave Schorr

Track Official Storm Reporting

Follow the path of the latest hurricane on a Google Map.

Google Map hacking started for me in early March 2005, when I became aware of some of the great hacks that were already being created. My interest was particularly piqued after seeing the beta release of Adrian Holovaty's Chicagocrime.org web site, as described in "Examine Patterns of Criminal Activity" [Hack #18]. I immediately realized the myriad other applications for this new mapping technology. To be more precise, I determined that it would be beneficial to develop a storm-reporting mapping site, which you can visit today at *http://www.stormreportmap.com/*, as shown in Figure 3-7.

Figure 3-7. The weather on Google Maps

You can click on a marker to see more details. For example, Figure 3-8 shows a report of hail in Sioux, Nebraska.

Another interesting feature is the hurricane tracking maps. As shown in Figure 3-9 you can see the tracks of tropical storms.

Clicking on the marker icons gives you more information about the storm at that point. In Figure 3-10, we see that Irene has been bouncing between a tropical storm and a tropical depression.

The data source for the web site is the National Oceanic & Atmospheric Administration's (NOAA) National Weather Service (NWS) Storm Prediction Center (SPC), which can be found online at *http://spc.noaa.gov/*. One of

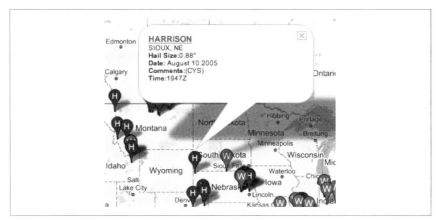

Figure 3-8. Hail in Nebraska

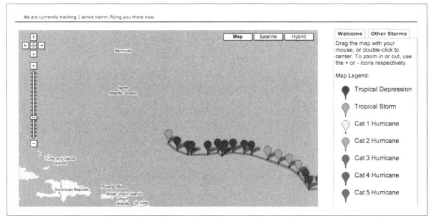

Figure 3-9. Hurricane-tracking maps

the top products that the SPC maintains is their Storm Report tracker at *http://spc.noaa.gov/climo/*. This product takes reports from trained weather spotters, emergency and first responders, and local residents, and then maps them to an unattractive, static page. Moreover, the reports also don't give much in the way of comprehensible locations, aside from latitude/longitude coordinates, and the county and state where the storm was reported. Additionally, since each report is submitted into the database as a separate event, there are times when several tornado reports received are actually all from the same tornado. Due to these shortcomings in the original product, and because of its general popularity, I felt that my project might enhance the product's basic functionality.

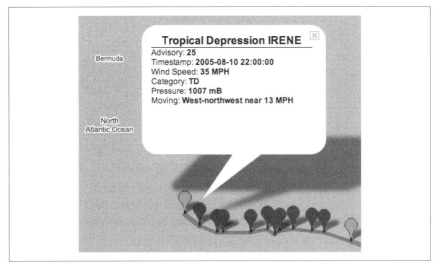

Figure 3-10. Good night, Irene!

Getting the Data

The SPC began collecting storm report data in mid-1999. Unfortunately, they did not begin putting the data into a web-friendly format until early 2004. Therefore, without parsing through three different versions of web sites, the project will only show storm report data from early 2004 on.

The data is obtained through a *Comma Separated Values* (CSV) file that is posted along with each update. This very friendly format allows me to parse through the file, convert it into an array, format it to my liking, and push the contents out as an XML file. If you are getting your data from a third-party site through an XML or RSS feed, it's important to realize that bandwidth often costs money.

Before beginning this project, I realized that obtaining the data I want and in the timeframe I wanted it might present a problem for the remote SPC web site. Our assumptions using information obtained from the site were the following:

- The current day's map is updated every 15 minutes.
- Yesterday's map is updated in 3-hour increments.
- Once a map is more than 2 days old, it is no longer updated.

I couldn't develop a project that would simply leech off the SPC web site's data for every visit to my site—it's disrespectful, lazy, and, most of all *slow*. I determined that the best model would be to use a back-end database to store all the requested data and load the most current data using a series of timestamps.

Here's how the site handles the data refresh when a user visits the site:

1. The site loads the report data for the request.

2. A timestamp indicating when the data was last updated for each day is stored in the database.

3. Since each page load requires that the database load the report data, the site also checks to see when the data was last updated.

4. The site updates today's data, if more than 60 minutes have elapsed between the stored timestamp and the current timestamp.

5. The site updates yesterday's data, if more than 24 hours have elapsed between the stored timestamp and the current timestamp.

6. For historical data, no timestamp checking is done, because the most current data is already loaded, based on previous assumptions.

7. The page displays the data to the user.

This model drastically reduces the traffic and bandwidth sent to the remote SPC web site, and I would recommend using it for any site that uses regularly updated third-party data from remote web sites.

The Hack

When the Google Maps API was finally released, I decided to check out its functionality firsthand. Since the original site was weather related and hurricane season was just beginning to get in the swing of things, a hurricane tracker using the new API was in order.

The Hurricane Track Map uses the Google Maps API to develop a Google Map without jumping through all the hoops that the pre-API XSLT methods required. The catch is that there is quite a bit more JavaScript development that you will need to include. Google has gone to great lengths to try and give enough documentation for a novice developer to get started, but even some veteran programmers have trouble getting it to work correctly.

This code snippet shows just how you can use the GXmlHttp class from the Google Maps API to load XML data from a file on your server. As usual, you cannot retrieve remote files from other sites using AJAX; only files within your domain or host can be loaded, which is another good reason to cache the data in your own database first.

```
var request = GXmlHttp.create( );
request.open("GET", "data.xml", true);
request.onreadystatechange = function( ) {
  if (request.readyState == 4) {
    markers = [];
    points = [];
```

```
        infoHtmls = [];
        categorypoly = [];
        var xmlDoc = request.responseXML;
        var markers = xmlDoc.documentElement.getElementsByTagName("marker");

    // Loop through the XML document and grab the data contained
    // with the tags. Store that data into an array.

        for (var i = 0; i < markers.length; i++) {
            points[i] = new GPoint(parseFloat(markers[i].getAttribute("lng")),
                        parseFloat(markers[i].getAttribute("lat")));
            name = markers[i].getAttribute("name");
            type = markers[i].getAttribute("type");
            advisory = markers[i].getAttribute("advisory");
            timestamp = markers[i].getAttribute("timestamp");
            windspeed = markers[i].getAttribute("windspeed");
            pressure = markers[i].getAttribute("pressure");
            moving = markers[i].getAttribute("moving");
            point = points[i];
    // Append a hurricane category rating on it based on the
    // Wind Speed.
            if (type == "Tropical Depression") {category = "TD";}
            else if (type == "Tropical Storm") {category = "TS";}

            else { // Its a hurricane
                if (windspeed >= 74 && windspeed <= 95) {category = "1";}
                else if (windspeed >= 96 && windspeed <= 110) {category = "2";}
                else if (windspeed >= 111 && windspeed <= 130) {category = "3";}
                else if (windspeed >= 131 && windspeed <= 155) {category = "4";}
                else {category = "5";}
            }
            categorypoly[i] = category;

    // Call to the createMarker function to create the marker
            var marker = createMarker(point, name, type, advisory, timestamp,
                        windspeed, category, pressure, moving);

    // Overlay the markers on the map
            map.addOverlay(marker);
        }
```

The createMarker( ) function is called in order to build the info window for that particular marker. Also, this function assigns a custom icon to the marker, depending on whether the storm is classified as a tropical storm, a tropical depression, or a category 1 through 5 hurricane.

Next, our code adds a polyline to go along with the markers. This is valuable, because hurricane tracks are very unpredictable, and often make loops and turns before they make landfall or get pushed back out to sea.

```
var pointset = [];
// Loop through the array of points created above. Each point, based
```

```
// upon the category it received will receive a line segment color as
// well as the width.
    for (q=0; q < points.length; q++) {
        pointset.push(points[q]);
        if (categorypoly[q] == "TD") {color = "#660099";size = 5;}
        else if (categorypoly[q] == "TS") {color = "#333399";size = 7;}
        else if (categorypoly[q] == "1") {color = "#33FFFF";size = 9;}
        else if (categorypoly[q] == "2") {color = "#33FF66";size = 11;}
        else if (categorypoly[q] == "3") {color = "#FFFF66";size = 13;}
        else if (categorypoly[q] == "4") {color = "#FF9933";size = 15;}
        else {color = "#FF3333";size = 17;}
// Add point to the GPolyline so the map can draw it.
        map.addOverlay(new GPolyline(pointset, color, size));
        pointset = [];
        pointset.push(points[q]);
    }
```

See Also

- See *http://code.stormreportmap.com/* for more source code and references.
- All source code is released under the GNU General Public License. You may use and publish as you wish without any copyright notice being retained or transferred. If you wish to contact me, I can be reached at *webmaster@stormreportmap.com.*

—Anthony Petito

H A C K Track the International Space Station
#21

Track the International Space Station and the Space Shuttle in near-real time.

You can track anything on Google Maps—all you need is a source of data. Tom Mangan created his own site to track the Space Shuttle and International Space Station (ISS) at *http://gmaps.tommangan.us/spacecraft_tracking.html.*

The site tracks the location of the ISS and, when it is in orbit, the Space Shuttle, as shown in Figure 3-11. The excitement can come from being able to spot the Shuttle and ISS from the ground, and in watching on the map as they rendevous. When you first load the page you should get one or two markers, depending on whether the Shuttle is in orbit. If you leave the page open the markers leave a trail of where the ISS and Shuttle have been. Over the course of about 90 minutes (actually, 91.55 minutes for the ISS, according to the Wikipedia page at *http://en.wikipedia.org/wiki/International_Space_Station),* the characteristic sine wave shape of low Earth orbits appears. No, objects in space don't bounce around like tennis balls; this represents the effects of representing a three dimensional orbit onto a flat map. The first rule of cartography is that you always distort something!

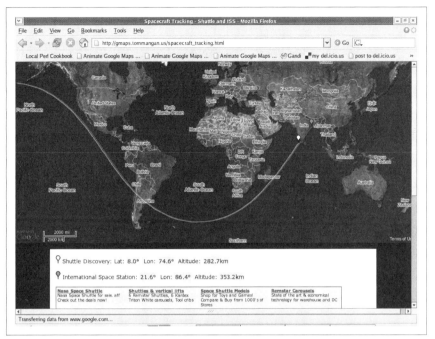

Figure 3-11. Shuttle and ISS tracking, with an amusing note

Google's AdSense ads are often the funniest part of a page. Here we have a link to "NASA Space Shuttle for sale. Check out the deals now!" I don't think I want to buy an affordable spacecraft on eBay! Maybe in a few years.

How It Works

Most of the work happens in the JavaScript in the site's autoUpdate( ) function. autoUpdate( ) is called as soon as the page loads.

```
<body style="background-color: #000; text-align: center;"
    onload="autoUpdate( );">
```

The autoUpdate function uses the GXmlHttp class from Google Maps to fetch the *iss.js* file from the server. You can take a look at the file at *http://gmaps.tommangan.us/iss.js*.

```
-48.6;-11.7;369.8;-51.6;-31.9;291.1
```

This shows the latitude and longitude of the ISS first, and then that of the shuttle. The code reads the file, then splits the results into the array coords with the split method. The rest of the method is housekeeping to do a sanity check on the returned result, then adds the points to the current arrays of results for the Shuttle and ISS.

```
function autoUpdate( ) {
    var request = GXmlHttp.create( );
```

```
    request.open("GET", "iss.js", true);
    request.onreadystatechange = function( ) {
      if (request.readyState == 4) {
        var response = request.responseText;
        coords = response.split(';');
        var valid = (coords[0]&&coords[1]&&coords[3]&&coords[4]
            &&coords[0]>-90&&coords[0]<90&&coords[1]>-180
            &&coords[1]<180&&coords[3]>-90&&coords[3]<90
            &&coords[4]>-180&&coords[4]<180);

        if (valid) {
          map.clearOverlays( );
          var sPoint = new GPoint (coords[4],coords[3]);
          var sMarker = new GMarker (sPoint,pinWhite);
          if (coords[4] < -174) { sTrack=[]; }
          sTrack.push (sPoint);
          map.addOverlay(sMarker);

          var issPoint = new GPoint (coords[1],coords[0]);
          var issMarker = new GMarker (issPoint,pinRed);
          if (coords[1] < -174) { issTrack=[]; }
          issTrack.push (issPoint);
          map.addOverlay(issMarker);

          refreshCoords( );
          drawTrack( );
        }
      }
    }
    request.send(null);
    window.setTimeout ('autoUpdate( )', 60000);
  }
```

The final trick is the last line of autoUpdate( ):

```
    window.setTimeout ('autoUpdate( )', 60000);
```

This tells the window to timeout after 60,000 milliseconds, i.e., one minute. When it times out it calls autoUpdate( ) and starts the cycle again.

There is a script running on the server that queries the NASA site for the current position of the Shuttle and ISS, and then writes that out the *iss.js* file. You can use these same techniques to do dynamic updating of your own maps.

If you are the sort of person who goes in for space shuttle tracking, you'll like a couple of Tom's other projects at *http://gmaps.tommangan.us/*. He has a map that shows the current known locations of all of the SR 71 Blackbirds and aerial photos of Area 51. Both projects use his TPhoto extension to the Google Maps API, which lets you embed your own images within Google Maps [Hack #55].

See Also

- NASA's Satellite Tracking Page, which includes applications to track many different satellites, although not with Google Maps: *http://science.nasa.gov/realtime/*.

Witness the Effects of a Nuclear Explosion

Sometimes a map can reveal truths we'd rather not know.

For over 50 years, the human race has lived under the shadow of the threat of nuclear war. Eric A. Meyer's HYDESim (High-Yield Detonation Effects Simulator) web site, which uses Google Maps in a somewhat novel way to illustrate the blast effects of a nuclear detonation. You can see the results for yourself at *http://meyerweb.com/eric/tools/gmap/hydesim.html*. Figure 3-12 shows the default view, which illustrates the effect of a 150 kiloton explosion at ground level in downtown Manhattan.

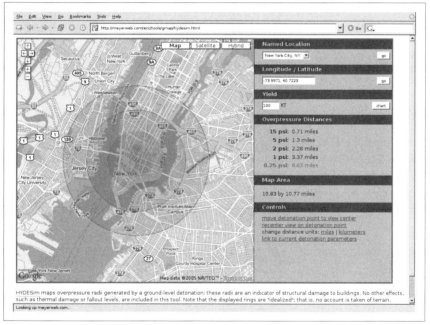

Figure 3-12. Depiction of the blast wave of a 150-kT nuclear explosion in downtown Manhattan

The blast effect of a nuclear explosion is usually reckoned in terms of *overpressure*, which is a measure of how much force is exerted on people and buildings at a given distance away from ground zero. On the map, this is shown as four concentric rings of decreasing intensity, which spread outward from the hypothetical explosion site, representing overpressures of 15 psi, 5 psi, 2 psi, and 1 psi, respectively. The display on the left shows the blast radius for .25 psi overpressure as well, although this ring is not shown on the map.

What exactly do these figures mean, though? The descriptions shown in Table 3-1 are taken from section 5 of the Nuclear Weapons FAQ at *http://nuclearweaponarchive.org/Nwfaq/Nfaq5.html*.

Table 3-1. Destructive effects of atmospheric overpressure

Overpressure	Structural effects	Human injuries
1 psi	Window glass shatters.	Light injuries from fragments occur.
3 psi	Residential structures collapse.	Serious injuries are common, fatalities may occur.
5 psi	Most buildings collapse.	Injuries are universal, fatalities are widespread.
10 psi	Reinforced concrete buildings are severely damaged or demolished.	Most people are killed.
20 psi	Heavily built concrete buildings are severely damaged or demolished.	Fatalities approach 100%.

Although the results are simplified, they sure don't look pretty—at that location and yield, such a nuclear explosion would literally wreck all of downtown Manhattan. What's worse, this map doesn't take the effects of heat or radiation into account. (On the other hand, this map doesn't take the attenuating effects of terrain and weather into account, either.) Although the destructive effects of nuclear weapons are hardly news to anyone, it is still kind of morbidly interesting to be able to see them on a map. Additionally, the site allows you to see the effects on certain other U.S. cities listed in the drop-down box at the upper right, and, if you happen to know the latitude and longitude of a place that particularly interests you, you can enter them into the coordinates box below that.

If you live in the States and don't happen to know the coordinates of, say, your hometown, you can look up a specific address on the Geocoder.US web site at *http://geocoder.us/*.

Finally, you can adjust the yield of the hypothetical explosion, which is measured in kilotons of TNT. By experimenting, we can see that a 1 megaton nuclear explosion over the Brooklyn Bridge would destroy most of Manhattan, Queens, and Brooklyn. Fortunately, these high-yield nukes have been phased out of most of the world's military stockpiles. On the other hand, we can see that even a relatively "small" detonation on the order of 5 kilotons could wreak utter mayhem in significant parts of the city.

The Code

From a technical standpoint, what makes this hack interesting is this bit of JavaScript code, which you can find for yourself by viewing the source of the aforementioned web page:

```
var base = new GIcon( );
base.image = "radii.png";
base.shadow = 't.png';
base.shadowSize = new GSize(1, 1);

var GZ = new GIcon(base);
GZ.image = "crosshair.png";
GZ.iconSize = new GSize(13, 13);
GZ.iconAnchor = new GPoint(6, 6);
GZ.infoWindowAnchor = new GPoint(6, 6);

var p15 = new GIcon(base);
p15.iconSize = new GSize(det.radius.p15*2/mpp, det.radius.p15*2/mpp);
p15.iconAnchor = new GPoint(det.radius.p15/mpp, det.radius.p15/mpp);
p15.infoWindowAnchor = new GPoint(det.radius.p15/mpp,
    det.radius.p15/mpp);

var p5 = new GIcon(base);
p5.iconSize = new GSize(det.radius.p5*2/mpp, det.radius.p5*2/mpp);
p5.iconAnchor = new GPoint(det.radius.p5/mpp, det.radius.p5/mpp);
p5.infoWindowAnchor = new GPoint(det.radius.p5/mpp, det.radius.p5/mpp);
```

This code, which you'll find in the buildOverlays( ) function, uses the standard GIcon marker object from the Google Maps API to render the blast radius rings using the same semi-transparent *radii.png* image. Each one is sized separately, according to the blast radii calculated from the detonation yield in the Detonation( ) constructor (not shown here), and the mpp variable, which stores the map scale at the current zoom level. Additionally, a crosshair icon is created to represent ground zero itself.

The upshot is that when the map is loaded, or whenever the detonation location is moved, the individual blast radius markers are stacked on top of one another at the same location on the map. The semi-transparent circles then give the visual impression of blast intensity decreasing, as it moves away from ground zero. The result, which perfectly conveys the desired information, is a very clever use of the Google Maps marker icons, which are usually used to represent grocery stores or yard sales! The same technique could be used to represent any kind of data via Google Maps that involves concentric radii of decreasing intensity. One immediately thinks of volcanic explosions or earthquake damage as candidates for this kind of interface, but there are probably less destructive topics that could be illustrated the same way.

Certainly, the prospect of nuclear war, or even of an isolated nuclear explosion in a populated area, is a terrifying one. So far, humanity has managed to show considerable restraint in its application of nuclear weapons, but an estimated 20,000 nuclear warheads still exist in the world's military arsenals. Ridding ourselves of this menace remains one of the most important outstanding issues in international politics. Hopefully, access to the kind of information offered by the HYDESim site will bring home to people how tragic the possibilities are, and just how imperative it is that the menace never becomes a reality.

See Also

- The Nuclear Weapons FAQ (*http://nuclearweaponarchive.org/Nwfaq/ Nfaq0.html*) answers a lot of common questions about nuclear weapons.

- The Atomic Archive's New York example (*http://www.atomicarchive.com/ Example/Example1.shtml*) illustrates a situation much like the one shown in Figure 3-12, only in much more detail.

- Wikipedia's List of Nuclear Accidents at *http://en.wikipedia.org/wiki/ List_of_nuclear_accidents* makes for an interesting read and illustrates just how close we've come over the years to serious accidental nuclear explosions.

HACK #23   Find a Place to Live

Why slog through endless listings of apartments that all look the same, when you can pick and choose based on where you actually want to live?

Finding a place to live, particularly in large cities, can be a huge pain. Locating a place at a price you can afford is enough of a challenge, but, even when you can locate such places, they're often not situated where you actually want to live. Real estate and rental listing sites like Craigslist.org go a long way towards easing this pain by offering searches against listings based on keywords and price brackets, but often even the search results themselves are still daunting. Where the heck are all these places? How close are each of these apartments to the grocery store? To public transit? To my friends' houses? The listings often include neighborhood names, or even street addresses or nearby intersections, but if you're not particularly familiar with the area, these names might not mean anything to you.

Paul Rademacher's HousingMaps site offers an inventive start on a solution to this problem: take one part Craigslist.org real estate listings, one part Google Maps API, and stir!

What to Do?

The front page of HousingMaps, which you can find at *http://housingmaps.com/*, shows a Google Maps view of the United States and Canada, as seen in Figure 3-13. The green icons on the map mark many of the major urban areas served by Craigslist, and clicking one opens a call-out, from which you can select real estate for sale, rentals, rooms for rent, and sublets or temporary housing for that city.

If you find this view a bit confusing—or find the icons hard to click, as in the northeastern United States, where the icons are bunched a bit close together—then you can select the metropolitan area of your choice from the drop-down box at the top left, and then use the links above to narrow your search. (Alternatively, you can recenter with a mouse drag or double-click, and then zoom in! This is Google Maps, after all.) Finally, another drop-down box at the top allows you to indicate price ranges of properties to show on the map.

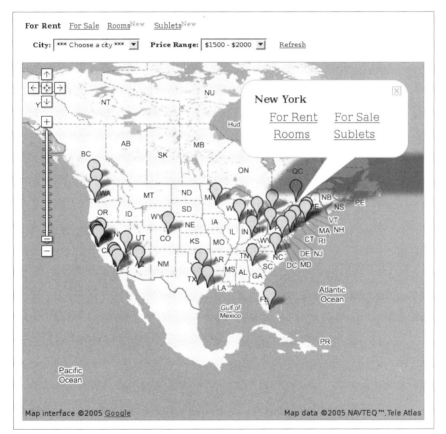

Figure 3-13. Why live anywhere when you could live, er, anywhere?

After selecting a type of listing for a given city, you're taken to a view of the available properties of that type in that city. Since I've been looking for a cheap short-term sublet in north Brooklyn, I select *sublets* in New York City, and then use the zoom and pan controls to focus in on that area. Yellow icons identify listings with photos, while red icons identify those without. I started by clicking one of the yellow icons on the map, as shown in Figure 3-14. A Google Maps info window pops up, showing the details of the property, including contact details and any photos.

Figure 3-14. A search for rentals in north Brooklyn using HousingMaps

A list of identifiable properties for that city and type is shown on the right side, sorted by price. Clicking on one of the icons recenters the map on that property and opens its call-out, while clicking on the adjacent link takes you directly to that entry in Craigslist. Additionally, you can apply the same filters to your search that Craigslist offers, such as keywords, pets permitted, and the presence of photos in a listing. Finally, there's a "permalink" option that allows you to bookmark a particular search for future use once you've zeroed in on the part of town and the search filters you're interested in. Does this beat paging through mind-numbing lists of rentals that all look the same or what?

How It Works

How does this miracle of modern technology function? Part of the answer lies in the RSS feeds offered by Craigslist for each category they provide. The Brooklyn sublets, for example, are listed at *http://newyork.craigslist.org/brk/sub/*. At the bottom of the page, there's a link labelled RSS, which points to *http://newyork.craigslist.org/brk/sub/index.rss.* This file contains an XML document that provides a machine-readable version of the 15 most recent listings for that category. Here's a snippet:

```
<item rdf:about="http://newyork.craigslist.org/brk/sub/87294481.html">
<title>***Bedroom Avail in Apt with Garden- Aug Sublet*** (Williamsburg)
$650 3bd</title>
<link>http://newyork.craigslist.org/brk/sub/87294481.html</link>
<dc:rights>Copyright 2005, craigslist.org</dc:rights>
<dc:language>en-us</dc:language>
<dc:date>2005-07-27T14:52:39-04:00</dc:date>
<dc:type>text</dc:type>
</item>
```

The main thing to note, of course, is the URL in the <link> element. That HTML page is the rental listing itself and, buried within it, are a few choice bits of HTML comments that Craigslist puts in every page:

```
<!-- START CLTAGS -->
<!-- DO NOT EDIT these unless you're really feeling brave and want your posting
messed up. You have been warned. -->
<!-- CLTAG xstreet0=Boerum Street --><!-- CLTAG xstreet1=Bushwick Ave -->
<!-- CLTAG city=Brooklyn --><!-- CLTAG state=NY -->
```

These comment tags, of course, contain enough information to plot the approximate location of the rental on a map! We'll show how to do this for U.S. street addresses with Geocoder.us in "Find the Latitude and Longitude of a Street Address" [Hack #62]. The practical upshot is that, on the server side, the HousingMaps web site periodically spiders the Craigslist RSS feeds, finds new listings, and scrapes the location data out of each one. (The downside is that if there isn't any location information in the listing, it's awfully difficult to show it on the map!)

Finally, the site produces its own data file containing the listing information, links to photos, and, of course, the location data, which is then fed into the Google Maps interface in your web browser to produce the lovely maps you see before you, using XMLHttpRequest. Of course, now that Google has released a proper API for Google Maps, there are easy ways to do this yourself, as we'll also see later on in the book.

See Also

- Monkey Homes (New York, NY): *http://monkeyhomes.com/map/maps.php*
- Colorado Future (Denver, CO): *http://www.coloradofuture.com*
- ApartmentRatings.com (nationwide U.S.): *http://www.apartmentratings.com*

HACK   # Search for Events by Location

#24   Events listed in the EVDB event database can easily be plotted on a Google Map.

Using a generic search engine isn't a good way to find out about events such as musical performances or garage sales. You can't specify that only event descriptions are wanted, and even if you could, the results aren't displayed in a way that organizes them usefully in time and space.

Wouldn't you like to be able to type keywords ("U2", "pug meetup", etc.) into a specialized event service, and get back not only a list of textual descriptions, but also a map showing event locations and a calendar highlighting event dates? Well, that's what EVMapper does. You can try EVMapper for yourself at *http://mapbureau.com/evmapper/*. Figure 3-15 is a screenshot of the results of the "pug meetup" search.

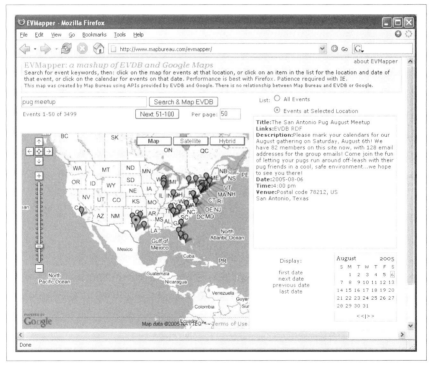

Figure 3-15. Pug meetup locations

You can click on a map dot, or an event listing, or a highlighted calendar date, and details about the event at that place or time will be displayed. If there is more than one, a list is displayed instead. Whenever an event is selected, and however the selection took place, its location will be marked on the map by the big balloon and its date will be marked by a little red square on the calendar. You can also click your way through the events in time.

How It Works

EVMapper is a mashup of two services: EVDB and Google Maps. EVDB (*http://evdb.com*) is the Events and Venues Database, a free site that allows anyone to submit or search for events. An EVDB search displays a list of events; events can also be organized into personal calendars. However, maps are not currently part of the experience at the EVDB site.

EVDB provides a RESTful API to the event database (*http://api.evdb.com*). When a user enters a query into EVMapper, an /events/search call is made to the API; for example:

```
http://api.evdb.com/rest/events/search?app_key=...&keywords=pug+meetup
```

The XML returned by EVDB contains descriptions of the matching events. The descriptions specify place by name (e.g., city, state, and sometimes ZIP Code or street address), not latitude/longitude, so EVMapper needs to do the geocoding. EVMapper implements the simplest possible geocoding method, which is adequate to demonstrate the idea of event mapping: it looks up city/ state in a GNIS database covering the United States only. The Geographic Names Information System is the official repository of place names in the United States. You can query the GNIS at *http://geonames.usgs.gov/*. As of this writing, EVDB has recently begun to provide lat/long coordinates with some event descriptions, and EVMapper will soon exploit this development with dispatch.

EVMapper uses RDF, rather than EVDB's specialized XML, for its internal data. RDF makes EVMapper's representation and processing of events fully extensible, since RDF is built from an open-ended series of vocabularies, each for its own application domain. RDF datasets freely mingle vocabularies for as many domains as are relevant to the application at hand. In future, EVMapper may aggregate events from a variety of sources, not just EVDB. New bits of RDF vocabulary, asserting things like tonnage of ships for shipwrecks or Richter Scale values for earthquakes, will be added as needed, with no need to disturb the underlying implementation. Of course, translators from other formats may be required, as was the case for EVDB.

EVMapper is implemented in Fabl (*http://fabl.net*), a programming language for which RDF is the native data representation.

See Also

- The World Wide Web Consortium's RDF Primer at *http://www.w3.org/ TR/rdf-primer/*.

—Chris Goad

Track Your UPS Packages

HACK
#25

With Google Maps and a simple Greasemonkey user script, you can watch
your UPS packages travel across the country.

Anyone who's received a package delivered by UPS, or any other large ship-
ping company, probably has had the experience of wondering where the
heck the package is right now, and when exactly it's going to arrive. By
entering the package's tracking number into a form on the UPS web site,
you can get back a list of the cities which the package has traveled through
to date. Of course, this is enough information to allow us to visualize the
package's progress on a map!

The Hack

As usual, the trick of mashing up Google Maps with information from
another site, such as that from the UPS tracking form, involves a bit of con-
tortion, to get around security restrictions in the browser. One solution to
this problem (at least for Mozilla Firefox users) is to use a Greasemonkey
user script to modify the contents of a web page to include a link to a map of
the things on that page. The Greasemonkey approach [Hack #27] is exactly the
one taken by Matthew King, when he decided he wanted to visualize the
path traversed by his new laser printer, on its way from the warehouse to his
hometown.

First, you'll need to be running Mozilla Firefox. You'll also want to install
the latest version of the Greasemonkey extension from *http://greasemonkey.
mozdev.org/*, if you haven't done this already; see "Add Google Maps to Any
Web Site" [Hack #27] for more information on how this works. To install the
UPS tracking user script, visit *http://www.thrall.net/~mking/maps/upstrack.
user.js* in Firefox, and then select Tools → Install User Script from the menu
bar. A confirmation window will pop up, in which you can simply click OK.

Now you're ready to track your UPS packages! Visit the UPS package tracking form at *http://www.ups.com/content/us/en/index.jsx*, enter a tracking
number, click the checkbox to accept the terms and conditions of use, and
then click the button marked Track. A summary page will load, with a
"View package progress" link. Click this link as well. You should get a
results page that looks something like Figure 3-16. This particular example
shows the course of a box of O'Reilly's *Mapping Hacks* sent from the company's warehouse in Tennessee to our old house in San Francisco.

So far this looks just like the regular UPS package details page, with a list of
cities, dates, and status messages. However, if you look closely, you'll see
that the Greasemonkey script you installed earlier has added a special link to

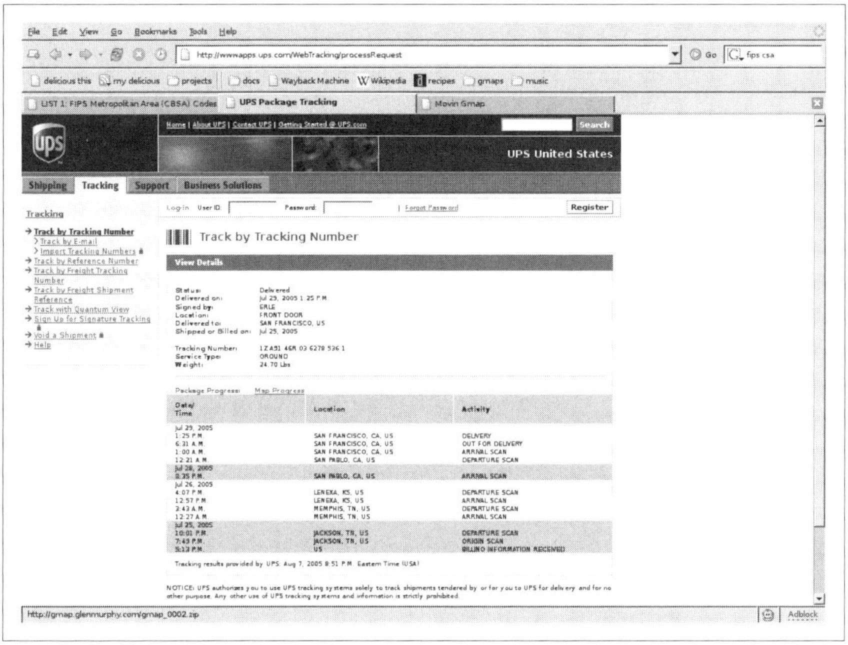

Figure 3-16. The UPS package tracking details page, augmented by Greasemonkey

this page that reads simply "Map Progress." Go on, click it! A new window should open, showing a map of your package's progress across the country, as shown in Figure 3-17.

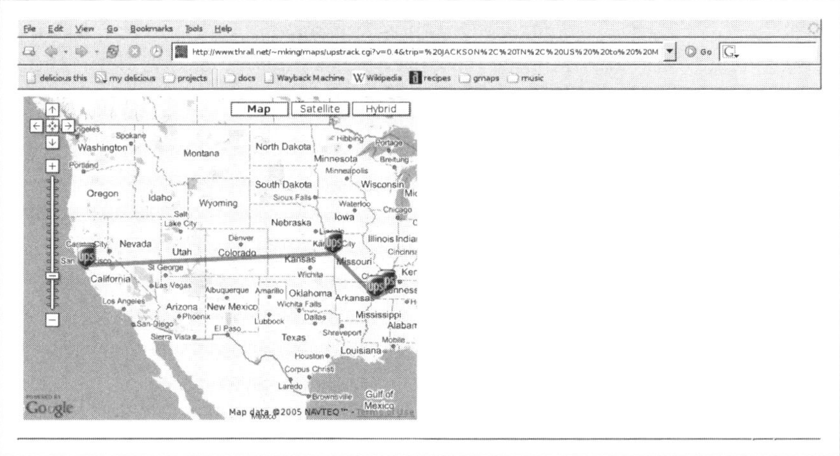

Figure 3-17. The Google Maps representation of a package's travels

If you don't have a package of your own to track, you can always try out Matt King's example page at *http://www.thrall.net/~mking/maps/ups_sample.html*.

The Code

The Greasemonkey code for this hack is actually really simple and offers a good example of how to use Greasemonkey to pick elements from an existing page on the Web and use them to insert new elements into the same page. This first chunk of code from *upstrack.user.js* extracts all the locations from the UPS detailed results page:

```
var lastLoc = null;
var loc = null;
var locations = new Array;
var allDivs, thisDiv;
allDivs =
    document.evaluate("//div[@class='modulepad']", document, null,
                      XPathResult.UNORDERED_NODE_SNAPSHOT_TYPE, null);
for (var i = 0; i < allDivs.snapshotLength; i++) {
    thisDiv = allDivs.snapshotItem(i);
    var html = thisDiv.innerHTML;
    html = html.split(/[\t\n\r]+/).join(' ');
    html = html.replace("<br> ", '');
    if (html.indexOf(', US') == -1)
        continue;
    loc = html;
    if (loc == lastLoc)
        continue;
    locations[locations.length] = loc;
    lastLoc = loc;
}
```

The code starts by creating an empty array of locations and then passes an XPath to Firefox's document.evaluate( ) method to find all of the HTML div elements of the class modulepad, which apparently contain the location strings. The script then iterates over each div node, extracting the location string, cleaning it up a bit, and then pushing it on to the array of locations, checking each one to make sure that it's not redundant with the locations already stored.

The next bit of code in the script handles the insertion of the Map Progress link into the results page:

```
if (locations.length > 1) {
    locations.reverse( );
    var locStr = locations.join(" to ");
    allDivs =
        document.evaluate("//span[@class='brownbold']", document, null,
                          XPathResult.UNORDERED_NODE_SNAPSHOT_TYPE, null);
    for (var i = 0; i < allDivs.snapshotLength; i++) {
        thisDiv = allDivs.snapshotItem(i);
        var html = thisDiv.innerHTML;
        var estr = escape(locStr).replace(/\    //g, '%2F');
        html += '     '
```

```
        + '<a href="http://www.thrall.net/~mking/maps/upstrack.cgi?'
        + 'v=0.4&trip=' + estr +
        '" target="_blank">Map Progress</a>';
    thisDiv.innerHTML = html;
  }
}
```

In this section, the code checks to see if any locations were found, and, if so, joins them with the string " to ", yielding something like `NASHVILLE TN to KANSAS CITY MO to SAN FRANCISCO CA` in the `locStr` variable. The script then looks for `div` elements of the class `brownbold`, which presumably holds the "Package Progress:" text displayed on the page above the list of locations, and inserts a link to Matt King's *http://www.thrall.net/~mking/maps/upstrack.cgi* script into the div's `innerHTML`, passing a URL-escaped rendition of `locStr` as an HTTP GET parameter. This results in the Map Progress link that you can click to show the map in a new browser window. The server-side script geocodes each location and returns a Google Map with markers based on the UPS logo over each location, with colored polylines connecting them—thus describing the path of your package.

Hacking the Hack

You'll note that this code also ensures that the location is within the United States, which means it won't work if the package's origin or destination is outside the States. If you live outside the U.S. (and are feeling adventurous), you might try removing or commenting that line out in your local copy of *upstrack. user.js* (buried somewhere in your Mozilla user directory) and then restarting Firefox to see if it does indeed work for you.

HACK #26 Follow Your Packets Across the Internet

Ever wonder where your network traffic goes when you visit a site on the 'Net?

Not long after the Internet began to be widely used in our society, a new word began to gain currency among the public to evoke the experience of being able to find information and communicate with people from all over the globe, and that word was *cyberspace*. In fact, the word "cyberspace," taken from the term *cybernetics*, a technical term for human-computer interfaces, has been so overused that it comes across as trite or hackneyed today. All the same, the word conjures up an image of sweeping digital vistas, waiting to be explored and homesteaded, and so has a great deal of potency—which is probably why the word became a cliche in the first place.

The fact, however, is that the Internet works so beautifully and, usually, so transparently, that most people don't take the time to consider that cyberspace and meatspace (as we hackers sometimes jokingly refer to the Real World) are actually connected. Obviously, every web server, DSL router, cable modem, dial-up service, and so on, is located somewhere on the planet. But who knows where?

From Clicks to Bricks

As it happens, the Whereis service at *http://www.parsec.it/whereis/* knows where Internet addresses are hosted in the real world, sometimes with astonishing accuracy. The front page of the site, clearly modeled after Google's, offers a simple search box, where you can type in an Internet domain name or an IP address in dotted-quad format (e.g., 192.168.1.1). Clicking the locate button takes you to the view shown in Figure 3-18, with a Google Map showing a marker over the most probable physical location of that Internet address. Clicking on the marker pops up some basic information about the address, including the country and locale that it's believed to be physically located in or near.

Whereis uses the standard Google Maps API to display the map on the results page. Embedded within a JavaScript block on the results page is a call to the GMarker() constructor, which specifies the physical coordinates of the Internet address and generates the marker that you see on the map.

What's particularly interesting about Whereis is how accurately it identifies the approximate location of high-speed residential connections, such as DSL and cable modems. If you have such a connection, try putting in your own IP address at home. If you don't happen to know what your IP address is at home—and it may be assigned dynamically—you can use an online service like *http://www.whatismyipaddress.com/* to find out what public IP address you're appearing from, and then cut and paste that address into the Whereis search box.

What's even more interesting about Whereis is that when it fails, as it might if your Internet provider uses an upstream web proxy (which AOL has been known to do). As a result, Whereis may decide that you're in, say, Reston, Virginia, even though the sign outside your house says "Welcome to Rapid City, Iowa!" Note also that what Whereis tries to return is the physical location of the hardware hosting the domain, not the place that the web site or even the domain name purports to represent, which is why web sites such as *zooleika.org.uk* and *www.freemap.in* turn up in Fremont, California, rather than in London or Mumbai. Also, it's conceivable that some large web sites might be hosted in different locations, with different IP addresses for the same domain name, which might result in different locations being returned on different tries for a single address.

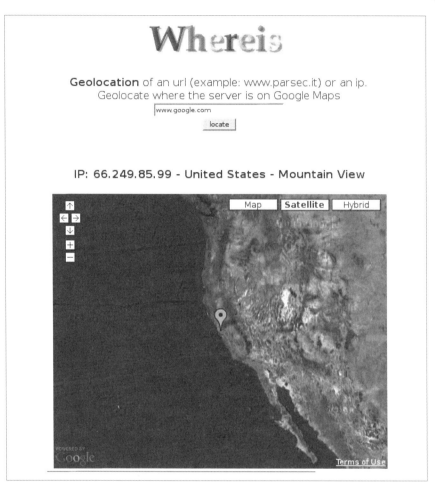

Figure 3-18. Whereis correctly places www.google.com in Mountain View, California

How It Works

The fact that Whereis does as well as it does seems nothing short of miraculous, under the circumstances. The Internet Address and Naming Authority (IANA), licenses a number of organizations around the world to manage the allocation of IP addresses and domain names. Each of these organizations maintains its own public database of address assignments, which typically can be accessed through the *whois* service on the 'Net. The problem is that each *whois* database returns results that have different information and are formatted in different ways. Not only that, but even once you've got, say, a mailing address for the owner of a given range of IP addresses, you still don't necessarily know where that place is in the world, in terms of latitude and longitude, which means you can't yet put it on a map or say what else is nearby.

So, the problem of physically locating an IP address turns out to be quite difficult—so difficult, in fact, that there aren't any worthwhile free-as-in-freedom sources of this information on the 'Net that are more precise than the country level. Mapping IP addresses to countries can be useful for collecting statistics on international visitors to your weblog, but it's no good for making decent maps. Instead, Parsec Tech s.r.l., the maintainers of the Whereis service, would seem to be using MaxMind's GeoIP database, which, as you can see, does offer pretty impressive results. You can learn about Max-Mind's products, which, interestingly enough, are used first and foremost for credit card fraud prevention, at *http://www.maxmind.com/*.

Hacking the Hack

Seeing where your favorite web sites actually live in the real world can be quite fascinating, but doesn't it make you curious to see how your requests get there in the first place? It definitely did for me, so I decided to hack the hack, by building a traceroute mapping service on top of Whereis. In technical parlance, the term traceroute is used to describe an attempt to discern which computers an Internet Protocol packet travels through on the way to its destination, after the Unix network diagnostics tool designed for that purpose. (A very similar tool ships with Windows, but its name has been abbreviated to *tracert*.)

The *traceroute* utility works as follows: all traffic sent over the Internet is broken up into packets, and each packet that's sent is marked with the IP address of the sender and the intended receiver. Additionally, each IP packet is marked with a Time-to-Live (TTL), which specifies how many network hops the packet can travel through. Each time a computer forwards the packet towards its destination, the TTL value in the packet header is decremented by one, and if it ever reaches zero, a message is sent back to the sender informing it that the receiver was unreachable. This feature of the Internet Protocol is designed to allow network engineers to detect loops and other routing problems.

traceroute piggybacks on this process, by first sending out a test packet to a given destination with a TTL of 1, and then a packet with a TTL of 2, and so on. Each time, the computer at each successive network hop along the way drops the TTL to zero and bounces the packet, thereby revealing its IP address. The process continues until the TTL value reaches the number of network hops to the destination, at which point the entire route is known. The time taken to perform each step provides an estimate of round-trip network latency and can be used to identify bottlenecks in a network route.

Fortunately, *traceroute* has a sufficiently simple output format that the results can easily be parsed in JavaScript by a web browser—and that's exactly what the Google Maps traceroute at *http://mappinghacks.com/ projects/gmaps/traceroute.html* does. Start by running traceroute *<hostname>* from your *nix or OS X terminal, or tracert *<hostname>* from the Windows command line, where *<hostname>* is an Internet domain name or an IP address. Copy the output to the clipboard, then go back to your web browser and paste the results into the text box on the right, as shown in Figure 3-19. Finally, click "Trace your packets!" and watch the hosts between you and your chosen destination appear on the map, one by one. Clicking on any of the markers that show up opens an info window that shows the country and locale, the servers hosted there, and the reported network latency to that host.

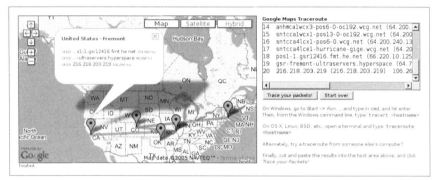

Figure 3-19. The route from New York City to googlemapshacks.com

On Windows, you can get to the command-line interface by going to Start → Run, typing in cmd, and then clicking OK.

Under the hood, when you click Trace, a JavaScript function parses the individual entries from the supplied *traceroute* output by looping over it with a regular expression. Next, it sends each IP address to Whereis via asynchronous XMLHttpRequest( ), and then uses another regular expression to scrape the coordinates out of the JavaScript in the returned HTML page. As the results come back, a marker is created on the map for each unique location, using Google Maps GMarker objects. Some care is taken to note when Internet hosts are listed as being at the same location, so as to avoid redundant overlapping markers. Additionally, a line is drawn between each successive location with GPolyline overlays, to mark out the path of your packets as they speed through the ether. The code runs to over 180 lines, so we don't have room to print it here, but you can always view the source of the page in your browser if you're curious to see how it works.

Try it with a few different hosts and see what sort of results you get. You might see certain patterns emerge, such that your packets may have to run through a number of specific hops just to get out of your ISP. For variety's sake, you might try mapping traceroute results from any of the online traceroute services listed at *http://traceroute.org/*. Finally, if you map network routes that cross the Pacific Ocean, you may discover an interesting flaw in Google Maps polylines, as shown in Figure 3-20, which is that they can't cross the International Date Line! Oops!

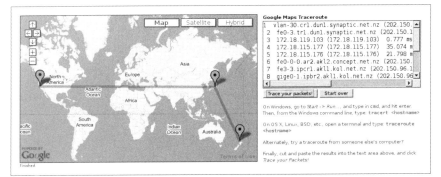

Figure 3-20. Hey, wait! You're going the wrong way!

Add Google Maps to Any Web Site

#27   Greasemap adds informative Google Maps to almost any page on the Web.

There are lots of sites on the Web that don't have maps but could really use them. Any web page with an address or a set of latitude and longitude coordinates is a candidate for a potentially useful map. Let's say, for example, that you want to visit O'Reilly's global headquarters to purchase the next hot Animal book straight from the bookstore in the reception lobby. You could go to *http://www.oreilly.com/oreilly/contact.html* and get the address, but what good does that do you? At the very least, you'll have to copy the address to your clipboard, and then go to *http://maps.google.com/* in another browser window, paste the address in there, and so on. Isn't there some way your web browser could just do this for you?

Greasemap to the Rescue

As it happens, there is a way—if you're running Mozilla Firefox. Firefox supports an extension called Greasemonkey, which allows custom Java-Script-based *user scripts* to, well, monkey with the contents of any page you view in your browser. As you can imagine, there is a wealth of possibilities inherent in the Greasemonkey concept.

Vinq.com's Greasemap is one such user script for Greasemonkey. Greasemap augments any web page you visit, by searching the page for street addresses and clearly marked geographic coordinates. If it finds any, Greasemap provides a clickable message bar across the top of the page, notifying you that a map is available. Clicking on the message bar adds an IFrame to the top of the page, in which a Google Map is loaded, displaying all the locations found on that page.

The maps from Google remain interactive; you can zoom in, pan around, and so on. The map will be one wide map if there are multiple locations found, or two smaller maps—an overview map and a zoomed in map—if there is just one location found on the page.

Installing Greasemap

Installing Greasemap takes a few short steps and should be almost painless.

1. Download and install Greasemonkey (*http://greasemonkey.mozdev.org/*). When you first try to install Greasemonkey, you may see a thin bar at the top of Firefox that says "Firefox prevented an extension from loading." Click the button at the right side of that bar, then "Allow extensions from that site." Once you've done this, try installing Greasemonkey again; it should work the second time around.

2. Restart Firefox. This allows Firefox to load the newly installed extension.

3. Visit the Greasemap homepage at *http://www.vinq.com/greasemap/*. About halfway down the page, you'll see a link to install the Greasemap script. Right-click this link, and then choose the Install User Script option to install the Greasemap script in your browser.

To uninstall Greasemap, go to the Tools → Manage User Scripts menu in Firefox, select Greasemap, and click the Uninstall button. You can also use this panel to temporarily disable it.

You can also temporarily disable Greasemap by disabling Greasemonkey itself, by clicking the Greasemonkey icon in the lower-right corner of your browser. The icon should turn gray, indicating that Greasemonkey is deactivated. Clicking the icon again reactivates Greasemonkey.

To upgrade Greasemap, first uninstall it, then follow Step 3 above to install the latest version. Unfortunately, there's no way to avoid uninstalling first—this is a limitation of Greasemonkey.

Taking Greasemap Out for a Spin

Once you've got Greasemap installed, getting a map for any location shown on a web page becomes a snap. Figure 3-21 shows the Greasemap version of O'Reilly Media's contact page, with the message bar at the top of the page.

Figure 3-21. O'Reilly Media's contact page, with the Greasemap message bar

Clicking on the message bar loads a Google Map in an Iframe at the top of the page, with a marker placed on the map for each location found on the page, as shown in Figure 3-22. Clicking a marker on the map highlights the matching location on the right side of the frame, and clicking the "Big map in new window" link does just what it says: it opens a larger version of the same map in a new browser window. From this larger map, you can click on the markers to get an info window that allows you to search for directions to that place, as shown in Figure 3-23.

Figure 3-22. O'Reilly Media's contact page plus the Greasemap frame

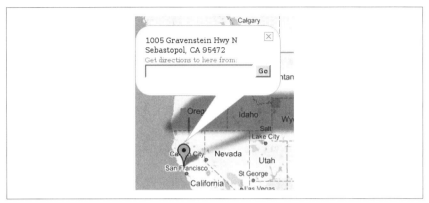

Figure 3-23. Search for driving directions in a new browser window with a single click

Instead of a whole lot of frustrating cutting and pasting, and opening new browser windows, Greasemap turns the process of finding directions to a location shown on a web page to a mere three clicks of the mouse button.

 Sometimes Greasemap reports more locations in the message bar than it actually shows on the map. The reason for this is that although Greasemap is fairly liberal about identifying locations on a web page, occasionally not all of them can be identified with actual geographic coordinates when it comes time to generate the map.

Addresses aren't the only thing that Greasemap can illustrate on a map. Several other types of location, such as *geourl.org*-style ICBM tags can be detected and mapped, as well. For example, Figure 3-24 shows the "location" of Rich Gibson's home page at *http://www.testingrange.com/*. Although there aren't any addresses directly visible on Rich's site, there *is* an HTML meta element embedded in the page that specifies a latitude and longitude, that Greasemap can identify and plot on a Google Map.

Figure 3-24. Rich's home page, automatically identified and mapped by Greasemap

How Greasemap Identifies Locations

Greasemap uses JavaScript *regular expressions* to identify locations in a web page. The following styles of location reference are currently supported:

1600 Amphitheatre Parkway, Mountain View, CA 94043
> At the moment, only U.S. addresses are supported. The ZIP Code is optional.

<meta name="geo.position" content="41.328,-110.292">
> This style of HTML meta element is used by sites that are indexed from *geourl.org.*

<meta name="ICBM" content="41.328,-110.292">
> This is an alternate form of the same.

N 42 25.159 W 071 29.492
> Degrees and decimal minutes are often used as geocache coordinates on *geocaching.org.*

geo:lat=... *and* geo:long=...
> This W3C-derived style of geotagging is frequently used on sites such as del.icio.us and Flickr. See *http://www.flickr.com/photos/tags/geotagged/* for examples.

Since the Google Maps API doesn't offer address lookups, Greasemap currently turns U.S. street addresses into latitude/longitude coordinates on the server side, using the Census Bureau's TIGER/Line data with the Geo:: Coder::US Perl module. Canadian and UK addresses should be coming soon.

If you're interested in having Greasemap identify other kinds of addresses or coordinates, have a look at the JavaScript source at *http://www.vinq.com/ greasemap/.* If you wind up modifying the Greasemap source to include your favorite way to specify a location, please send us the code! We're always looking for new ways to improve the usefulness of this tool.

See Also

- Geo::Coder::US can be found on the Web at *http://geocoder.us/.* See "Find the Latitude and Longitude of a Street Address" **[Hack #62]** for more info on how to use the web service based on it.

- Mark Pilgrim's *Dive Into Greasemonkey* provides an excellent introduction to creating and improving Greasemonkey scripts. You can read the entire book online at *http://www.diveintogreasemonkey.com/.*

—Mark Torrance

How Big Is That, Exactly?

HACK #28

Explore the size of geographic regions in terms of those you already know.

A Google search for "roughly the size of" returns 398,000 results. Certainly this suggests that, when it comes to visualizing the size of faraway places, we feel the need to refer to the unknown in terms of the familiar. Take this newspaper quote, for example:

> …when the Amazon shrank a record 11,200 square miles, an area roughly the size of Belgium, or the American state of Massachusetts….

I read that and get a vague sense of confusion and think, "Wow, I bet the people in Belgium and Massachusetts know what that means, but I sure don't." There's more:

> "Huge iceberg menaces Antarctica…roughly the size of the island of Jamaica." (*http://www.theregister.co.uk/2005/05/20/iceberg_penguin_menace/*)

> "The largest-known iceberg was from this region. It was roughly the size of the state of Rhode Island." (*http://www.factmonster.com/ipka/A0781668.html*)

> "Months later, after I discussed what I had seen with the oceanographer Curtis Ebbesmeyer, perhaps the world's leading expert on flotsam, he began referring to the area as the 'Eastern garbage patch.' But 'patch,' doesn't begin to convey the reality. Ebbesmeyer has estimated that the area, nearly covered with floating plastic debris, is roughly the size of Texas." (*http://www.naturalhistorymag.com/1103/1103_feature.html*)

A search for "roughly the size of" reveals interesting things. The fact that the writer needed to find something, anything, to use to provide a measure of spatial context hints at something odd and interesting. An "Eastern garbage patch…roughly the size of Texas"? The image is vivid.

The Hack

The statement "roughly the size of…" demands the ability to compare the unknown with a known quantity. At *http://www.mappinghacks.com/projects/gmaps/size_of.html* you can select the outline of a state or country and pin it onto the map. Pick the shape from a drop-down box then scroll around on the map until you find a familiar place and click. Figure 3-25 shows an outline of Pennsylvania on top of Hungary.

State boundaries can have an historical basis, but often are rather arbitrary. There is no particular reason for us to respect the work of our forebearers, and with Google Maps we don't need to! Figure 3-26 shows an outline of the state of Delaware, rotated 90 degrees clockwise and pinned over the San Francisco Bay area.

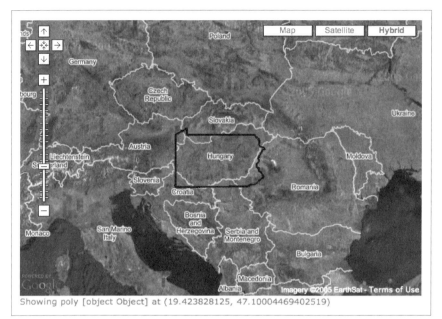

Showing poly [object Object] at (19.423828125, 47.10004469402519)

Figure 3-25. Hungary is roughly the size of Pennsylvania

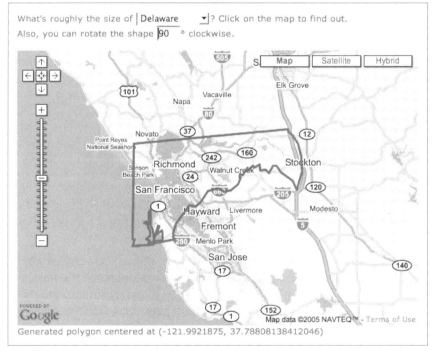

What's roughly the size of |Delaware ▾|? Click on the map to find out.
Also, you can rotate the shape |90 ° clockwise.

Generated polygon centered at (-121.9921875, 37.78808138412046)

Figure 3-26. Delaware is roughly the size of the Bay Area

Depending on how you maneuver the outline, Delaware is roughly the size of the San Francisco Bay Area. Or perhaps the Bay Area is roughly the size of Delaware. Once you start doing comparisons like this, you need a fully declensed language, like Latin, so you can specify which place is nominative and which one accusative. (Oddly, neither would be locative.)

Pinning a state or country onto the world expands our understanding of geography. For example, people don't appreciate how very long Chile is. Figure 3-27 shows Chile on top of the west coast of California—it goes from the southern tip of Alaska to the bottom of Baja California!

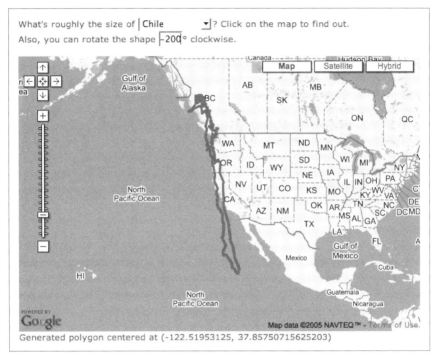

Figure 3-27. Chile flipped over and pinned to the west coast of North America

This image of Chile has been flipped, so southern Chile is near Alaska and northern Chile over Baja. The latitudes roughly match, and there is a general correspondence in climate. The north of Chile includes the Atacama desert, the driest place on earth. In parts of the Atacama, there has been no rainfall in recorded history. Baja California is not quite that dry, but it is pretty darn dry! The central part of Chile is a ripe agricultural region, analogous to California, then tending toward forests in the Southern Lakes district, which is evocative of the Inland Passage of Canada and Alaska. (Again, we have that nominative and accusative question: which one is analogous to the other, and which one is the defining instance?)

When we rotate Chile and lay it over the whole of the United States, it reaches most of the way from California to Florida, as shown in Figure 3-28.

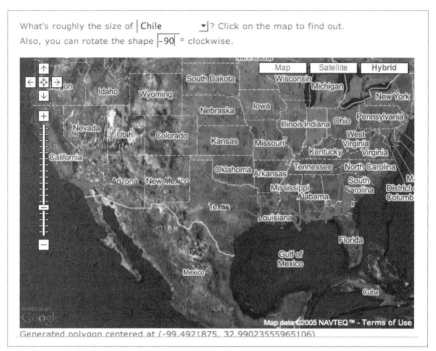

Figure 3-28. Chile shows her length

You don't need Google Maps to demo this, but the ease with which the Google Maps API handles everything on the client side (from rendering the map background to overlaying the boundary outlines to handling the user interaction), made this interesting idea an implementation in just a few hours.

The Code

We started by taking outlines of our example regions from common sources in ESRI Shapefile format. We then used a simple Perl script to extract these outlines and calculate the bounding box of the coordinates in the outline. Taking the average of the corners of the bounding box, we estimated a centerpoint for each region, and then calculated the offset of each coordinate in the perimeter from that center point. This allows us to draw the outline of the country or state around any arbitrary point that a user might click on the map.

Also, we took this opportunity to quantize the coordinate values—essentially snapping them to a grid of an arbitrary size—and then removed the duplicate coordinates to get the region's outline down to a number of points that's manageable for Google Maps. Additionally, we scaled the longitudinal distances by the cosine of the center latitude, so that the areas display at more or less the right size anywhere on the map. These doctored outlines were then put in individual text files on our server. The JavaScript uses the GXmlHttp class from the Google Maps API to fetch the file for a given country or state from our server:

```
function loadPolygonData (url, displayNow) {
    if (!url)
        url = document.forms['selectPoly'].area.value;
        var xmlHttp = GXmlHttp.create();
        msg.innerHTML = "Fetching " + url;
        xmlHttp.open('GET', url, true);
        xmlHttp.onreadystatechange = function () {
        msg.innerHTML = "Fetching " + url + "(readyState "
        + xmlHttp.readyState + ")";
        if (xmlHttp.readyState == 4) {
            shape = parsePolygonData( xmlHttp.responseText );
            if (displayNow) {
                var center = map.getCenterLatLng();
                drawPolygon(null, center);
            }
        }
    }
    xmlHttp.send(null);
}
```

The URL of the file that gets fetched is pulled from the following select box:

```
What's roughly the size of
    <select name="area">
    <option value="size_of/california.txt">California</option>
    <option value="size_of/texas.txt">Texas</option>

    <option value="size_of/minnesota.txt">Minnesota</option>
    <option value="size_of/pennsylvania.txt">Pennsylvania</option>
    <option value="size_of/delaware.txt">Delaware</option>
    <option value="size_of/rhode_island.txt">Rhode Island</option>
    <option value="size_of/chile.txt">Chile</option>
    <option value="size_of/italy.txt">Italy</option>

    <option value="size_of/mexico.txt">Mexico</option>
    <option value="size_of/australia.txt">Australia</option>
    <option value="size_of/india.txt">India</option>
    </select>? Click on the map to find out.
```

As one example, the points file for California is at *http://mappinghacks.com/ projects/gmaps/size_of/california.txt* and starts out like this:

```
-3.93254 4.72960
-0.58090 4.72519
-0.58141 1.73040
3.44982 -2.02319
4.08442 -2.96202
3.77594 -3.31706
3.77654 -3.71225
```

This data is processed with the parsePolygonData( ) function:

```
function parsePolygonData (txt) {
    var rePoint = /^(\S+)\s+(\S+)$/igm;
    var match, pts = [];
    msg.innerHTML = "Parsing polygon data...";
    while (match = rePoint.exec(txt)) {
        var lon = parseFloat(match[1]),
            lat = parseFloat(match[2]);
        pts.push(lon, lat);
    }
    msg.innerHTML = "Click anywhere on the map to continue.";
    return pts;
}
```

This bit of code defines a regular expression to read the pairs of points as longitude and latitude, and push them onto an array called pts[]. Next, the drawPolygon( ) function is called when a user clicks on the map:

```
function drawPolygon (overlay, point) {
    msg.innerHTML = "Got click at " + point;
    if (point && shape) {
        var angle = parseInt(document.forms["selectPoly"].rotate.value);
        var poly = makePolygon( point, angle, shape );
        // msg.innerHTML = "Showing poly " + poly + " at " + point;
        map.centerAndZoom(point, 13);
        map.clearOverlays();
        map.addOverlay(poly);
    }
}
```

The drawPolygon( ) function takes the angle that you are applying to turn the state or country outline, and then calls makePolygon( ) to generate a polygon represents the state or country borders. Finally, the polygon is added to the map with map.addOverlay( ), and the map is recentered and zoomed in. The mathematical core of the code is in the makePolygon( ) function.

```
function makePolygon (center, angle, ptsIn) {
    var ptsOut = [];

    if (isNaN(angle))
        angle = 0;

    var theta = - angle * Math.PI / 180;
    for (var i = 0; i < ptsIn.length; i += 2) {
        var x = ptsIn[i] * Math.cos(theta)
            - ptsIn[i+1] * Math.sin(theta)
            + center.x;
        var y = ptsIn[i] / phi * Math.sin(theta)
            + ptsIn[i+1] * Math.cos(theta)
            + center.y;
        var pt = new GPoint(x, y);
        ptsOut.push(pt);
    }
```

```
        var poly = new GPolyline(ptsOut, 'ff0000', 3, 1);
        msg.innerHTML = "Generated polygon centered at " + center;
        return poly;
    }
```

The makePolygon( ) function takes the requested angle, converts it from degrees to radians, and stores it in theta. The x and y coordinates are composed by scaling each point from the geographic outline by the horizontal and vertical components of theta, and then offsetting that point from the point where the user clicked on the map. These coordinates are used to create GPoint objects that are pushed onto an array, and then assembled into a GPolyline, which is returned and then displayed on the map by drawPolygon( ).

How Big Is "That Big"?

We would hope that this tool helps provide a bit of spatial perspective to address a weakness in geographical literacy. Problems of cultural referents remain. For example, it is said that one difference between America and England is that Americans think 100 years is a long time, and the English think 100 miles is a long way. Perhaps the tool needs the addition of a set of radio buttons, modeled after a Slashdot poll.

When faced with a 100-mile trip, I will:

- Happily drive down in the morning and back that night
- Try to schedule it for the best time
- Go for a week-long trip
- Consider it an absurdly extreme ordeal
- The Bentley hardly gets up to speed in 100 miles
- Cowboy Neal/I'm on a home release program, you insensitive clod

Humor aside, calibrating perceived distances is an important task. The Jhai Project *http://www.jhai.org/* is installing computers and Wi-Fi relays to allow people in remote villages to connect with each other and the world. Farmers can see what the current market prices are before deciding to take their goods to market, because a 10-mile trip can take hours, and the the difference between selling on a bad-price day and a good-price day has an enormous effect on the well-being of an extended family. By getting current market prices and dealing directly, farmers and craftspeople are able to double their income.

I can drive from Sebastopol, CA down to San Francisco International Airport, fly to Los Angeles, and *return* in less time than it takes to get to the nearest market town in the mountains of Laos. A mile (or kilometer) may be the same distance the world round, but it doesn't mean the same thing to me as it does to a Laotian farmer. Even though (for some people) our world is getting smaller every day, areas and distances still matter to humanity a great deal.

## CHAPTER FOUR

On the Road with Google Maps
Hacks 29–41

By now, you should be familiar with the basic use of Google Maps for finding driving directions. However, the flexibility of Google Maps offers plenty more opportunities for figuring out how to get from point A to point B. We'll see that Google Maps can assist you in finding the best gasoline prices, avoiding traffic congestion, and even avoiding the use of an automobile altogether!

In this day and age, one of the most useful tools of the digital cartographer is her *Global Positioning System*, or GPS, receiver. We're also going to explore several useful combinations of GPS and Google Maps, including loading routes from Google Maps into your GPS receiver, plotting your travels from the GPS receiver's tracklog within Google Maps, and how to use your GPS to make Google Maps of local wireless network coverage.

As a bonus, we'll also see how Google Maps saved one man from an expensive traffic fine!

HACK #29 Find the Best Gasoline Prices
Drive your mouse for cheaper fuel—and then catch a movie.

My friends in construction spend a lot of time driving up and down Highway 101, and they all know where the cheap gas is. I spend my time sitting in front of a computer, but thanks to *http://www.ahding.com/cheapgas/*, I also know where the cheap gas flows.

What a Gas!

The Cheap Gas site in Figure 4-1 uses data from *http://www.gasbuddy.com/*, which aggregates user reports of gas prices so that everyone can benefit. You can also contribute to the Gas Buddy web site by becoming one of their volunteer spotters, thus gratifying your natural human desire to tell other people something that they don't know.

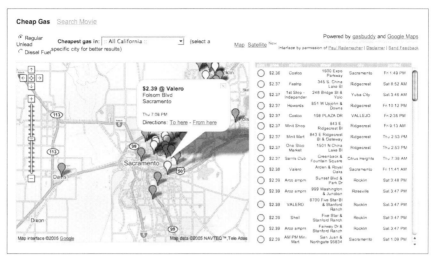

Figure 4-1. Where are the deals?

After you pick a city, the site lists gas stations on the side bar and markers on the map. The green icons represent the lowest half of gas stations by price and the red icons are the high half. As shown in Figure 4-1, each station has a marker with more information.

What is interesting about this example is the integration with *http://www.gasbuddy.com/*. GasBuddy.com provides the database of cheap gas, but is not run by cartographers, so Ahding.com was able to create the now-classic mashup.

What causes gas price variations? An interesting project in geospatial analysis would be to see if one could draw any conclusions about why there is such variation in prices from station to station. Overlaying different thematic layers and doing calculations based on multiple data sets is exactly what a Geographic Information System (GIS) is all about, but Google Maps has shown that there has been an enormous demand for an easy-to-use "put a push pin on a map" solution. That is now a solved problem!

 Once you get your fuel price woes straightened out, you can click on the Movies link at *http://www.ahding.com/movie/* and use the same basic interface to query the Internet Movie Database (*http://www.imdb.com*) to check out local movies.

GasWatch

Another low-cost-gasoline solution is GasWatch by Adrian Gonzales, which is available from *http://www.widgetgallery.com/view.php?widget=36500*. This is a widget that will run under Konfabulator for Windows and Mac OS X (the grass is greener on both sides) and show you the best prices for gas. "GasWatch shows you the lowest priced gas in your ZIP Code. It also provides a handy button to show a map to the gas station. Maps for Mac users provided by Google Maps."

To install the widget you need Konfabulator (*http://www.konfabulator.com/ download*). Konfabulator is a JavaScript environment for your desktop. People can write small programs called *widgets*, and you can run them under Konfabulator.

For Mac OS X, download the disk image (*.dmg*) file. When it is finished downloading, mount the *.dmg* by double-clicking on it. When the folder opens, drag the icon into your applications folder. Now you can download the GasWatch widget. Double-click and it will prompt for your ZIP Code, and then sit quietly on your Desktop, as shown in Figure 4-2, letting you know the current cheapest local gas prices.

Figure 4-2. Cheap gas on your desktop

Clicking on the Map button will bring up Google Maps with this address highlighted. This is a great example of the value to be gained from connecting different sources of data in new ways.

Stay Out of Traffic Jams
HACK #30   A few Google Maps mashups to keep you and your car out of trouble.

According to statistics published by the BBC in 2002, there are nearly half a million traffic jams in Britain every year—or more than 10,000 a week—and those numbers were on the rise. A quarter of Britain's main roads are jammed every day, and nearly 1 in 4 residents of the U.K, have to contend with heavy automobile traffic daily. In our car-obsessed United States, automobile commuters spent an average of 47 hours delayed by traffic congestion in 2003 alone, according to estimates published by the Texas Transportation Institute. In the ten largest metro areas in the States, that figure goes up to an average of 61 hours a year. That's two and a half whole days out of every year, spent by the average driver, just sitting in the car, idling in bumper-to-bumper gridlock!

Fortunately, the hackability of Google Maps offers hardy urban dwellers superior access to timely information in this fast-paced era! Almost as soon as Google's flashy road maps hit the Web, hackers went to work plotting out the miasma of traffic congestion that plagues the lives of so many in the urbanized western world.

Avoiding Gridlock in the United States

The best Googlified traffic maps of the States come from the Google-Traffic. com Traffic-Weather Maps site at *http://supergreg.hopto.org/google-traffic.com/*. Using RSS from the Traffic.com web site, "Super" Greg Sadetsky has assembled an informative service that reports the locations of traffic conditions in major U.S. cities. From the front page, you can select your city of interest, and click the Go! button to be taken directly to the map. Figure 4-3 shows the current traffic conditions in Philadelphia.

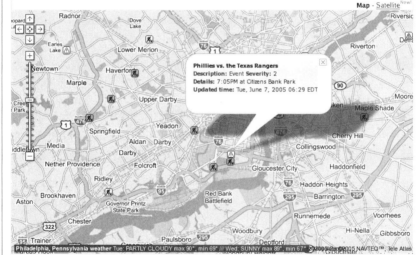

Figure 4-3. A Google-Traffic.com traffic map of Center City, Philadelphia

Custom icons show the type of delay—either construction or some kind of incident—and the color of the icon indicates the severity of the delay, from yellow to red. Clicking on any of the icons loads a callout that displays the details of the traffic delay. Miraculously, the Schuylkill Expressway (I-76) is clear this morning—but it's early yet, only about 6:30 A.M.—while the Broad Street exit of I-95 should plainly be avoided, especially later this evening when baseball fans will flock to Veterans Stadium to watch the home team lose to the Rangers.

Naturally, you can click on the Satellite link to get the same view of current traffic conditions, laid over satellite imagery, instead of road maps. (Although it's not entirely clear what utility this feature actually offers, it's still pretty darn cool.)

You can link to these maps, bookmark them, or embed them on your own page in an HTML iframe, using the following URL format, substituting your city of interest for "Philadelphia,+PA":

```
http://supergreg.hopto.org/google-traffic.com/traffic.php?csz=Philadelphia,+PA
```

Traffic details for 23 major cities are offered on the site, including Atlanta, Baltimore, Boston, Chicago, Dallas, Detroit, Houston, Los Angeles, Miami, Minneapolis, New York, Orlando, Philadelphia, Phoenix, Pittsburgh, Providence, Sacramento, San Diego, San Francisco, Seattle, St. Louis, Tampa, and Washington, D.C. As a bonus, weather information for the selected city is also pulled from an RSS feed and is embedded in a small horizontal bar at the bottom edge of the map. If you don't care for this feature, you can turn it off by adding &weather=0 to the URL for your city.

Avoiding Gridlock in the United Kingdom

The opening of the BBC Backstage service, which offers access to RSS feeds of many different kinds of information from the BBC, was almost perfectly timed with the initial release of Google Maps UK. It didn't take long at all for several hackers to leap to the challenge of plotting the BBC's traffic feeds on Google's new road maps of Britain. One solid example is Andrew Newdigate's TrafficMeister at *http://gtraffic.datatribe.net/*, which offers the by-now-familiar Google Maps view of the entire UK, with custom, clickable icons indicating the type of delay. Figure 4-4 shows an example of roadwork near Southampton.

Another interesting take on the same idea can be found on Alistair Rutherford's gTraffic site at *http://www.gtraffic.info/*, which uses colored icons to indicate the severity of the delay. Additionally, the gTraffic site displays the latest alerts in chronological order down the right side of the page. Figure 4-5 shows the same roadwork delay near Southampton on gTraffic.info.

Potentially even more useful to residents of the United Kingdom, where petrol is more expensive and private automobiles not quite the institution they are in the States, is the drop-down box at the top of the page that offers a Transport option. Figure 4-6 illustrates the increasingly dismal state of British rail in the modern era of transport privatization.

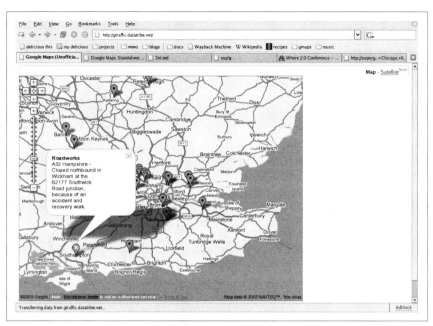

Figure 4-4. A TrafficMeister map of the southeastern UK

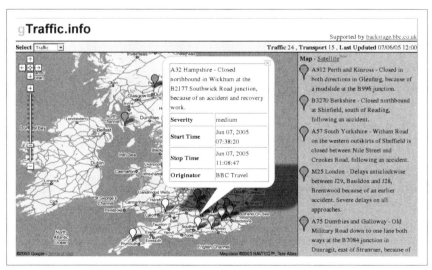

Figure 4-5. A gTraffic.info map of the southeastern UK

A similar take on this sad state of affairs can be found on Duncan Barclay's site at *http://backstage.min-data.co.uk/travel/*, where you can also view either road or rail delays. Figure 4-7 shows the same delayed train service, this time on the *min-data.co.uk* site. Interestingly, on this map, the marker has been

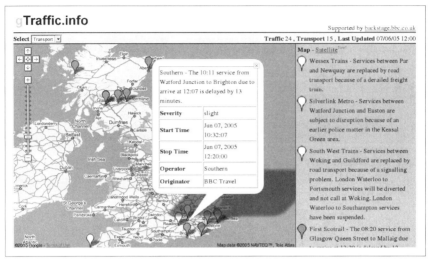

Figure 4-6. Delayed train service to Brighton

placed at Watford Junction, where the train departed from, rather than Brighton, where its arrival has been delayed.

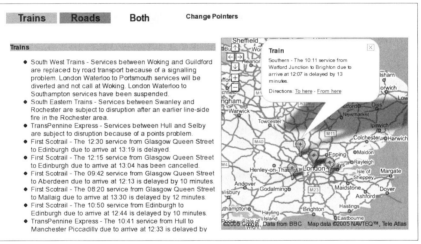

Figure 4-7. Delayed train service from Watford Junction

But, Wait, There's More!

The eagle-eyed reader will probably have already discovered this, but at least a couple of sites have gone as far as remixing Google Maps with the BBC's webcams of traffic hotspots in surveillance-happy London. gTraffic.info has a CCTV option in the drop-down on the upper left; Figure 4-8 shows the situation this morning outside St. James's Park, along Piccadilly.

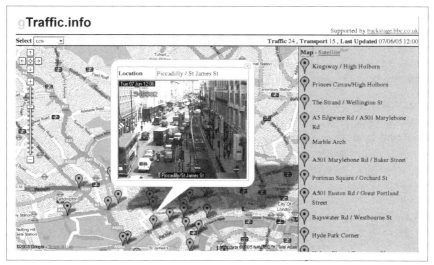

Figure 4-8. It's a circus out there!

The amazing gmaptrack site offers a similar view at *http://www.gmaptrack.com/map/locations/24/44*, where you can also click a link to see the image at its source on the BBC London Jam Cams web site. On either site, you can click the links on the right to view the camera image in a callout over the map location—probably best to take a bicycle this morning!

Hacking the Hack

Several other web sites that offer this kind of experimental traffic map can be found on the BBC Backstage web site at *http://backstage.bbc.co.uk/*. Although web-based maps of traffic conditions are nothing new, the ease with which hackers have been able to remix RSS feeds of traffic reports with Google's stylish mapping interface is a testament to the possibilities inherent in open systems loosely joined by open protocols, even before Google published its Maps API!

HACK
#31

Navigate Public Transportation

Finding your way around local public transit just got a lot easier.

You have an appointment in town somewhere, and you've just discovered from "Stay Out of Traffic Jams" [Hack #30] that it's definitely not worth driving this morning. You fire up your local public transit authority's web site, download their sketchy schematic map of the subway or bus system, and then discover to your chagrin that the map gives you no idea of which stop on which route is actually closest to your destination. Does this sound familiar? If the Google Maps hackers get their way, your experience will soon be a thing of the past.

As of this writing, Google Maps–enhanced public transportation maps are only available for a few cities in North America. Here's a rundown of what's available.

Vancouver

The first stop on our tour of Google Maps transit mashups is David Pritchard's Vancouver Transit Map for the public transportation system in Vancouver, BC. The Vancouver Transit Map lives on the Web at *http://www.david.enigmati.ca/maps/transit.html*. As you can see from Figure 4-9, the site uses Google Maps polylines to depict the major transit routes in town.

Figure 4-9. Public transit in Vancouver, BC

The transit line stops are depicted with circles, which open an info window showing the name of the stop and the intersecting bus lines. The text labels showing the names of major stops at different zoom levels are also clickable, and make for a nice touch in terms of the map's readability.

Boston

Matt King's Boston Subway Station Map at *http://www.thrall.net/maps/mbta.html* takes something of a similar approach, as you can see in Figure 4-10. Instead of the station labels on the map, along the top we get a row of color-coded drop-down boxes, organized by subway line, to help find individual stations.

Clicking any of the station markers opens an info window with the station name, street address, and navigational links. The "To here" and "From here" driving directions links are pretty self-explanatory, but the "Zoom in" and "Zoom out" navigation links are special. If the map is zoomed out, clicking "Zoom in" will cause the map to iteratively zoom in, one level at a time, on a delay interval, so that you can situate the subway stop in the larger geographic context of Boston. Once zoomed in, the "Zoom out" link

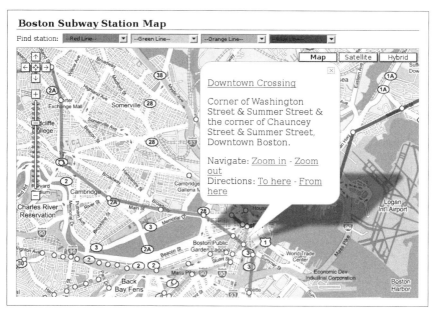

Figure 4-10. Subway stations in Boston, MA

performs the reverse operation. This progressive zoom-in/zoom-out is referred to by digital cartographers as *ballistic zoom*.

Seattle

Chris Smoak's Seattle Bus Monster site at *http://www.busmonster.com/* is probably the most feature-rich of the Google Maps transit mashups we've seen so far. The site has three basic sections: Bus Stops, Routes, and Traffic Conditions. In the Bus Stops section, you type in an address, intersection, or landmark to find bus stops near that location, as shown in Figure 4-11. Clicking on an individual bus stop shows, almost miraculously, the expected arrival times for the next few buses on that route (if available).

In the Routes section, you can type in route numbers to view routes, stops along those routes, and current bus locations. The Traffic Conditions section shows hundreds of traffic cams in the area.

Perhaps the most remarkable feature of this site is that, in the Routes view, you can click on a particular bus stop and set an "alarm" for that scheduled bus arrival. Once you've created the alarm, you can click on the alarm icon in the info window, and you'll be prompted for a number of minutes lead time and an email address to send the alarm to. If your cellular provider relays email to your phone as text messages—and most do—you can enter the email address of your phone and be notified in real time when the bus is on its way!

Figure 4-11. Public buses in Seattle, WA

The Bus Monster site makes heavy use of the XMaps extension to the Google Maps API [Hack #64].

New York City

Naturally, the Big Apple, with one of the most extensive public transportation systems in North America, wouldn't be without at least one Google Maps transit mashup. Will James is responsible for the NYC Subway Map at *http://www.onnyturf.com/subwaymap.php*. The basic functionality of this map is similar to that of other maps—click on a station, and an info window pops up, with the station name and one or more icons provide links to the MTA's web page for the relevant subway lines that stop at that station, as shown in Figure 4-12.

What's exceptional about the NYC Subway Map is that, unlike the other transit mashups, it doesn't use the Google Maps GPolyLine class to depict the subway lines. Instead, Will decided that the variety of colors in the standard MTA subway map meshed poorly with the default color scheme of Google Maps, and that the map would look better—and be more readable—if he made his *own* background tiles. An additional map type control marked "SUBWAY" at the top-right corner of the map, allows you to switch back and forth between that and the traditional Google Maps backgrounds. Will's process for generating custom Google Maps background tiles is described in Chapter 7.

Chicago

Adrian Holovaty's Chicago Transit Authority map page (*http://www.holovaty. com/blog/archive/2005/04/19/0216* deserves special mention for being one of the

Figure 4-12. Subway stations in New York City

earlier Google Maps mashups. Instead of providing an integrated interface using the Google Maps API, the CTA map relied on a Firefox extension to integrate Adrian's custom map tiles into Google Maps on the client side at the right time and place (namely, zoom level 5 over Chicago). Unfortunately, as of this writing, the extension no longer works, probably due to subsequent changes to the Google Maps interface.

Where's My City?

Don't live in any of these places? Can't find a Google Maps transit mashup for your hometown? Perhaps that's a sign that you should finish this book and then go out and make your own!

HACK #32 Locate a Phone Number

Perform reverse lookups with Google Phonebook and Google Maps.

Have a phone number, but you don't know where it originates? You can use Google to get an address, and then Google Maps to pinpoint it. Your search engine is a phone book? Why not? Phone numbers are just another thing that can be searched on!

When you enter a phone number into the search box on *http://google.com*, the first link is to the Google Phonebook (assuming that the number is found). For example, doing a search on the U.S. phone number (707) 827-7000 brings up the results shown in Figure 4-13. The Google phone book is very forgiving. You can search for 707 827-7000 or 707-827-7000 or even 7078277000 and Phonebook will still work.

> Interestingly enough, you can't search for a phone number directly through the Google Maps search box: you have to go through the regular Google Search first!

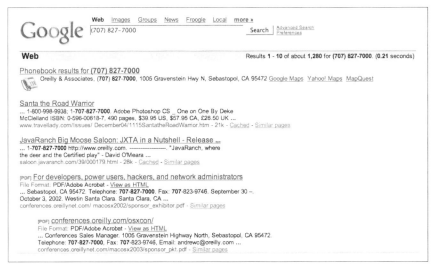

Figure 4-13. Google Phonebook results for (707) 827-7000

The Google Phonebook is mapping-service agnostic, showing links to this address in Google Maps, Yahoo! Maps, and MapQuest. If you click on the Google Maps link, you can do a local search for something common, such as pizza, and then click on "Link to this page" near the top right of the page to get a page like Figure 4-14.

The point isn't to get information on pizza, but to show that when you click on "Link to this page," Google Maps loads the URL for the current map in your browser. That URL includes the latitude and longitude of the center of your search area as the sll parameter, which stands for *search lat/long*. Look at the address bar in Figure 4-14, and you can see the URL query string ?q=pizza&sll=38.411170,-122.841720. So, phone number (707) 827-7000 is located at 38.411170 N, 122.841720 W. That location isn't perfect, but it is pretty darn good. See "Inside Google Maps URLs" [Hack #7] for more on the structure of Google Maps URLs.

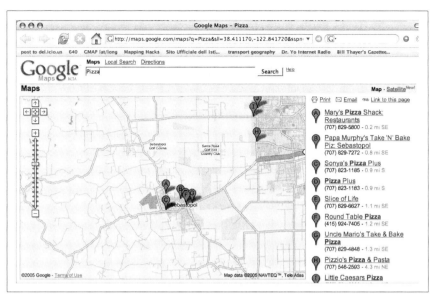

Figure 4-14. Pizza near (707) 827-7000

Another thing to note about that original Google search for the phone number in Figure 4-13, is that a search for a phone number also does a standard Google search. This can be interesting because it pulls things up in a new way. The first Google link for O'Reilly's phone number is a Road Warrior's Christmas list. Who would have thought that?

Reverse lookup availability appears to vary over time. At one point, a reverse lookup on my home phone number pulled up my street address. As of this writing, it just returns the city and ZIP Code. Other residential phone numbers that I've tested still work, and business listings still pull up a full address.

 ## Why Your Cell Phone Doesn't Work There

Trouble getting a signal? Google maps and the FCC database can help.

I live almost in the shadow of a 30.2-meter cell phone tower, and I have to go out on the porch to get decent reception. What is up with that? I know the exact height of the tower, thanks to Mobiledia. You can go to its site at *http://www.cellreception.com/towers/index.html* and browse for cell towers by city or state. When I look up Sebastopol, California, I get the map in Figure 4-15.

I live near the *S* in Sebastopol, so you'd think I'd have pretty good coverage 2.5 blocks from the tower. Clicking on the overlay marker brings up information

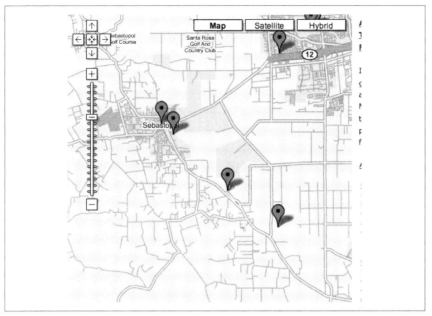

Figure 4-15. Cell towers near Sebastopol, CA

on the owner of the tower, as shown in Figure 4-16. So my problem appears to be that there is a tower, but my cell provider doesn't have gear up there.

You can click on the overlay marker because marker labels are HTML and support links. Mobiledia defines marker text with this line of code:

```
var html="<h1><a href='http://www.cellreception.com/towers/details.php?id=" +
id + "'>" + name + "</a></h1><br>" + address + "<br>" + city + ", " + state;
```

This builds a URL that calls a script on its site with more details. This is an example of how you can include links and arbitrary HTML in pop-up markers. Mobiledia uses the FCC database of antennas, and as explained on the site:

> The FCC does not require every antenna structure to be registered, and the map may not list all the towers in the area. Additionally, many carriers have sold their tower assets to third party companies, and leasing agreements are unknown. If this is the case, the best way to determine carrier coverage is by reading comments in the local area.

So it is possible that my provider rents space on the tower, but since the best way to determine coverage is to read the comments, I think it is safe to just assume that my calls don't go to the most convenient tower.

On the right sidebar is a "Cell phone reception search." Enter a ZIP Code and it pops up a reader forum on reception, or in reality more likely the *lack* of reception. You can also search for dead spots and add your own reviews.

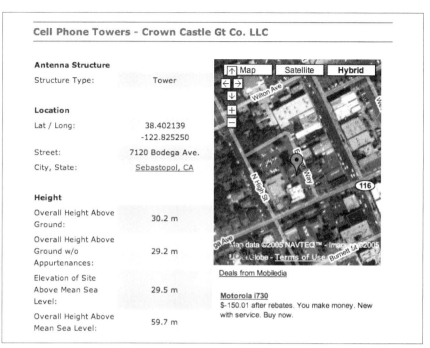

Cell Phone Towers - Crown Castle Gt Co. LLC

Antenna Structure

Structure Type: Tower

Location

Lat / Long: 38.402139
                       -122.825250

Street: 7120 Bodega Ave.

City, State: Sebastopol, CA

Height

Overall Height Above
Ground: 30.2 m

Overall Height Above
Ground w/o   29.2 m
Appurtenances:

Elevation of Site
Above Mean Sea   29.5 m
Level:

Overall Height Above
Mean Sea Level: 59.7 m

Map   Satellite   Hybrid

Deals from Mobiledia

Motorola i730
$-150.01 after rebates. You make money. New
with service. Buy now.

Figure 4-16. Ah, that would be why I don't have service

Another neat feature of the site is that you can get HTML that lets people search the reception and tower databases from your site. Just go to *http://www.cellreception.com/add/index.html* and fill out the form, and they send links to an HTML form that you can embed in your own web page.

HACK #34 Publish Your Own Hiking Trail Maps

Tell your own stories with a mix of social software and cartography.

We've all found ourselves climbing through hillside brambles on a hot sunny day thinking, "That's the last time I trust that trailhead pamphlet." Or worse, wanting to show a friend a special place you found on a hike a few months ago but now can't quite place.

If you're a hiker, mountain biker, rock climber, weekend warrior, amateur geologist, scout troop leader, endorphin junkie, equestrian, pedestrian, rock climber, birder, or simple romantic, then have we got a hack for you! The site, which lives at *http://ning.com/BayAreaHikingTrails*, looks like Figure 4-17.

Bay Area Hiking Trails (BAHT), written by Saumi Mehta and May Woo, allows you to capture and publish your trail maps with comments, GPS tracklogs, and photos. Even better, you can easily overlay your GPS track-logs on Google Maps via the API and provide a visual representation of your

Figure 4-17. Bay Area Hiking Trails

hike, bike, or ride alongside all these other goodies. But that's only the start. You can also offer these annotated trail maps to friends or strangers for rating and reviewing. You can even look for new hiking friends and fellow enthusiasts. How's that for social?

All right, so that may not be enough. Let's take it one step further. No single social map can cover all scenarios of what you might want to do with it. With just a little bit of PHP knowledge, BAHT enables you to easily change or extend the user input forms so that you can record your own specialized data: birds seen, bikers met, geocaches planted, or geocaches found. You can also go further and change the HTML layout, add new features, or introduce new kinds of objects for your users to edit. Perhaps you are employed by a local parks service to identify invasive plant species and want a new kind of form input to describe those. Or you're a mountain biker who wants to have a slightly specialized social mapping application to document the rockiness, steepness, or exposure of certain trails.

BAHT is extensible for such uses because it is built on the Ning Playground, which is a free online system that enables you to clone, mix, and run full-blown social web apps like BAHT without worrying about a bunch of pesky details. The Ning Playground handles user account management, system administration, hosting, and bandwidth nightmares, not to mention the tedium of performance and scalability issues.

If you don't know PHP, you can still do a lot with BAHT or any social application running on Ning. If you want to copy BAHT to create Malibu Hiking Trails, Bay Area Rock Climbs, Yosemite Mountaineering Routes, or Sonoma Bike Rides, just select the application and choose Clone It on the righthand sidebar to instantly create your own running version of the application, with an exact copy of the code behind the copied application, ready to be customized. You just change the title to apply the app to the place, interest, or activity you want. Now you're all set to start adding your own relevant trails, rocks, mountains, rides, or romantic spots, and invite your friends and neighbors to do the same.

If you know PHP, then it gets even better. You can go under the hood of the app by clicking on "view source," and, with those PHP skills, change the user input forms, add or delete features, or make the app anything you want.

BAHT combines the benefits of gadgets, data, and the real world experience of you and others to help you find and share the perfect place. You can compare your trips against your friends' trips—or blend different trips together to get a composite view of some new trip you've never thought of before.

BAHT helps you return to your favorite places over and over and easily find new favorites. It dissolves boundaries between the professional and the amateur by letting you create your own maps and your own mapping services. Ultimately, perhaps its most powerful role is that it helps you and your friends more easily share something valuable and important: this hugely complex and beautiful natural world we live in. I look forward to seeing what kinds of new projects you invent based on this starting point.

—Anselm Hook

Load Driving Directions into Your GPS

From Google straight to your Global Positioning System receiver, thanks to GPSBabel.

GPSBabel (*http://www.gpsbabel.org*) makes it possible to convert driving directions from Google Maps into various formats usable by other software and devices. This is possible because Google encodes the coordinates of the entire route in the JavaScript that is sent to the Google Maps client and used to generate the route that is put on the map.

The first step is, of course, to get Google Maps to make some driving directions. We'll use one of the examples given on the Google Maps home page. Enter "JFK to 350 5th Ave, New York" and hit the Search button. After a short calculation, a map like that in Figure 4-18 appears, with the route highlighted.

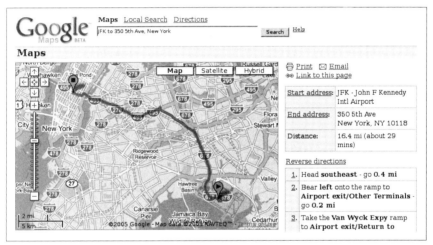

Figure 4-18. Directions from JFK to Fifth Avenue

Now, we need to get the output into a predictable format. To do that, we first need a URL that contains everything we need to recreate our route. Fortunately, Google provides a tool to do just that! Click "Link to this page." The displayed map won't change, but the URL in the address bar will contain your query and the parameters needed to return to this map at this zoom level.

The last step is to modify that URL to output the JavaScript that the Google Maps client uses internally. To do that, just add &output=js to the end of the URL in your address bar and hit Enter. Your URL will look like this (but all on one line):

```
http://maps.google.com/maps?q=jfk+to+350+5th+ave,+new+york&spn
    =0.103861,0.199934&hl=en&output=js
```

The observant reader will note that the instructions "JFK to 350 5th Ave, New York" are included in that URL, with spaces having been replaced with plus signs. With this information you can skip the steps of looking up an address, clicking on "Link to this page," and changing the URL to include &output=js, and instead just enter the URL of the JavaScript page straight into your browser. Here is a link to the page containing the points for directions from JFK to San Francisco International Airport the hard way:

```
http://maps.google.com/maps?q=jfk+to+sfo&spn
    =0.103861,0.199934&hl=en&output=js
```

The resulting page will appear mostly blank, but the HTML source contains all the data we need to extract the coordinates of the route. Save that page to your local hard disk with the File → Save As menu option. If you are using Internet Explorer, make sure to select Web Page, HTML Only from the "Save as type" drop-down. Saving as Web Page, Complete will cause the file to be rewritten as non-compliant XHTML, which GPSBabel will not be able to read. Give the file a name—we'll call ours *nyc.htm*—and hit the Save button.

Now we have a file to feed to GPSBabel. What can we do with it? One thing we can do is to load this route to a handheld GPS unit. These have limits on the number of points, so we can use GPSBabel to reduce the route Google Maps has computed for us to a smaller number of points. GPSBabel comes with a GUI frontend, but the real power lies in the command-line interface. For our example, we must use the command-line interface because the GUI does not support filters. Start a command prompt; make sure that GPSBabel is in your path, and switch to the directory where you saved your map file as *nyc.htm*. Connect a supported Magellan or Garmin GPS receiver to *com1:* or a serial or USB port. If you are running Linux, this is likely to be */dev/ttyS0* or */dev/ttyS1*. If you are using Mac OSX with a USB adapter, it may be */dev/cu.usbserial0*.

Assuming you used *com1:*, type the following all on one line and hit Enter. Otherwise, replace *com1:* with the name of your serial or USB port. For a Magellan GPS receiver:

```
c:\> gpsbabel -i google -f nyc.htm -x simplify,count=30 -o magellan -F com1:
```

For a Garmin GPS receiver:

```
c:\> gpsbabel -i google -f nyc.htm -x simplify,count=30 -o garmin -F com1:
```

That's it! GPSBabel will read the driving directions produced by Google Maps, pick the 30 most salient points along the route, and upload the new route to your GPS receiver. Now you can follow along on this route as you walk, bicycle, or drive!

One other thing you might want to do is to save those points to a GPX file so that you can include them on your own Google Map, or upload them to a site like *http://gpsvisualizer.net/*. The Topografix site at *http://www.topografix.com/gpx.asp* describes the GPX format:

> GPX (the GPS Exchange format) is a light-weight XML data format for the interchange of GPS data (waypoints, routes, and tracks) between applications and Web services on the Internet.

This command will convert all of the points, without simplifying them, into a GPX file:

```
c:\> gpsbabel -i google -f nyc.htm -o gpx -F nyc.gpx
```

You can also reduce the number of points from this GPX file and load them into your GPX. The following command will load the points from *nyc.gpx*, select the 30 best fit points and upload them to a Garmin GPS on *com1:*.

```
c:\> gpsbabel -i gpx -f nyc.gpx -x simplify,count=30 -o garmin -F com1:
```

Naturally, this is analogous to the earlier command we used to go directly from Google Maps output to the GPS receiver, except that this time the input file is in GPX format.

GPSBabel is such a great tool that any Google Maps hackers should consider becoming Babelheads!

See Also

- The GPSBabel page at *http://www.gpsbabel.org/*.
- Another implementation can be found at *http://www.elsewhere.org/GMapToGPX/*.

—Ron Parker

Get Driving Directions for More Than Two Locations

HACK #36
Going from here to there is okay, but going from here to there to another there to here is better.

In "Load Driving Directions into Your GPS" **[Hack #35]** we saw how to compute a route and load it into a GPS. The hack showed how to directly create a URL that will fetch the Google Maps file that contains the route points. GPSBabel can parse the points out of a route file and you can do whatever you would like with this information.

This suggests a script that takes a list of locations that Google can understand and then generates driving directions between each point. In addition to normal locations such as "San Francisco, CA to Denver, CO," Google Maps can generate driving directions based on latitude and longitude. The results of searching for directions from 38, -121 to 39.526421, -119.807539 are shown in Figure 4-19.

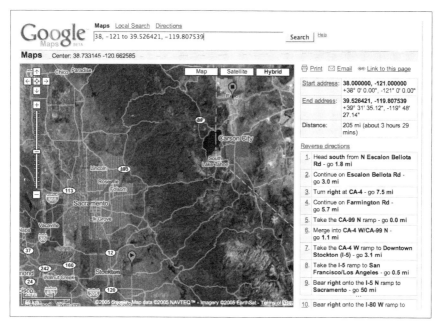

Figure 4-19. Directions from latitude/longitude to latitude/longitude

Lat/long routes don't always work. There are some places that are just a bit too far off of the beaten track for road-based routing to be effective. If you try 38, -121 to 39.731482, -119.53537, you get "We could not calculate driving directions between 38, -121 and 39.731482, -119.53537." Since 38, -121 worked in the first example, Google must have a problem with 39.731482, -119.53537. A glance at Figure 4-20 shows that Google should be forgiven for this routing difficulty. Apparently the engineers didn't anticipate helicopter-based mountain-top expeditions.

But lat/long–based directions work often enough to be interesting. Great, but why would you want to get driving directions for multiple points or for lat/longs? Let's say you want to drive from San Francisco to Denver; you can generate the route in Figure 4-21 with the query SFO to DEN, using an airport-to-airport search. Why do you need more than one set of directions?

You've got everything you need—1,299 miles, and you are there. But it turns out you want to stop in Moab for some of that Slickrock action. You can't (yet) enter a request to Google for multipart driving directions, such as SFO to Moab, UT to DEN, but with this hack you can get something similar. Download the Perl script called *takeme.pl* from *http://mappinghacks.com/*

Figure 4-20. You can't always get driving directions to a lat/long

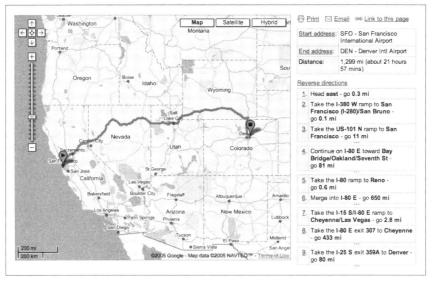

Figure 4-21. San Francisco and Denver are just a click apart

projects/gmaps/takeme.html. The script can accept any combination of locations that Google can understand and GPS waypoints stored in GPX format. For example:

```
$ perl takeme.pl SFO to wy_small.gpx to Moab, UT, to DEN
```

The program returns the combination of driving directions from each point to the next, as well as a simplified list of lat/long points.

```
new route segment 37.61830, -122.38632 to 38.57320, -109.55060
 San Francisco Airport
 to  Slick Rock Capitol


 -------------------------------------------------------------------
 Head    west
 0.5| mi (734 meters) for 1 min
 -------------------------------------------------------------------
 Take the  I-380 W
 ramp to   San Francisco (I-280)/San Bruno
 0.1| mi (197 meters) for 12 secs
```

You might want to specify multiple locations, including a detour to visit friends, or you might want to trick the routing algorithm into using a route that it considers sub-optimal. Here's a real life example of tricking a routing algorithm: my dad and step-mom had just gotten a Prius with a navigation system—they had had it less than two weeks. My dad, while quite bright, is not particularly technical. One day they were driving and playing with the navigation system. My dad said, "Don't set it to go to our destination until you get to this turn—it will take us a bad way from here."

My nontechnical dad had figured out the tool in under a week. Without knowing how, he was dynamically gaming the system's shortest-path algorithm by artificially increasing the weight of one segment by adding the cost of turning around to get back to that segment. He made that segment less attractive to the routing algorithm by inserting another segment in between himself and the dreaded slower path. Specifying intermediate points (or desired side trips) adds local knowledge to the cost calculation used in the routing system. In Google Maps terms, it sure would be nice to have "do not use this segment" checkboxes next to each step in the route, followed by "recalculate my route without the checked segments," but until that happens, you can use the *takeme.pl* tool!

HACK #37 View Your GPS Tracklogs in Google Maps

Plotting your GPS tracklogs on Google Maps allows others to see where you've been.

Sharing tracklogs and waypoints from your GPS receiver became a lot easier with the invention of the *GPX* format, which is an open XML standard that encodes your GPS wanderings to a file readable by many applications. The best waypoints are pubs—so why not plot them on Google Maps, as in Figure 4-22?

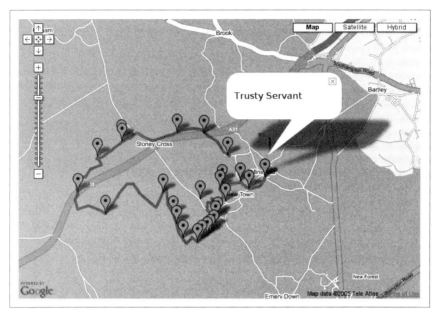

Figure 4-22. Some waypoints of London pubs, shown in Google Maps

You can go to *http://www.tom-carden.co.uk/googlegpx/* and upload your own GPX format file. Any waypoints appear as marker pins, and the start and end of tracks will be marked with pins, as shown in Figure 4-23.

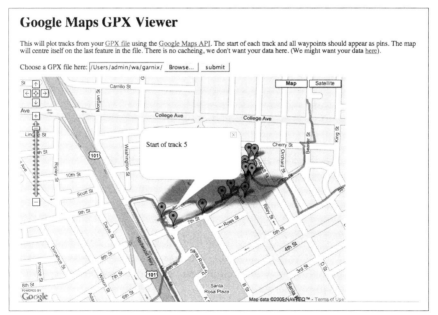

Figure 4-23. A bit of a "derive" captured on the GPX viewer

Processing GPX Tracks to Reduce Complexity

There are several ways to process a GPX file into something Google Maps will understand, and we demonstrate two methods here. Using server-side processing, you upload the file from your browser and process it on your server (in this case using Ruby) and return a script that displays the data. Alternatively, you can put the GPX onto your own server and use some JavaScript to open it, process it on the client side, and pass it to Google Maps. The usual caveats for passing information around in a browser apply—there are restrictions on what scripts are allowed to access—but old friends like the iframe element and new friends like XMLHttpRequest can help us here.

No matter what method you use to process the GPX data, a GPX file will typically contain thousands of points—far too many for Google Maps to handle. Why is this? When you display polylines in Google Maps, your vectors are rendered into an image file on Google's servers. The more points, the more time it takes to generate the images. Except this isn't the whole story—Google only does this if you aren't using Internet Explorer. IE has a built-in vector language called VML, which renders the vectors very quickly in the browser.

Being fans of Firefox and Mozilla, for us it wasn't good enough to rely on IE. Therefore we thought up a way to selectively choose which points to display so we didn't have too many, yet had enough to show the route without slowing Google down. A seemingly obvious solution would be to simply drop every fifth point to reduce the number of points by 20%—but the problem is that one of those ignored points might be the crucial part of a turn or otherwise cause distortions of the route.

Consider another scheme in which points are intelligently dropped on straight lines but not on complex bends. In this scenario, successive points in a straight line add little information to a route and may be forgotten. Points that turn direction quickly would then be kept as they are more important than those that only reinforce a straight line. The key here is determining the amount of change in direction in order to pick those points that should be displayed.

You could simply choose an angle and choose successive points based on whether the path they mapped out deviated more than that angle, and it's a good choice. The problem, however, is that a GPX file may have 1,000 or 10,000 points within it, and these must be mapped down to a sufficiently small number of points to actually plot in both cases because Google Maps can't plot too many. And so we developed an adaptive algorithm that gets a good number of points to display.

Before describing the algorithm, we should be honest and point out that this hack doesn't choose points based on angle, but something a little more crude that is effectively equivalent. Instead of angle, it is the difference vector between successive line segments. What does that mean? Perhaps the diagram shown in Figure 4-24 will help.

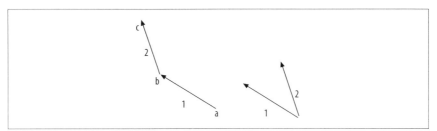

Figure 4-24. One method for simplifying tracklogs for display

Consider three trackpoints recorded by your GPS unit, where you travel from *a* to *b* to the bottom of *c*. Take the vector 2 between *b* and *c*, so that it starts at *a* and you can compare the vector 1 between *a* and *b* to it. Notice the dashed line between them. This dashed line is the difference between the vectors. It's like the angle between them but both quicker to compute and sufficient, because we only need a rough guess to figure out the change in direction.

There is one final fact we must admit, which is that these vectors are laid out in linear latitude and longitude. So when you're in London one degree in latitude is a different absolute length (say, in meters) than one degree in longitude. You could equalize these but for our purposes it doesn't matter that much.

Back to that adaptive algorithm: we choose a small number as a threshold for the length of that dashed line. Then, for every successive pair of line segments in a GPX track we see if the dashed line is bigger than our threshold. If it is bigger, then we include the point; otherwise, we forget about it. By going through the entire GPX file, we may decide to forget 100 points but have 4,000 left. This is far too many for Google to plot. We therefore make our small number a bit bigger and try again, this time dropping more points. We repeat this cycle until we have less than 200 points and then use those points to plot in our track.

This algorithm has been implemented with both a server-side Ruby back-end and JavaScript client parsing.

Converting GPX to JavaScript Calls Using Ruby

Here is the Ruby script to place server side, if that's the way you want to plot your GPX files. We recommend using Apache and mod_ruby to run it, and much documentation is available for both.

```ruby
#!/usr/bin/ruby

# make sure we can speak CGI and XML:
require 'cgi'
require 'rexml/document'
include REXML

cgi = CGI.new

print cgi.header("type"=>"text/html")

stringfile = cgi['gpxfile']

doc = Document.new stringfile.read

# Put the header of the HTML file:

puts '<!DOCTYPE html PUBLIC "-//W3C//DTD XHTML 1.0 Strict//EN"
  "http://www.w3.org/TR/xhtml1/DTD/xhtml1-strict.dtd">
<html xmlns="http://www.w3.org/1999/xhtml">
  <head>
    <script type="text/javascript">
      function addPoints() {'

count = 201
trackcount = 0
diff = 0.000000001
firstpt = ''
lastpt = ''

# For each track point in a segment
doc.elements.each('gpx/trk/trkseg') do |e|
  count = 201
  diff = 0.000000001

# So long as the total count of points to draw is less than 200
  while count > 200

    output = '          parent.gpxtrack(new Array('
    first = true

    oldlon = 0.0
    oldlat = 0.0
    oldvx = 0.0
    oldvy = 0.0
    count = 0
```

```
    # For each point in a segment
    e.elements.each('trkpt') do |pt|
      lat = pt.attributes['lat'].to_f
      lon = pt.attributes['lon'].to_f
      # Always add the first point
      if first
        output+= pt.attributes['lat'] + ',' + pt.attributes['lon']
        first = false
        count = 1
        firstpt = 'parent.addpin(' + pt.attributes['lat'] + ',' +
         pt.attributes['lon'] + ', "Start of track ' + trackcount.to_s + '");'
      else
        vx = oldlon - lon
        vy = oldlat - lat

        # If the point is bigger than our small value
        if ((oldvx - vx)*(oldvx - vx))+((oldvy - vy)*(oldvy - vy)) > diff
          # Then add it
          count += 1
          output += ',' +  pt.attributes['lat'] + ',' + pt.attributes['lon']
          oldvx = vx
          oldvy = vy
          oldlat = lat
          oldlon = lon
        end
      end

    end

    # Make our small distance value 5 times bigger and try again
    diff *= 5

  end

  if count > 1
    puts output + '));'
    puts firstpt
    trackcount += 1
  end

end

# Now, for each waypoint plot it with the description:
doc.elements.each('gpx/wpt') do |e|

  lat = e.attributes['lat']
  lon = e.attributes['lon']

  str = ''

  e.elements.each('name') do |wpt|
    str += wpt.get_text.value + '<br>'
  end
```

```
      e.elements.each('cmt') do |wpt|
        str += wpt.get_text.value + '<br>'
      end

      e.elements.each('desc') do |wpt|
        str += wpt.get_text.value
      end

      puts '          parent.addpin(' + lat + ',' + lon + ',"' + str + '");'

    end

    # put the end of the HTML
    puts '      }'
    puts '
        </script>
      </head>
    <body onload="addPoints();">
    <p>uploaded successfully as far as we can tell</p>
    </body>
    </html>'
```

Once that script is in a suitable location, you need an HTML page with a little JavaScript to hook it up to.

Supporting HTML and JavaScript for GPX Viewing

We start with the most basic Google Maps instance, modified to support VML and Internet Explorer.

```
    <!DOCTYPE html PUBLIC "-//W3C//DTD XHTML 1.0 Strict//EN"
       "http://www.w3.org/TR/xhtml1/DTD/xhtml1-strict.dtd">
    <html xmlns="http://www.w3.org/1999/xhtml" xmlns:v
       ="urn:schemas-microsoft-com:vml">
      <head>
        <title>Google Maps GPX Viewer</title>
        <style type="text/css">
        v\:* {
          behavior:url(#default#VML);
        }
        </style>
        <script src="http://maps.google.com/maps?file=api&v=1&key
          =YOUR_KEY_GOES_HERE" type="text/javascript"></script>
      <script type="text/javascript">
      //<![CDATA[
      var map;
      function addMap() {
        map = new GMap(document.getElementById("map"));
        map.addControl(new GLargeMapControl());
        map.addControl(new GMapTypeControl ());
        map.centerAndZoom(new GPoint(0.0, 0.0), 16);
      }
```

```
    //]]>
   </script>
   </head>
   <body onLoad="onMap();">
     <div id="map" style="width: 740px; height: 500px; margin: 10px 0 0 0;">
   </div>
   </body>
   </html>
```

The Ruby code described above expects to receive a GPX file from an HTML multipart form. That form should look something like this:

```
<form name="gpxupload" action="ruby/upload-gpx.rbx"
  enctype="multipart/form-data" method="POST" target="sekrit">
  <label for="gpxfile">Choose a GPX file here:</label>
  <input type="file" name="gpxfile" />
  <input type="submit" value="submit" />
</form>
```

You can see that this form is being submitted to a frame called sekrit. That's pretty straightforward to add to the HTML too:

```
<iframe width="740" height="200" border="1"
  name="sekrit" id="sekrit"></iframe>
```

And once those items are in your HTML file, all that remains is to add the following JavaScript after the addMap() function.

```
// whenever a waypoint element is encountered (used by Ruby and JS parsers)
function addpin(lat,lon,text) {
  if (lat && lon) {
    var p = new GPoint(lon,lat);
    var marker = new GMarker(p);
    if (text) {
      // supplied text is wrapped in a <p> tag but can contain other html
      var html = "<p>" + text + "</p>";
      GEvent.addListener(marker, "click", function() {
        marker.openInfoWindowHtml(html);
      });
    }
    map.addOverlay(marker);
    map.centerAndZoom(p,4);
  }
}

// whenever a trkseg element is encountered (only used by Ruby parser)
function gpxtrack(track) {
  if (track) {
    if (track.length >= 4) {
      var points = [];
      for (i = 0; i < track.length; i+=2) {
        points[points.length] = new GPoint(track[i+1],track[i]);
      }
      map.addOverlay(new GPolyline(points));
```

```
        map.centerAndZoom(points[0],4);
    }
  }
}
```

Client-Side Implementation

Instead of parsing the GPX on the server side, and returning some Java-Script to an `iframe`, which calls functions in its parent, we can actually use JavaScript to do the whole job—fetch the GPX file and parse it, too. The one problem with this approach is that JavaScript is only allowed to access files hosted on the same domain as the web page it runs in. To get around this, we implemented a PHP proxy that bounces remote GPX files off our server to let JavaScript have it's way with them.

To see this in action, add the following to the JavaScript after the gpxtrack( ) function above.

```
// this is called on submit from an html form
function fetchfile( ) {

  // disable the form (there's probably a nicer way to do this)
  document.getElementById("submitbutton").disabled = true;
  // find the URL from the form (you might want to check that it's a valid
URL)
  var url = document.getElementById('gpxfile').value;

  // create an XMLHttpRequest object, using Google's utility which
  // abstracts away the browser differences
  var request = GXmlHttp.create( );

  // fetch the URL via a proxy script on your server
  // (otherwise you can only fetch URLs from the same domain
  //  as the javascript is server from)
  request.open("GET", 'proxy.php?url='+URLencode(url), true);

  // tell the request what to do if the file is successfully received
  request.onreadystatechange = function( ) {
    if (request.readyState == 4) {
      var xmlDoc = GXml.parse(request.responseText);
      if (xmlDoc) {

        var lastPoint; // for centring the map on the last thing of interest

        var trks = xmlDoc.documentElement.getElementsByTagName("trk");
        for (var i = 0; i < trks.length; i++) {

          var trksegs = trks[i].getElementsByTagName("trkseg");
          for (var j = 0; j < trksegs.length; j++) {

            var trkpts = trksegs[j].getElementsByTagName("trkpt");
```

```
var points; // array to contain GPoints
var count = 201;
var diff = 0.000000001;

while (count > 200) {

  // empty the points array
  points = [];

  // we always add the first point
  var first = true;

  // characteristics of the last GPoint added to the points array
  var oldlon = 0.0;
  var oldlat = 0.0;
  var oldvx = 0.0;
  var oldvy = 0.0;

  var lat;
  var lon;
  for (var k = 0; k < trkpts.length; k++) {
    lat = parseFloat(trkpts[k].getAttribute("lat"))
    lon = parseFloat(trkpts[k].getAttribute("lon"))
    if (first == true) {
      points[points.length] = new GPoint( lon, lat );
      first = false;
      count = 1;
    }
    else {
      vx = oldlon - lon;
      vy = oldlat - lat;
      dx = oldvx - vx;
      dy = oldvy - vy;
      if ( (dx*dx)+(dy*dy) > diff ) {
        count += 1;
        points[points.length] = new GPoint( lon, lat );
        oldvx = vx;
        oldvy = vy;
        oldlat = lat;
        oldlon = lon;
      }
    }
  } // for

  // if we have >200 pts, we'll try again using a bigger threshold
  diff *= 5.0

} // while

map.addOverlay(new GPolyline(points));
lastPoint = points[0];
```

```
        } // for j (each trkseg)

      } // for i (each trk)

      var wpts = xmlDoc.documentElement.getElementsByTagName("wpt");
      for (var i = 0; i < wpts.length; i++) {
        var text = "Waypoint info:<br/>"
        for (var wpt = wpts[i].firstChild; wpt; wpt = wpt.nextSibling) {
          // different browsers handle xml attributes differently
          // this should present waypoint attributes as key:value pairs
          if (wpt.text) {
            text += wpt.nodeName + ": " + wpt.text + "<br/>";
          }
          else if (wpt.nodeType != 3) {
            text += wpt.nodeName + ": " + wpt.firstChild.nodeValue + "<br/>";
          }
        }
        addpin( parseFloat(wpts[i].getAttribute("lat")),
                parseFloat(wpts[i].getAttribute("lon")),
                text );
      }

      map.centerAndZoom(lastPoint,4);

    }
    else {
      alert("xmldoc seems to be null: " + xmlDoc);
    }
  }
}
  request.send(null);
  document.getElementById("submitbutton").disabled = false;
}

// this is ugly, and possibly there's a better way to do
// it with some "proper" javascript. I found it on the web...
function URLencode(sStr) {
  return escape(sStr).replace(/\+/g, '%2B')
      .replace(/\"/g,'%22').replace(/\'/g, '%27');
}
```

You can remove the iframe since we're using XMLHttpRequest this time, and change the HTML form to the following:

```
<form name="gpxform" onsubmit="fetchfile(); return false;">
  <label for="gpxfile">Type the (valid) URL of a (valid)
      GPX file here:</label>
  <input type="text" name="gpxfile" id="gpxfile" value="http://" />
  <input type="submit" value="submit" id="submitbutton" name="submitbutton" />
</form>
```

The PHP proxy we used in *proxy.php* looked like this:

```php
<?php
    // note that this will not follow redirects
    // you really should validate the URL too
    readfile($_GET['url']);
?>
```

And that's it!

Other Possibilities

There are a lot more things you can do with this. A few of the most obvious include:

- Fix the waypoint metadata JavaScript parser to work in Safari.
- Implement the waypoint metadata parsing in Ruby.
- In Ruby, save the resulting file on your server, so the maps are linkable.
- With JavaScript or Ruby, accept a URL in a query string, and then fetch it via HTTP so that the maps are linkable.
- For the Ruby version, submit the file using `XMLHttpRequest` and return a bit of JavaScript to eval, instead of futzing around with `iframe`.

See Also

- How to use Google Maps' XSLT voodoo to process the GPX file: *http://cse-mjmcl.cse.bris.ac.uk/blog/2005/07/26/1122414882406.html*
- How to modify the pin icon/contents: *http://maps.kylemulka.com/ gpxviewer.php*
- A standalone VB version: *http://www.planetsourcecode.com/vb/scripts/ ShowCode.asp?txtCodeId=61857&lngWId=1*

—Tom Carden & Steve Coast

H A C K **Map Your Wardriving Expeditions**
#38 Found Wi-Fi nearby? Put it on a map!

My interest in Wi-Fi is what got me started with GIS. I had been following the early 802.11 devices and was psyched to read about new modern and cheaply made wireless equipment in the news—and then actually see them on the shelves of various stores. Businesses of all sizes and millions of households started buying and installing these devices all over the place. I wondered where these things were being installed, and just how many were around.

Not long afterwards, I learned that there were people who would go out in their cars with GPSs and laptops, recording the locations of these wireless signals. These *wardrivers*, I learned, weren't breaking into these networks, but were comparing findings such as the funny names for some of the networks and the locations of the increasingly popular local wireless hotspots. I figured I had to try this out, and after about five minutes, I was hooked.

I was still curious about what my findings looked like. I had to figure out not only how to plot them, but also how to plot them on a map and on the Web. After a while, and with another curious person, Eric Blevins, we put together *http://WiFiMaps.com*.

WiFiMaps.com is a web-based geographic map of where Wi-Fi has been installed. The locations are updated by the users, who upload their wardriving scans of various areas. In turn, the site uses TIGER, Mapserver, and a host of other open source and otherwise free tools to plot street-level maps of Wi-Fi installations for those who wonder.

You too can do the same thing—and not just the wondering part, but also the where part. We'll do some wardriving and use a PHP script to parse the data found, and then plot the Wi-Fi spots on Google Maps.

The Hack

For collecting Wi-Fi data, I generally use Netstumbler, available from *http://www.netstumbler.com*, which is popular among wardrivers. For free 'nix operating systems, Kismet (*http://www.kismetwireless.net/*) is the tool of choice, while on Mac OS X, there's both MacStumbler (*http://www.macstumbler.com/*) and KisMAC (*http://kismac.binaervarianz.de*). In this hack, we'll be exporting data from these programs in the *WiScan* log format, which all four programs should happily generate. WiScan is a tab-delimited text file with its own characteristics, and perhaps there are other wardriving packages that also export to this format.

So, go out for a wardrive! If you are in a densely populated area, even a 20-minute wardrive can produce thousands of points. Be safe! Don't be tempted to access any of the networks you find while wardriving unless you have permission from the owner, or you are at a public hotspot. Also, pay attention to the road while collecting data—not your laptop.

The Code

We have four components to mapping the data you've just collected: the HTML form, the plain and simple Google Maps code, the wacky PHP parser bits, and some interesting local data to plot. You'll need access to and permission for a web server with PHP, and to be familiar enough with those to get the code situated.

Let's start with the HTML upload form, which will allow us to send our WiScan log to the server to be mapped. Call this file *index.html*:

```html
<html>
    <head>
        <title>Wi-Fi Data on Google Maps</title>
    </head>
    <body>
        <form enctype="multipart/form-data"
            action="post.php"
            method="post">
        Send this file:
        <input name="userfile" type="file">
        <input type="submit" value="Send File">
        </form>
    </body>
</html>
```

This is quite simple, and I may have even not included some extra functionality. This seemed to work okay, however. Then we can go to the Google Maps default JavaScript setup described in Chapter 2. I decided to add the large zoom control and the map type control, so you can switch between street maps and satellite imagery.

```
Map.addControl(new GLargeMapControl());
Map.addControl(new GMapTypeControl());
```

Next is the magical PHP code. We'll keep some sanity here by paring things down by MAC address and doing an average on the various points. This will give us a pseudocenter for placing our markers. We also use a spatial average to generate the starting map. Where you would normally put the following line in your JavaScript:

```
map.centerAndZoom(new GPoint(-122.141944, 37.441944), 4);
```

... replace it instead with the PHP code shown here:

```php
<?php
    // PHP WiScan parser

    // Strips-off header and entries with no lat/lng
    function stripulate($line) {
            if ( ereg("^#", $line) ) { return 0; }
            if ( ereg("^[NS] 0.0000", $line) ) { return 0; }
            return 1;
    }

    // self parsing accumulator
    function splitotron($line) {
```

```
                    global $MAC;
                    global $center;

                    // Change N/S to +/-
                    $line = ereg_replace("^N ", "", $line);
                    $line = ereg_replace("^S ", "-", $line);

                    // Strip-off parenthesis
                    $line = ereg_replace("[ )\t(]+", "\t", $line);

                    // Change E/W to +/-
                    $line = ereg_replace("^([0-9.-]+)\tE\t", "\\1\t", $line);
                    $line = ereg_replace("^([0-9.-]+)\tW\t", "\\1\t-", $line);

                    // Split by tabs
                    $cols = preg_split("/\t/", $line);

                    // Add lats with same MAC
                    $MAC[$cols[4]]["lat"] += $cols[0];

                    // Add longs with same MAC
                    $MAC[$cols[4]]["lng"] += $cols[1];

                    // We'll just make them equal here
                    $MAC[$cols[4]]["ssid"] = $cols[2];

                    // Accumulate how many per MAC
                    $MAC[$cols[4]]["cnt"] ++;

                    // Add 'em all together for the center
                    $center["lat"] += $cols[0];
                    $center["lng"] += $cols[1];

                // Accumulate for the center
                    $center["cnt"] ++;

        }

// Deal with the upload
$name = $_FILES['userfile']['name'];
if (copy($_FILES['userfile']['tmp_name'], "tmp/$name")) {
        $uploadfile = file("tmp/$name");

        // Apply Stripulate function to the uploaded data
        $uploadfile = array_filter($uploadfile, "stripulate");

        // Apply Splitotron to the uploaded data
        $uploadfile = array_map("splitotron", $uploadfile);

        // Generate centerpoint for map
        $centerlat = $center["lat"] / $center["cnt"];
        $centerlng = $center["lng"] / $center["cnt"];
        echo "map.centerAndZoom(new GPoint({$centerlng},{$centerlat}),2);";
```

```
// Generate points and markers
foreach ($MAC as $mac => $unique) {
        $divlat = $unique["lat"] / $unique["cnt"];
        $divlng = $unique["lng"] / $unique["cnt"];
        echo "var point = new GPoint({$divlng}, {$divlat});\n";
        echo "var marker = new GMarker(point);
        \nmap.addOverlay(marker);";
        }
}

?>
```

Once you have these scripts in place, you will need to create a temporary directory with appropriate write permissions. You should then be able to call up your PHP script, upload a WiScan file, and have the results displayed on a Google Map, which might look like Figure 4-25.

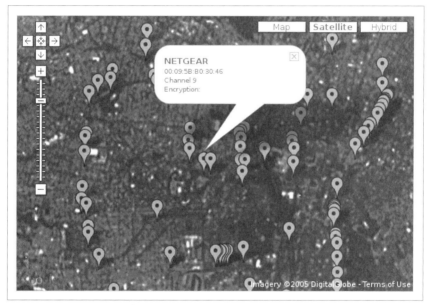

Figure 4-25. Some results from a wardriving expedition

Hacking the Hack

If you're using Kismet, you can have it generate logfiles in its custom XML format and use a combination of JavaScript and XSLT to translate the log entries directly into HTML for the info window, without the need for PHP. You can see an example of this online at *http://mappinghacks.com/projects/gmaps/kismet.html*. Since you can view source on that page to see its inner workings, we'll just cover the juicy bits. Here's a somewhat simplified snippet of a Kismet XML log:

```
<wireless-network wep="false"
      first-time="Sat Nov 27 16:35:00 2004"
      last-time="Sat Nov 27 18:21:56 2004">
   <SSID>linksys</SSID>
   <BSSID>00:11:22:33:44:55</BSSID>
   <channel>6</channel>
   <encryption>None</encryption>
   <gps-info unit="metric">
     <min-lat>6.2069</min-lat>
     <min-lon>-75.5629</min-lon>
     <max-lat>6.2078</max-lat>
     <max-lon>-75.5618</max-lon>
   </gps-info>
</wireless-network>
```

Each wireless-network element in the log contains details about each network seen, including a gps-info element that describes the area in which the network was detected. We can use an XSLT stylesheet to turn each of these entries into HTML:

```
<?xml version="1.0"?>
<xsl:stylesheet version="1.0" xmlns:xsl="http://www.w3.org/1999/XSL/Transform">
   <xsl:template match="wireless-network">
      <div style="width: 200px; max-height: 75px;">
         <div style="font-size: 125%; font-weight: bold;">
            <xsl:value-of select="SSID" />
         </div>
         <div style="font-color: #ccc">
            <div><xsl:value-of select="BSSID" /></div>
            <div>Channel <xsl:value-of select="channel" /></div>
            <div>Encryption: <xsl:value-of select="encryption" /></div>
         </div>
      </div>
   </xsl:template>
</xsl:stylesheet>
```

The stylesheet identifies a log entry by looking elements in the log called wireless-network, and then outputs an HTML div element, using the values of the SSID, BSSID, channel, and encryption elements from inside each log entry. The HTML that would result from the XSLT transformation of the example log entry using this stylesheet would look something like this:

```
<div style="width: 200px; max-height: 75px;">
  <div style="font-size: 125%; font-weight: bold;">linksys</div>
  <div style="font-color: #ccc">
    <div>00:11:22:33:44:55</div>
    <div>Channel 6</div>
    <div>Encryption: None</div>
  </div>
</div>
```

On our map page, we fetch the Kismet log using GXmlHttp and feed it to a function called mapFeed( ). This function uses the JavaScript DOM API to find all the wireless-network entries and then looks inside each one to find the minimum latitude and longitude of the network's coverage area. For each network node with geographic information, a GPoint object is created with its coordinates, which is passed to another function, addMarker( ), to create a marker on the map for that node.

```
function mapFeed (xml) {
    var items = xml.documentElement
                    .getElementsByTagName("wireless-network");

    map.clearOverlays();

    for (var i = 0; i < items.length; i++) {
        var gpsinfo = items[i].getElementsByTagName("gps-info");
        if (gpsinfo.length == 0) continue;

        var lon = gpsinfo[0].getElementsByTagName("min-lon")[0]
                            .childNodes[0].nodeValue;
        var lat = gpsinfo[0].getElementsByTagName("min-lat")[0]
                            .childNodes[0].nodeValue;
        var x = parseFloat(lon);
        var y = parseFloat(lat);
        if (x && x != 90 && y && y != 180) {
            var point = new GPoint(x, y);
            var marker = addMarker(point, items[i]);
            map.addOverlay(marker);
        }
    }
}
```

The addMarker( ) function is almost painfully simple:

```
function addMarker (point, xml) {
    var marker = new GMarker(point);
    GEvent.addListener(marker, "click", function () {
        marker.openInfoWindowXslt( xml, "kismet2marker.xsl" );
    });
    return marker;
}
```

The supplied point is used to create a new GMarker, and then a click event is added to that marker, and the marker is returned. Later, when a user clicks on the marker, the event handler calls marker.openInfoWindowXslt( ), which fetches our XSLT stylesheet from the server, applies it to the DOM element containing the log entry for that wireless node, and then takes the resulting HTML and sticks it into a new info window over the marker. The result is quite elegant, because instead of having to assemble the HTML layout of the info window in JavaScript (which can get quite messy), we can use an external XSLT stylesheet to cleanly separate our logic and our presentation. If we want to add other data from the logfiles to the info window, we can do so by updating the XSLT without ever having to touch the JavaScript again.

The JavaScript in this example could stand some improvement. For example, we could fetch the maximum lat/long for each node and average them with the minimum lat/long for a more accurate position. We could also display a different marker based on the contents of the encryption field, so that we could see, at a glance, which networks were open and which were closed. We could add some logic to track the maximum and minimum coordinates of our logfile and set the map center and zoom level appropriately [Hack #58]. Finally, as wardriving logs tend to pick up lots of points quickly, we might want to look into using "Show Lots of Stuff—Quickly" [Hack #59] as a means of speeding up the map display.

—Drew from Zhrodague

HACK #39 Track Your Every Move with Google Earth

Ever wanted to have your own spy in the sky watching your every move, tracking you wherever you go?

Google Earth, formerly known as Keyhole, is the desktop-based big brother to Google Maps, offering 3D overviews of major cities, mountains, and other terrain, as well as local businesses and information, driving directions, and maps. Its features are far too numerous to mention here, but you can find out more and download a free version at *http://earth.google.com/*. Tragically, although it's based on the OpenGL standard, Google Earth is, as of this writing, supported on Windows only.

One of Google Earth's most interesting features is the ability to bookmark a particular view of a place or places, and then export that view to other Google Earth users via the Keyhole Markup Language (KML) format. The XML-based KML format is good for adding static content to Google Earth (e.g., bridges, monuments, or buildings), but how do we map things that move?

Fortunately, Google Earth has something called a *Network Link*, which we'll look at a bit more in a second. The upshot is that we can use it to read in a *.kml* file that holds our position every few seconds. We also have a GPS system that updates our position every few seconds. The hack we're going to attempt is to constantly get the values from the GPS system into the *.kml* file. This is surprisingly easy to do on Linux, but we're running Google Earth on Windows, where things are slightly more, er, entertaining.

First, the tools we're going to use: Google Earth (and its Network Link feature), Firefox, one Garmin GPS receiver with a serial cable, a copy of Garnix for MS-DOS, two *.bat* files, *ping*, possibly some sticky tape, string, and a bit of luck. We'll talk about the other bits of software, like GPSBabel, but even if you don't have all this stuff—i.e., you have a different brand of GPS receiver—there should still be enough here to get you hacking around any problems.

Peering into the Keyhole

Let's have a closer look at the *.kml* file we're going to be creating. Start up Google Earth, zoom into someplace near home, and press Ctrl-N to add a new Placemark. Call it something useful like "Me" and click OK. The Placemark will appear on the map, as well as in the Places section over on the left. Right-click on the Placemark and select Save As. Save it as *me.kml* (not *.kmz*) into somewhere really easy to get to, as we'll be writing DOS *.bat* files in a while, so somewhere close to the root drive with a short name is preferable. I made a folder called *c:\geo* and used that.

If you open your *.kml* file in Notepad, or any other text editor, you'll something along the lines of the following:

```
<?xml version="1.0" encoding="UTF-8"?>
<kml xmlns="http://earth.google.com/kml/2.0">
<Placemark>
  <name>Me</name>
  <LookAt>
    <longitude>-2.189175686596352</longitude>
    <latitude>53.0420501867381</latitude>
    <range>769.3231615683798</range>
    <tilt>-8.237346562804484e-011</tilt>
    <heading>-0.002462111503350637</heading>
  </LookAt>
  <styleUrl>root://styleMaps#default+nicon=0x307+hicon=0x317</styleUrl>
  <Point>
    <coordinates>-2.19004490258348,53.04134242507396,0</coordinates>
  </Point>
</Placemark>
</kml>
```

The values we're primarily concerned with are the <longitude>, <latitude> and <coordinates> elements. These should match each other, as the place we are looking at and the point we're at should be the same. I normally set the tilt and heading values to be 0 when I generate *.kml* files with code.

Back to Google Earth, right-click the Placemark, and then delete it—back to square one. We're doing this because it's just no rock-n-roll fun as a "normal" Placemark: we'll make ours far more dynamic, by loading it in as a Network Link!

From the top menu bar, pick Add → Network Link. Once more, pick a useful name, e.g., "Me", and then hit the Browse button and locate the *me.kml* file we just saved. At the moment, it's still acting as a normal Placemark, so change the time-based Refresh When option to Periodically and make the period every 10 seconds. Finally (for fun) tick the Fly to View on Refresh checkbox, then press OK.

What do we have? Google Earth loading in the same KML file over and over again, every 10 seconds, going to the same location over and over again. The next step is fairly obvious: we want to update the values in that *.kml* file every few seconds from some gnarly code we've thrown together. If you're so inclined and outfitted, try firing up your favorite development environment and having it spit random values into the KML file—and then sit back and watch as Google Earth tries to fly all over the place!

Back Down to Earth

Of course, we want *your* location, not some random one. We'll be using your Garmin GPS receiver to get your position and the cable you probably felt you were paying far too much money for (unless it came with your receiver or you built it yourself, in which case, good for you) to connect it to your PC.

We also need some software that'll fetch your longitude and latitude from the GPS device. You would think that would be a simple task, but unless my search engine fu is failing me badly, I couldn't find anything that just got our location from the device. Lots of applications for downloading waypoints and tracklogs, loads of neat scripts for Linux, but Windows programs for lat and long in an easy to use format? No such luck.

The closest I could find was the MS-DOS binary version of Garnix from *http://homepage.ntlworld.com/anton.helm/garnix.html*. Download it and unzip it into your *c:\geo* folder, or where ever you decided to put your *.kml* file. You'll need to edit the *GARNIX.CFG* file in Notepad to read as follows:

```
port:        "com4";
deg_min_sec;
datum:       "WGS84";
;grid:       "UTM";
;zone:       "33";
;
;See datum.cfg for datum names
;See grid.cfg for grid and zone names
```

Replace com4 with whatever com port your GPS device connects on—usually somewhere from *com1* through *com4*—and make sure the semicolon is removed from the front of the deg_min_sec line. If you don't know what com port your GPS uses, and you own Google Earth Plus, connect your GPS, turn it on and then pick Tools → GPS Device, which will probably figure out which port it's connected on. Alternatively, you can experiment with EasyGPS from *http://www.easygps.com*.

With your GPS system connected to your PC, go outside until you get a GPS reading locked in and have your lat/long position. If you can't go outside, try hanging the GPS unit out the window, maybe attach it to a stick or pole—this is where the sticky tape and string comes in! (And you thought we were kidding about that?) If none of those options are possible, then there's a slightly less exciting one: most GPS units have a demo mode, hidden somewhere in the settings menu. If you turn that on, it'll start making up positions for you.

Open up a command window by clicking Start → Run and then type in cmd, and click OK. Then change to the correct directory and test out Garnix as follows:

```
c:\> cd c:\geo
c:\geo\> garnix -x
```

With luck you'll get a response along the lines of:

```
Device ID:      eTrex Software Version 2.14
Device Time:    17:06:31-2005/07/23

Current Position (WGS84):
Latitude    53deg  6min  2.43sec
Longitude   -2deg 11min 55.59sec
```

Different devices may give slightly different results. We'll have to deal with this later on, but it only takes a little tinkering.

> If you can't get connected with Garnix, all is not lost. As long as your GPS system is cofnnected on com ports 1 to 4 you can use G7To(W) from *http://www.gpsinformation.org/ronh/#g7to*. The command line you'll need to use is:
>
> ```
> c:\geo\> G7tow -n -i G45P
> ```
>
> *n* is the serial port your unit is attached to. The output is different from Garnix, so you'll need to hack the JavaScript shown later. Alternatively, you can try using GPSBabel, as described later on in the hack.

Now we have the information, but not in a useful format. There are a few options; for example, you could download the source code and hack it around to output the numbers in decimal format, or even take it a step further and write out the whole *.kml* file. (Please email us if you do this!) You could probably throw together some regular expressions in Perl to perform mysterious voodoo coding to automagically convert the output or, as we're going to do now, turn to Firefox and code up a quick solution in JavaScript.

Before we do that, back to the command line once more, to do this:

```
c:\geo\> garnix -x > results.txt
```

This writes the information into a text file, which we can use for testing. You can return indoors now or pull the GPS back through the window and switch it off; we'll not be needing it for a while.

The Code

Next, we need to turn the output from Garnix into something Google Earth can use. To keep things simple(ish) we're going to use JavaScript and open the page in Firefox to run it. In the same folder as everything else, create an *index.html* file and copy the code below into it. Alternatively, you can download the code from *http://googlemapshacks.com/projects/gmaps/tracking/*.

```
<!DOCTYPE HTML PUBLIC "-//W3C//DTD HTML 4.01 Transitional//EN">
<html>
<head>
    <meta http-equiv="refresh" content="10">
    <title>geo convert</title>

<script>
var readfile = "c:\\geo\\results.txt";
var writefile = "c:\\geo\\me.kml";
var fAlt = "750";
```

The above code sets up the HTML page to reload every 10 seconds and defines where we want to read and write the files to. The fAlt variable is the altitude we want the camera in Google Earth to hover above the surface. Different situations warrant different values, so it's best to play around to see what suits you best.

The next two functions deal with reading and writing files to the local drive. A certain amount of jumping through security hoops is needed to get Firefox to allow JavaScript to interact with the filesystem. At the end of the fnRead function we'll call the fnWrangleText function, which does the hard work.

When you run this page, just load it into Firefox as a file using File → Open File. You're not trying to load this as a web page—and indeed the file read/write will fail if you do. No web server is needed for this hack!

```
function fnWrite(sText) {
    try {
        netscape.security.PrivilegeManager.
enablePrivilege("UniversalXPConnect");
    } catch (e) {
        alert("Permission to save file was denied.");
    }
    var file = Components.classes["@mozilla.org/file/local;1"]
                    .createInstance(Components.interfaces.nsILocalFile);
```

```
        file.initWithPath( writefile );
        if ( file.exists() == false )
            file.create( Components.interfaces.nsIFile.NORMAL_FILE_TYPE, 420 );
        var outputStream =
            Components.classes["@mozilla.org/network/file-output-stream;1"]
                    .createInstance( Components.interfaces.nsIFileOutputStream );
        outputStream.init( file, 0x04 | 0x08 | 0x20, 420, 0 );
        var result = outputStream.write( sText, sText.length );
        outputStream.close( );
    }

    function fnRead( ) {
        try {
            netscape.security.PrivilegeManager.
    enablePrivilege("UniversalXPConnect");
        } catch (e) {
            alert("Permission to read file was denied.");
        }
        var file = Components.classes["@mozilla.org/file/local;1"]
                        .createInstance(Components.interfaces.nsILocalFile);
        file.initWithPath( readfile );
        if ( file.exists() == false )
            alert("File does not exist");
        var is = Components.classes["@mozilla.org/network/file-input-stream;1"]
                        .createInstance( Components.interfaces.
    nsIFileInputStream );
        is.init( file,0x01, 00004, null);
        var sis =
            Components.classes["@mozilla.org/scriptableinputstream;1"]
                    .createInstance( Components.interfaces.
    nsIScriptableInputStream );
        sis.init( is );
        var readText = sis.read( sis.available( ) );
        fnWrangleText(readText);
    }
```

The next part is where it gets interesting. First of all, we'll create pointers to the two textboxes that'll we'll use to see what's going on.

```
    function fnWrangleText(sText) {
        var sInput = document.getElementById('txtInput');
        var sOutput = document.getElementById('txtOutput');
```

We want to get to the values right at the end of the text. There are all sorts of ways to do this, but I happen to find this the easiest to follow. We're going to remove all the line breaks and extra spaces to make the text just one long line. Next, we turn the text into an array, using the spaces that are left as the divider, so that each word becomes its own element in the array.

```
        sText = sText.replace(/\s+/g, " ");
        sInput.value = sText;

        var aText = sText.split(" ");
```

The information we want is held in the *last* eight words, or elements, as they are now; therefore, we can count back from the end to get at the data we want. Sometimes, there will be a space at the very end, which we have to take into account. If we count back from the end, we see that "53deg" (using the example output from above) is the 7th word from the end, planning for the extra space we count 8 back to get at it. For the latitude we need the 8th, 7th, and 6th words from the end, then the 4th, 3rd, and 2nd for the longitude. The division of minutes by 60 and seconds by 3,600 allows us to combine all three values into decimal degrees.

```
var fLatDeg = parseFloat(aText[aText.length-8]);
var fLatMin = parseFloat(aText[aText.length-7])/60;
var fLatSec = parseFloat(aText[aText.length-6])/3600;
var fLat = Math.abs(fLatDeg) + fLatMin + fLatSec;
if (fLatDeg < 0) fLat *= -1;

var fLonDeg = parseFloat(aText[aText.length-4]);
var fLonMin = parseFloat(aText[aText.length-3])/60;
var fLonSec = parseFloat(aText[aText.length-2])/3600;
var fLon = Math.abs(fLonDeg) + fLonMin + fLonSec;
if (fLonDeg < 0) fLon *= -1;
```

One last check shown below makes sure we have a valid number for the latitude and longitude. It's possible that your output from Garnix is slightly different from that shown above, so you may need to change the values needed to count back from the end. Sometimes you may also get a clash when you attempt to read the file just as Garnix is writing it, which will just cause us to skip an update using the code below.

```
if (isNaN(fLon) || isNaN(fLat)) {
    sOutput.value = fLatDeg + ' ' + fLatMin + ' ' + fLatSec + ' : '
                  + fLonDeg + ' ' + fLonMin + ' ' + fLonSec;
    return;
}
```

Finally the important bit: we construct the contents for our *.kml* file, putting the new values into it, then we send it to the fnWrite( ) function to save it back out.

```
sOutput.value = '<?xml version="1.0" encoding="UTF-8"?>\n';
sOutput.value = sOutput.value + '<kml xmlns="http://earth.google.com/
kml/2.0">\n';
sOutput.value = sOutput.value + '<Placemark>\n';
sOutput.value = sOutput.value + '  <name>Me</name>\n';
sOutput.value = sOutput.value + '  <LookAt>\n';
sOutput.value = sOutput.value + '    <longitude>' + fLon + '</longitude>\n';
sOutput.value = sOutput.value + '    <latitude>' + fLat + '</latitude>\n';
sOutput.value = sOutput.value + '    <range>' + fAlt + '</range>\n';
sOutput.value = sOutput.value + '    <tilt>0</tilt>\n';
sOutput.value = sOutput.value + '    <heading>0</heading>\n';
```

```
         sOutput.value = sOutput.value + '  </LookAt>\n';
         sOutput.value = sOutput.value +
             '  <styleUrl>root://styleMaps#default+nicon=0x307+hicon=
                   0x317</styleUrl>\n';
         sOutput.value = sOutput.value + '  <Point>\n';
         sOutput.value = sOutput.value +
             '     <coordinates>' + fLon + ',' + fLat + ',0</coordinates>\n';
         sOutput.value = sOutput.value + '  </Point>\n';
         sOutput.value = sOutput.value + '</Placemark>\n';
         sOutput.value = sOutput.value + '</kml>\n';

         fnWrite(sOutput.value);

    }
    </script>
    </head>
```

The onLoad attribute of the body element below starts the whole thing off.
The remainder of the HTML is just layout and formatting.

```
<body onload="fnRead()">
<table>
    <tr>
        <td>
            <strong>Input Text</strong><br />
            <textarea id="txtInput" cols="80" rows="3"></textarea>
        </td>
        <td rowspan="2" valign="top"><strong>Map Results</strong></td>
     </tr>
    <tr>
        <td>
            <strong>Output Text</strong><br />
            <textarea id="txtOutput" cols="80" rows="18"></textarea>
        </td>
    </tr>
    <tr>
        <td colspan="2"><strong>Save Results</strong></td>
    </tr>
</table>
</body>
</html>
```

We have Google Earth loading in the *.kml* file every 10 seconds and the
JavaScript page reading in the *results.txt* file and writing out the *me.kml* file
every 10 seconds. There's just one thing left to do, which is to grab the data
from the GPS unit every few seconds. Time to go back outside or put the
unit into demo mode! What we want to do is call the command garnix -x >
results.txt once every few seconds. We could, for example, write a *.bat* file
called *go.bat* and put the following in it:

```
garnix -x > results.txt
go
```

That'll run the command and then call itself again. However, that'll really mess us up: CPU usage will rocket up and, most of the time, the file will be in an open, deleted, or being-created state. As a result, our JavaScript will never get a look inside. We need to be able to pause the running for a short while.

Sadly, Microsoft didn't ship MS-DOS with a pause or wait command. There is a file called *sleep.exe* that's part of a 12MB resource kit, but I for one don't want to download 12MB worth of files just for one small application. It's cheeky, but here's what we'll do: we'll create a new file called *wait.bat* and enter this into it:

```
@ping 127.0.0.1 -n 11 -w 1000 > nul
go
```

We're going to ping ourselves as a way of inserting a delay in our script. (yes, seriously—we did say it was a hack!) The parameters we use are -w 1000, which sets the timeout to 1,000 milliseconds, and -n 11, which tells it to send off 11 pings. In principle, this should delay for about 10 seconds, since it won't pause after the last ping. With a bit of experimentation, you'll be able to calibrate how many pings you need for certain lengths of time.

Now, go back and edit the original *go.bat* file like this:

```
garnix -x > results.txt
wait
```

And we're all set!

Wire up the GPS unit and make sure it's on and connected. Then check that the correct com port is selected in the *garnix.cfg* file. Take a deep breath and type go from the Windows command line. A cycle should start with *go.bat* calling *wait.bat* and *wait.bat* after a delay calling *go.bat*. To stop it, type Ctrl-C.

Now, get all three things running: the *.bat* file cycle in the command shell, the *index.html* page reloading in Firefox, and, lastly, Google Earth reading in the *me.kml* file.

Hacking the Hack

Pre-cache the Google Earth data. I'll be the first to admit that needing a wireless connection when you're on the move isn't always ideal or even possible. First off, if you're planning a car trip or even a quick walk, you can go over the route in Google Earth first, and it'll cache the high-resolution images, roads, and other details you decide to enable. You can increase the size of the cache by going to Tools → Options → Cache. Stick the GPS unit and the laptop onto the dashboard, and off you go! You're just playing with the files in the local cache, so no Internet connection is needed.

Tracking with Perl

If the idea of using Firefox to read and write local files seems more than a bit weird to you, you might try obtaining a Windows version of Perl, such as ActivePerl (*http://www.activestate.com/*), and try running the following bit of Perl code with *perl.exe*:

```perl
my ($lat, $lon);
while (1) {
    sleep 10;
    unless (open GARNIX, "garnix -x|") {
        warn "Can't read from garnix: $!\n";
        next;
    }
    while (<GARNIX>) {
        if (/Lat\w+\s+(-?\d+)deg\s+(\d+)min\s+([\d.]+)sec/o) {
            $lat = abs($1) + $2 / 60 + $3 / 3600;
            $lat *= -1 if $lat < 0;
        }
        elsif (/Long\w+\s+(-?\d+)deg\s+(\d+)min\s+([\d.]+)sec/o) {
            $lon = abs($1) + $2 / 60 + $3 / 3600;
            $lon *= -1 if $lat < 0;
        }
    }
    close GARNIX;

    unless (open KML, ">me.kml") {
        warn "Can't write to me.kml: $!\n";
        next;
    }
    print KML <<End;
<?xml version="1.0" encoding="UTF-8"?>
<kml xmlns="http://earth.google.com/kml/2.0">
<Placemark>
  <name>Me</name>
  <LookAt>
    <longitude>$lon</longitude>
    <latitude>$lat</latitude>
    <range>750</range>
    <tilt>0</tilt>
    <heading>0</heading>
```

—continued—

```
    </LookAt>
    <styleUrl>
root://styleMaps#default+nicon=0x307+hicon=0x317
    </styleUrl>
    <Point>
      <coordinates>$lon,$lat,0</coordinates>
    </Point>
  </Placemark>
</kml>
End
    close KML;
}
```

As you can see, this code does basically the same thing as the JavaScript, but without the need for Firefox and the *results.txt* file.

However, if you're willing to use GPSBabel [Hack #35] instead of Garnix, you can actually get away with this simple batch script, since GPSBabel knows how to generate KML directly:

```
@echo off
:again
gpsbabel -i garmin,get_posn -f com1: -o kml \
    -F\tmp\me.kml
ping 127.0.0.1 -n 1 -w 1000 > nul:
goto again
```

Either way, by doing without Firefox, we lose the feedback provided by the browser window, particularly some of the nifty bits described in the "Hacking the Hack" section. Figuring out, for example, how to script FTP or *scp* to upload this file to a server without using Firefox will be left as an exercise for the user.

Let other Google Earth users follow along in real time. You're about to cycle across the country, so obviously you're going to be uploading your photos to Flickr and blogging your progress. It's all very well using the GPS and Google Earth to determine where you are, but what about letting other people know? We want to put our *.kml* file up onto the Internet so other people can connect to it with *their* Network Link.

It's time to update our *index.html* file. Edit the table at the bottom to look like this:

```
<table>
    <tr>
        <td>
            <strong>Input Text</strong><br />
            <textarea id="txtInput" cols="80" rows="3"></textarea>
        </td>
        <td rowspan="2" valign="top">
            <strong>Map Results</strong><br />
```

```
            <iframe id="iMap" width="300" height="400"></iframe>
        </td>
    </tr>
    <tr>
        <td>
            <strong>Output Text</strong><br />
            <textarea id="txtOutput" cols="80" rows="18"></textarea>
        </td>
    </tr>
    <tr>
        <td colspan="2">
            <strong>Save Results</strong><br />
            <iframe id="iSave" width="800" height="40"></iframe>
        </td>
    </tr>
</table>
```

To put the *.kml* file up onto the Internet, we're going to need a server and some server-side scripting. I'll use PHP as an example, but it should be easy enough to convert to any other language. Here's the PHP file, which we'll call *saveKML.php*, and which needs to be uploaded to a server someplace:

```
<?php
$kml = '<?xml version="1.0" encoding="UTF-8"?>';
$kml .= '<kml xmlns="http://earth.google.com/kml/2.0">';
$kml .= '<Placemark>';
$kml .= ' <name>Me</name>';
$kml .= ' <LookAt>';
$kml .= ' <longitude>'.$HTTP_GET_VARS['fLon'].'</longitude>';
$kml .= ' <latitude>'.$HTTP_GET_VARS['fLat'].'</latitude>';
$kml .= ' <range>750</range>';
$kml .= ' <tilt>0</tilt>';
$kml .= ' <heading>0</heading>';
$kml .= ' </LookAt>';
$kml .= ' <styleUrl>root://styleMaps#default+nicon=0x307+hicon=0x317</
styleUrl>';
$kml .= ' <Point>';
$kml .= ' <coordinates>'.$HTTP_GET_VARS['fLon'].','.$HTTP_GET_
VARS['fLat'].'</coordinates>';
$kml .= ' </Point>';
$kml .= '</Placemark>';
$kml .= '</kml>';
$fr = @fopen('me.kml', 'w');
@fputs($fr, $kml);
fclose($fr);
header('Content-Type: text/plain');
print 'saved';
?>
```

The above script takes two parameters, fLon and fLat, from the URL and uses them to build and save a KML file. You'll probably want to change the name in <name>Me</name> to your name, and change the *me.kml* to something else.

In order to upload the coordinates to the server, we'll add this line at the end of the fnWrangleText( ) function:

```
document.getElementById('iSave').src =
    'http://www.yourserver.com/urlPath/saveKML.php?fLat=' + fLat + '&fLon='
+ fLon;
```

Each time your *index.html* file reloads, it'll attempt to call the remote file and pass it your current location. If you happen to be near a Wi-Fi hotspot, your position will be updated. All your friends and family can add your *.kml* file as a Network Link set to update every 30 mins or so and use it to watch your daily progress.

An easier way of getting people to update a network link is to set up the Network Link as you'd want other people to use it, save it, then point people to *that* file rather than the actual *me.kml* file. Doing so will automatically subscribe them to the Network Link without any effort.

The file will look like this:

```
<?xml version="1.0" encoding="UTF-8"?>
<kml xmlns="http://earth.google.com/kml/2.0">
<NetworkLink>
  <description>
    Follow my cycle tour across the USA.
  </description>
  <name>My Road Trip</name>
  <Url>
    <href>http://www.yourserver.com/
        urlPath/me.kml</href>
    <refreshMode>onInterval</refreshMode>
    <refreshInverval>1800</refreshInverval>
  </Url>
</NetworkLink>
</kml>
```

If you don't have a server, you can still update your position by using a service such as Geobloggers.com using the following URL:

```
document.getElementById('iSave').src =      'http://www.geobloggers.com/
recordObject?objName=geoFlickrBot' +
    '&objKey=A56C-2256-FE23&fLat=' + fLat + '&fLon=' + fLon;
```

For your server to serve *.kml* files, you'll need to set up the correct MIME types:

```
application/vnd.google-earth.kml+xml kml
application/vnd.google-earth.kmz kmz
```

Use your favorite search engine to find out how to set up custom MIME types on your web server.

Add other people's photos into the browser window. Finally, add this line at the end of the `fnWrangleText( )` function.

```
document.getElementById('iMap').src =
    'http://www.geobloggers.com/mob/index.cfm?lat=' + fLat + '&lon=' + fLon;
```

If you have a connection to the Internet, Firefox will load the mobile phone version of Geobloggers into the other `iframe`. It shows you the nearest three photos to your current location along with the direction and distance to them. If you are wandering around a city, then every time you found some wireless access, you'd get updates of nearby photos to go and hunt out.

If you're stuck without Internet access, browse to *http://www.geobloggers.com/mob/* using your phone's web browser and enter your position via a form.

Add other people's photos into Google Earth itself. Besides having time-based network links, you can also have network links that update as you move around the Earth. Try adding a new network link to Google Earth, but this time set the location to *http://www.geobloggers.com/fullscreenBackend/dataFeed.cfm.* Set the View-Based Refresh to After Camera Stops, and make the delay four seconds. When you zoom into a location and then pause, after four seconds Google Earth will start to load in Flickr Photos from Geobloggers for the area you are looking at. Combine this with the hack just described and as you move around photos taken by Flickr users will appear.

If you want to see photos from just a single user add `?sUsername=[`*username*`]` onto the end of the URL. Alternatively, if you're viewing an area where you take a lot of photos yourself, you can add `?sExcludeUsername=[`*your username*`]` to the URL to get everyone else's photos.

—*Dan Catt*

The Ghost in Google Ride Finder
Generate street maps from Google's real-time taxi-mapping service.

One of the first Google Map Hacks was released by Google itself. The Google Ride Finder is ostensibly a mapping service to find nearby taxis and airport shuttles in major metro areas. While it's useless for getting a ride with these centrally booked services, it really functions as a very engaging advertisement for these companies. (And, while we're at it, don't we actually need the public transit Google Maps Hacks extended for live updates for sustainable transport alternatives?)

The real appeal is how Google Ride Finder demonstrates the use of real-time, updating spatial data. The immediacy of the Web, combined with geo visualization, has powerful possibilities. In this hack, that live data will be repurposed to reveal the street map "ghost" of airport shuttles and taxis, producing raw data that might be consumed by grassroots mapping projects such as OpenStreetMap (*http://www.openstreetmap.org/*).

The Google Ride Finder lives at *http://labs.google.com/ridefinder*. The initial view shown in Figure 4-26 is of North America, with push pins marking the areas for which they have data.

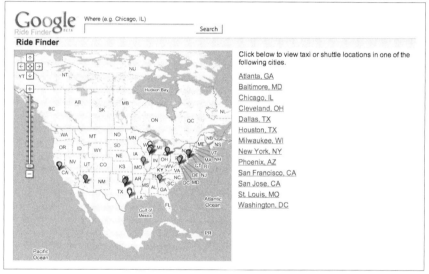

Figure 4-26. Ride Finder home page

If you zoom in to Chicago, you'll get a view like Figure 4-27. Each pushpin represents an individual vehicle, almost all of them taxicabs.

Finding the Data

Like Google Local searches, Google Ride Finder receives its annotations in their geodata format. To find the location of this feed, look in the JavaScript file *http://labs.google.com/ridefinder/data?file=ride_js*, referenced from the HTML source. The Update Vehicle Locations button calls `refreshMarkers( )`, which then calls `updateMarkers( )`. This function constructs the following URL:

```
var j="/ridefinder/data?marker=1&lat="+f+"&lon="+g+"&z="+m+
    "&src="+w+"&notes="+(new Date( )).getTime( );
```

Figure 4-27. Ride Finder in Chicago

In this bit of code, f and g are the lat/long center of the map, m is the zoom level, and w is hardcoded to 3. The notes argument is a timestamp, which seems to be appended to avoid hitting any cache. Constructing a URL with, for example, the center of Manhattan and scale 8, confirms that this is the feed for Ride Finder.

```
http://labs.google.com/ridefinder/data?marker=1&lat=40.750422
    &lon=-73.996328&z=8&src=3&notes=
```

Although each annotation within the feed corresponds to the location of an individual vehicle, no unique identifier is included to link two annotations across an update. It's possible to get near-matches by measuring spatial proximity in successive feeds, which update every five minutes according to Google. The interested reader is invited to give it a try and and see if you can build a poor man's real-time traffic monitoring application.

Accumulating the Data

Here, we're going to accumulate taxi positions over a few days and build up a street map of the city of your choice. Set the latitude and longitude of the data URL, derived from another source, such as *http://geocoder.us/*. Setting zoom to 8 is sufficient to cover a metro region. Append the current timestamp to avoid the cache.

Paste the following code into a file called *accumulate.pl*:

```
#!/usr/bin/perl

$dir = ".";
$date = time;
$lat = 40.750422;
$lon = 73.996328;
$url = " http://labs.google.com/ridefinder/data?"
            . "marker=1&lat=$lat&lon=$lon&z=8&src=1&notes=$date";
system("/usr/bin/wget -P $dir $url");
```

The variable $dir specifies where you will store the location data files. For example, ~/data will store them in the subdirectory named *data/* under your home directory. You want the script to run every five minutes in order to collect data. You can obsessively watch the clock and start the script yourself, or, under a *nix variant, you can use the scheduling feature of the modern operating system. Edit your *crontab* with the command crontab -e. This line will run the script every five minutes.

```
0-59/5 * * * * /home/ride_finder/accumulate.pl
```

Change */home/ride_finder* to match the directory in which you installed the *accumulate.pl* script.

Plotting the Data

After about 24 hours, you'll have enough data to start building ghost maps. This Perl script, *draw.pl*, simply strips the lat/long from the standard input and plots the points as an unprojected map. You'll also need the Image:: Magick module from the CPAN, which you can find at *http://search.cpan.org/ ~jchristy/PerlMagick/*.

```
#!/usr/bin/perl

use Math::Trig qw(deg2rad rad2deg asin);
use Image::Magick;
use POSIX qw(floor);

$lat = 40.750422;
$lon = -73.996328;
$d = 20;
$w = 1500;
$h = 1500;

sub latlon2xy {
    my ($lat,$lon) = @_;
    my @xy;
    $xy[1] = $h * ($north - $lat) / ($north - $south);
    $xy[0] = $w * ($lon - $west) / ($east - $west);
```

```
        return @xy;
}

$radius = 6378.1; #km
$lat = deg2rad($lat);
$lon = deg2rad($lon);
$arc = $d / $radius;

$north = rad2deg($lat + $arc);
$south = rad2deg($lat - $arc);
$west = rad2deg ($lon+asin(-1*sin($arc)/cos( asin(sin($lat)*cos($arc)) )));
$east = rad2deg ($lon+asin( sin($arc)/cos( asin(sin($lat)*cos($arc)) )));

my $img = new Image::Magick->new(size=> $w . "x" . $h, quality=> '100');
$img->ReadImage('xc:white');
while (<>) {
    @points = split "<location", $_;
    foreach $p (@points) {
        $p =~ /lat="(.*?)" lng="(.*?)"/;
        @xy = latlon2xy($1,$2);
        if ($xy[0] >= 0 && $xy[0] <= $w
                && $xy[1] >= 0 && $xy[1] <= $h) {
            $img->Set('pixel[' . floor($xy[0])
                        . ',' . floor($xy[1]) . ']'=>'#f00');
        }
    }
}
$img->Write(filename=>"out.jpg");
```

In order to run the hack, we'll assume you have the script in the current directory and the data you accumulated earlier in a subdirectory called *data/*. From there, run:

```
$ perl draw.pl data/*
```

The script writes the result to an image called *out.jpg* in the current directory. Set variables within the script for the lat/long center of the data feed, and a distance in kilometers of your choosing, which are used to calculate the extents of the map, and the width and height of the image. You want the lat/long to be close to the same as you selected in *accumulate.pl*. With lat/long translated to *x/y* coordinates, ImageMagick is employed to plot each point.

At first you may see just the barest outline of the city, with some major roads and bridges perhaps. With more days of data, individual streets will begin to form along lines of highest density, as suggested by Figure 4-28. (GPS in these vehicles can be inaccurate, resulting in a distribution over the actual street location, possibly bleeding into off-street space and buildings.) Peculiarities of taxi travel will become apparent, with routes to the airport overemphasized and route variations along socioeconomic and districting lines. Maybe you can spot drivers' favorite places for a coffee break.

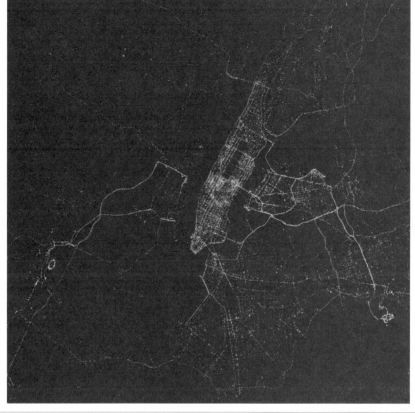

Figure 4-28. Ghost roads of New York

Hacking the Hack

For a neat variation, build an animated GIF with ImageMagick by grouping points by the hour, gradually revealing the street map ghost. Have fun!

See Also

- *crontab* tips are available at *http://www.everything2.com/index.pl?node_id=765412*

—Mikel Maron

HACK #41 How Google Maps Got Me Out of a Traffic Ticket

The democratization of research is demonstrated, and Google Maps serves the cause of justice by answering a basic, but disputed, factual question.

In January of this year, I was pulled over by a traffic officer for "disobeying a steady red," a.k.a. running a red light. I pleaded not guilty to the charge, and, nearly six months later, I went to court to find out the fate of my ticket violation. In the end, it was nearly down to my word against the officer's— but Google Maps saved the day!

There I was, on a bench waiting for my name to be called at the downtown Manhattan DMV hearings bureau. After hearing several testimonies from other drivers I knew this judge wasn't going to be sympathetic to my troubles. She heard driver after driver, but only one had a happy ending (from the driver's point of view).

So I was worried, because being found guilty would mean a $150 fine, plus $50 in penalties, and—worst of all—points on my license. I began to contemplate how it all happened since it had been so long. I jotted down some notes on a small piece of paper, and then came the moment of truth.

After my name was called, I gathered my belongings and made my way up to the stand where the ticketing officer joined me. The judge swore her in and asked for her testimony. The officer did just what I expected—after all, I had been listening to those prior testimonies—and began to describe the scene of the violation. In her story, I noticed one fatal flaw, which I wanted to exploit—but I had no proof whatsoever. The officer stated that the street I was on was a one-way westbound street, and that I was turning onto an avenue that was a two-way street separated by a concrete divider. The flaw was that I had actually been on a two-way street, not a one-way.

At last, the time came for my testimony, and I stated that I had been in midturn, when an oncoming vehicle came toward me very quickly, and I had decided not to make the turn until that SUV passed me. The Judge stopped and asked me how there could be an oncoming vehicle if the street was only one-way. I stated that it was actually a two-way street. The officer reiterated that it was a one-way. Who was the judge to believe? I was desperate for proof, so I did the obvious: I whipped out my notebook computer. I was very lucky to find an extremely bad connection via Wi-Fi. I pulled up Firefox and went to *maps.google.com*. I typed up the intersection and zoomed in as close as possible, as shown in Figure 4-29.

As you can see, Cathedral Parkway (a.k.a. 110th Street) has no arrow indicating the traffic directions. However, 109th and 111th do. I explained to the judge that this means that 110th is a two-way street. The traffic officer

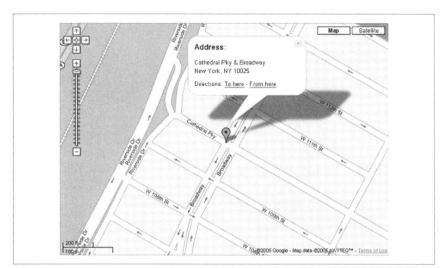

Figure 4-29. Does an absence of arrows mean that Cathedral Parkway is two-way?

begged to differ. She said perhaps an arrow was simply missing from the equation. So I called her bluff and showed the judge another intersection—the one at Times Square, as shown in Figure 4-30.

Figure 4-30. Everyone knows 42nd Street goes both ways

I asked Her Honor if she was familiar with 42nd Street. She nodded, and I continued by observing how all the neighboring streets have arrows to show the direction of traffic, with one exception: 42nd Street, which is well-known to be a two-way street. The judge replied that, due to the officer's poor memory, the violation would have to be dismissed.

Thank you, Google Maps: you rule!

See Also

- This story was originally posted on Gear Live. Gear Live is a web magazine devoted to the high-tech lifestyle, with news, previews, reviews, commentary, and the occasional tip on traffic law:

    http://www.gearlive.com/index.php/news/article/google_maps_helps_ fight_traffic_tickets_07160942/

- The ACLU has an informative publication called *Know Your Rights: What To Do if You're Stopped by the Police* at *http://www.aclu.org/ PolicePractices/PolicePractices.cfm?ID=9609&c=25*

    —Andru Edwards & Edwin Soto, http://www.gearlive.com

Google Maps in Words and Pictures

Hacks 42–50

The reason people love maps so much is that maps tell stories about places, and people love stories. Maps provide a narrative and a context for understanding the world around us. Even the most mundane maps tell a story; for example, a road or subway map's story is about how to get around quickly.

In this chapter, we're going to explore the narrative possibilities inherent in Google Maps. We'll see how Google Maps can be a reading aid, how satellite images don't always tell the full story, and how Google Maps can be mated with online photo services such as Flickr to establish a geographic context for the stories that our photographs tell. Finally, we'll look at the user-friendly end of the "geospatial web," where Google Maps can be used to produce and visualize feeds of information from other sources, to weave our story together into the many stories being told every day on the Internet.

HACK #42 Get More out of What You Read

If maps tell stories, what about the stories that tell maps?

"I lean against a USA Today paper box on Washington and Clark and think, 'Who the hell are you to make such a claim?'" That's the second sentence from the book *Bike Messengers and the Cult of Human Power* by Travis Hugh Culley. It is the story of Travis' work as a bicycle messenger in Chicago. Why did Travis pick that intersection? Did that just happen to be where he was, or does it have more meaning? Where is Washington and Clark?

Enter "Washington and Clark, Chicago, IL" in the location search box and we see in Figure 5-1 that the intersection is, well, in the middle of a lot of streets. That helps, maybe, a little. But I don't know Chicago, so all it means to me is a lot of streets.

Clicking on Satellite gives us the jackpot of Figure 5-2: the intersection is right smack in the middle of downtown.

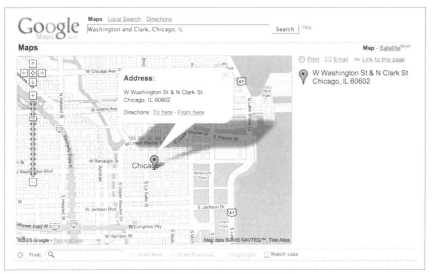

Figure 5-1. A map of Chicago showing the action in Bike Messengers and the Cult of Human Power

Figure 5-2. The satellite view gives us the big (or at least elevated) picture

Different zoom levels give us, well, different pictures. Figure 5-2 shows an overview of the whole city, but when we zoom way in as in Figure 5-3, we see a 4-block by 3 1/2–block window of downtown Chicago. Looking at that, I can almost smell the bus fumes.

Caught in the rush of plot, too often I'll let the details slide. Hollywood and Vine? Washington and Clark? Who cares? I just want to see what happens next! But if that is all that matters, why should authors bother with place

Figure 5-3. The satellite view tells another story

names? Why not simply write as if everything happened in the same grey protoplasmic sea? Context matters: the places where things happen shape what happens and what we think about what happens. Context feeds the mind.

Don't Believe Everything You Read on a Map

Learn how the selection of imagery can be extremely subjective.

It is easy to assume that maps are somehow true and objective representations of a place. After all, most of our interactions with maps have to do with practical affairs such as navigating the complex layout of a city. The truth, however, is that maps both reflect and create reality. This is most clear in the choices of what is, and is not, put on a map.

For example, chamber of commerce maps typically show lots of green for parks and greenbelts, but somehow neglect to point out the less desirable aspects of a community. Okay, you might say, the maps are subjective, but I can count on the aerial imagery, right? It is just a record of how things were. Alas, even there we have issues. There is a huge possibility for bias in the choices of images that will be displayed.

Figure 5-4 shows part of the Black Rock desert in Nevada, near the town of Gerlach. For most of the year this is an empty expanse where you can either hear yourself think or hear the people cruising about trying to set land-speed records in the armed-and-inebriated SUV-driving category. However, for a week, plus time before and after for set up and clean up, this is Black Rock City, home to the Burning Man festival. This particular image was taken during the setup period for the 2003 event.

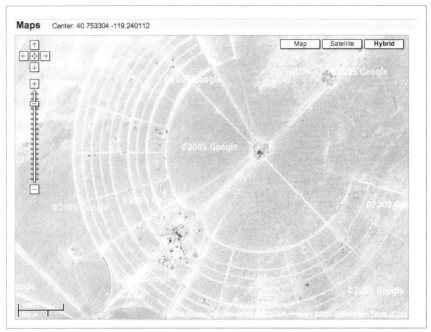

Figure 5-4. A bit of desert in Nevada, late summer

How did that happen to become the canonical Google representation of an area around 40.7549 N, 119.23608 W? I suspect that it wasn't pure chance! Was it an accident that the aerial photo in Figure 5-5 centered around 37.713532 N, 122.386075 W shows the San Francisco 49ers' football stadium near Candlestick Point State Park in the middle of a game?

On the other hand, the aerial photo in Figure 5-6 centered on 37.751367 N, -122.201239 W shows the nearby home of the Oakland Raiders, another football team, to be empty and configured for a baseball game??

The simplest explanation is that maps tell stories, and so these particular mapmakers configured reality through selection of imagery in order to tell a more entertaining story. After all, according to Muriel Rukeyser, "the universe is made up of stories, not atoms."

Some of the stories have a chilling message. Take a look at the imagery around 1600 Pennsylvania Avenue, Washington, D.C. You can count the trees on the White House grounds, but roofs are all obscured, as seen in Figure 5-7.

The White House suffers little in comparison to the Capitol. Clearly there is a large blobby thing at that end of the National Mall, but it isn't clear what it is. Congress is apparently more protective of its foliage than is the Executive Branch, as we can see in Figure 5-8.

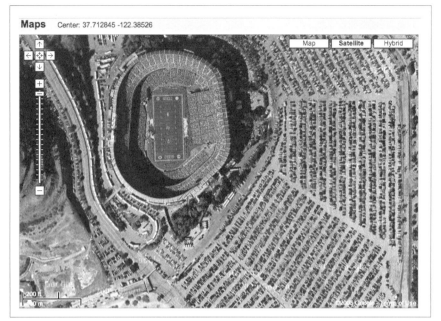

Figure 5-5. Near Candlestick Point State Park

Figure 5-6. The home of the Raider Nation in Oakland

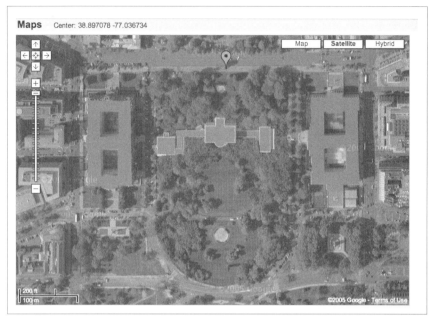

Figure 5-7. You can plan an Easter egg hunt, but don't plan to find any on the roof

Figure 5-8. Congress shall make no law, assuming you can find it

The Pentagon, as shown in Figure 5-9, appears to be the least protective of rooftop assets.

Figure 5-9. For once, the Pentagon appears to have nothing to hide

In some parts of the country, cornfield artists have expressed their support for the military. There are no obscured roofs in Figure 5-10, and I bet folks in uniform feel welcome in Bellevue, Nebraska. (At least, the ones who fly do!)

I'm tempted to make a comment about real national security versus "security theater," but there are so many strange things happening in the world that I don't understand that I'd best remain silent. At a recent conference, I was introduced to the phrase *kill chain*, as in "you can ignore him, he's not in the kill chain." Since I can't even figure out which Linux desktop is best, I have no chance at an intelligent opinion about national security or the kill chain.

Perhaps I'm better equipped for an appreciation of the two images of 1 Infinite Loop, Cupertino, CA 95014. The first, Figure 5-11, is taken from Google's satellite imagery, and the second, Figure 5-12, from Microsoft's Virtual Earth.

Was Apple bombed to rubble recently? Obviously, as of this writing, Microsoft's Digital Earth is using very old imagery of a small slice of Cupertino. This appears odd, since the imagery for other parts of the Bay Area seems much more current. It's almost as if…Microsoft…wants us to believe…that Apple…simply isn't there….No, in the end, fretting over conspiracy theories about how places are portrayed is unsatisfying.

Figure 5-10. "We honor those who serve America"

Figure 5-11. What Google thinks of this particular Infinite Loop

Figure 5-12. Apple appears to have disappeared

That doesn't make it necessarily wrong, however. After all, we live in a world where a telephone company with broadband business will intentionally block traffic to telecomm workers' union web sites during a strike. Perhaps it is enough to recognize the lesson that reality is a commodity, like any other, and that access to reality is sometimes mediated through more steps than might always be totally healthy for a free and democratic society.

You Got Your A9 Local in My Google Maps!

Use Greasemonkey to inject A9's Local Images into Google's much nicer map interface.

A9.com, Amazon's search company, has special trucks equipped with digital cameras and GPS units that run around selected cities. The trucks take street-level pictures of just about everything and then index that with the GPS and a geocoding application to add photographs to business listings. A9.com "brings Yellow Pages to life." Figure 5-13 shows the A9 Block View of the City Lights bookstore in San Francisco.

A9.com is pretty neat, but the mapping interface is a bit weak. If you have the Greasemonkey extension installed in the Firefox browser, you can install A9+Gmaps, a Greasemonkey user script that will load A9 images on top of your Google Maps.

> Installing Greasemonkey in Firefox is covered in detail in "Add Google Maps to Any Web Site" [Hack #27] and "Track Your UPS Packages" [Hack #25].

Figure 5-13. City Lights bookstore, according to A9.com

Once Greasemonkey has been installed in Firefox, you can get A9+Gmaps from *http://www.kokogiak.com/webtools/greasemonkey/a9imagesingooglemaps.html*. From that page, right-click on the link to a9gmap.user.js and select Install User Script. An installation window will pop up, as depicted in Figure 5-14.

Click on OK, and with a bit of luck you'll get a status window that says "Success! Refresh page to see changes." Now, when you search for a business on the Google Maps web site in an area covered by A9 Local, you'll be able to click on the icon and, a few seconds later, an A9 thumbnail will appear in your info window.

The A9+Gmaps Greasemonkey script is executed whenever a user is on a page in the *maps.google.com* domain. When the user clicks on an icon in the map, the script finds the newly opened info balloon and parses the HTML inside it to find the business name and address, if present. The script then sends that data out to A9.com, behind the scenes. When A9.com responds, the script parses A9's HTML to discover an image (if one exists), and gets the location and URL of the A9.com image and page. Finally, the script inserts a thumbnail image of that location into the Google Maps info window.

One caveat: this hack is largely based on screen-scraping and picking apart the respective Document Object Models on both sites. That means it's fragile and easily broken if either A9 or Google alter too much HTML layout. In

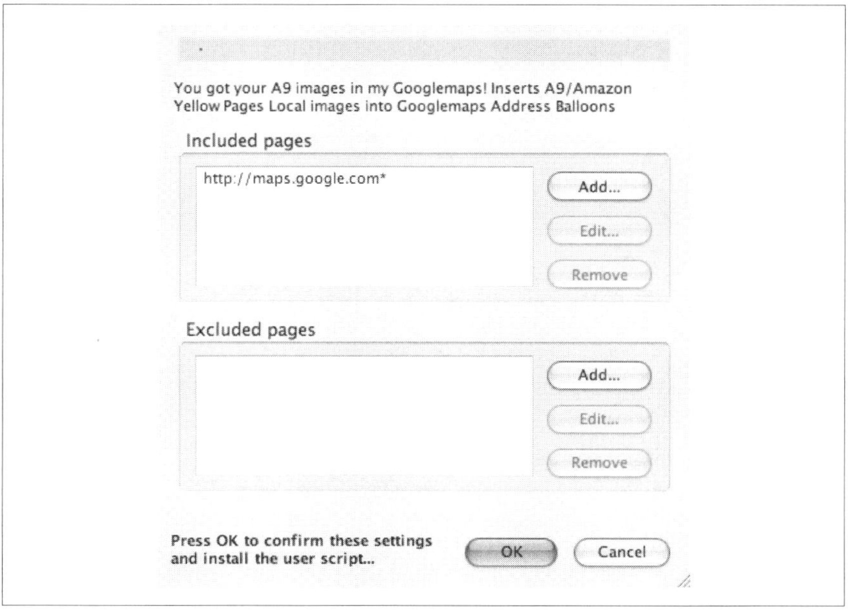

Figure 5-14. Installing a user script under Greasemonkey

the meantime, mashing up A9's street level photos with Google's map interface means that finding businesses and other locations is easier than ever.

—Alan Taylor

HACK Share Pictures with Your Community
#45
Use Flickrcity to set up a collaborative photo map.

Putting geolocated photos on a map is something geo-hackers have worked on for a long time. Now, using Flickr, Google Maps, and a little piece of glue called Flickrcity (*http://anti-mega.com/flickrcity/*), anyone can do this easily.

I started work on Flickrcity because I wanted to create a restaurant review site for Helsinki that anyone could contribute to. Flickr was the natural place to store photos and information; sites such as Geobloggers (*http://www.geobloggers.com/*) were using Flickr as a data source and had already created a standard for geotagging photos.

Flickrcity automatically filters on a tag of the name of the city and the tag *geotagged*. Using additional tags, or specifying a particular user, you can use Flickrcity for a variety of purposes.

To see all geotagged photos in a city, you can just go to the URL of the Flickrcity installation—e.g., for Helsinki, *http://anti-mega.com/flickrcity/helsinki.city*, as shown in Figure 5-15.

Figure 5-15. Photos geotagged in Helsinki

If you wanted to set up a collaborative restaurant review site for Helsinki, you would need to tag photos in Flickr with, say, "helsinki," "food," "geotagged," and the two location geotags [Hack #46]. Then you would construct a URL that would return these images with this tag query, such as *http://anti-mega.com/ flickrcity/helsinki.city?tags=food.* Figure 5-16 shows what this looks like.

If you just wanted to see all of my Helsinki photos, you would use a user query such as *http://anti-mega.com/flickrcity/helsinki.city?user=chrisdodo*, as Figure 5-17 demonstrates.

Of course, you can combine the two, to show just my food photos, as in *http://anti-mega.com/flickrcity/helsinki.city?tags=food&user=chrisdodo.*

If you're using the map for yourself, use a different tag for each project you want to create. If you want to set up a collaborative map, pick a tag name that isn't being used in Flickr and tell all your photographers to add that tag. Of course, others may see it and start using the tag too—Flickrcity gets even better with more geotagged photos.

I've set up Flickrcity installations for a few cities, and others have set up even more, but you can also download the code and set up Flickrcity for wherever you want. To do this, you will need a web server with Perl, some Perl modules (see the installation instructions on the web page for the list), and a little bit of webmaster knowledge.

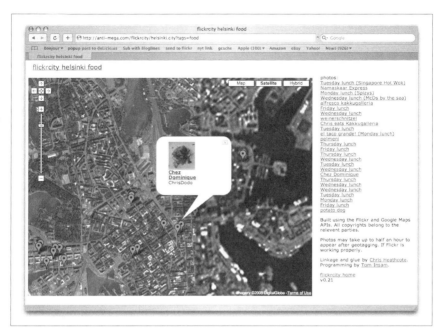

Figure 5-16. Photos tagged with food in Helsinki

Figure 5-17. Photos taken by chrisdodo in Helsinki

You will need to change a few things in the script (mainly the name of the city and the default Google map coordinates and zoom level), and a directory on the server to store cache files. Then put the script in a directory on your server suitable for housing CGI scripts, make the script executable, and it should work.

The script relies on the Flickr and Google Maps APIs, and if either service is slow or down, there may be problems. The first time you run the script, it will create a cache of data from Flickr, which will be slow, but it will run more quickly after that.

—*Chris Heathcote*

HACK #46   Browse Photography by Shooting Location
What a lovely photograph! Where was it taken?

Since the rise of digital photography, more people have been snapping more photos than ever. Web sites such as Flickr have sprung up to help people manage and publish their photos, and Flickr itself has gone one step further and allows its users to "tag" their photographs with keywords that indicate what's being depicted. These tags can help you figure out who and what is being depicted, but wouldn't it be nice sometimes—particularly in the case of those lovely landscape photos—to know where they were taken?

Tag, You're It

Fortunately, Flickr provides an API that allows you to query data from its system, and we can use this to find images that have been geotagged. Geotagged photos on Flickr have three special tags associated with them. First, they're tagged as `geotagged`, which allows us to find them using the Flickr API. Second, they have the tags `geo:lat=...` and `geo:long=...` associated with them, which gives us their geographic coordinates. Figure 5-18 shows one sort of map that can be made by mashing up the Flicker API and the Google Maps API.

In order to make use of the Flickr API, you need to sign up to Flickr, and then get yourself an API key from *http://www.flickr.com/services/api/*. Once you have a key, you can query Flickr using the `flickr.photos.search` call from their REST API, with a URL like:

```
http://www.flickr.com/services/rest/?method=flickr.photos.search&api_
key=[your API key]&tag_mode=all&tags=geotagged&per_page=20
```

This returns an XML document matching the latest photos tagged as geotagged. The XML looks something like the following:

```
<?xml version="1.0" encoding="utf-8" ?>
<rsp stat="ok">
    <photos page="1" pages="8553" perpage="5" total="42761">
```

Figure 5-18. A map of recent geotagged photos from Flickr

```
        <photo id="30221122" owner="47836075@N00" secret="11f6695a02"
               server="21"
          title="From Camera Server(SlabbersCam)0000/00/06,15:00:07"
          ispublic="1" isfriend="0" isfamily="0" />
        <photo id="30218138" owner="78211664@N00" secret="5a36fff7b3"
               server="21" title="P8010502" ispublic="1" isfriend="1"
               isfamily="1" />
        <photo id="30218130" owner="78211664@N00" secret="8bda841d8b"
               server="23"
          title="P8010498" ispublic="1" isfriend="1" isfamily="1" />
        <photo id="30211741" owner="59597347@N00" secret="bbadd69e06"
               server="21"
          title="Tiny Sea Cave" ispublic="1" isfriend="0" isfamily="0" />
        <photo id="30197466" owner="47836075@N00" secret="ea66947548"
               server="22"
          title="From Camera Server(SlabbersCam)0000/00/06,13:00:07"
          ispublic="1" isfriend="0" isfamily="0" />
      </photos>
    </rsp>
```

By querying the API for each particular photo, we can get the detailed tags for each one. For example, this URL returns the details of the "Tiny Sea Cave" photo above:

```
http://www.flickr.com/services/rest/?method=flickr.photos.getInfo&photo_id
  =30211741&api_key=[your API key]
```

The returned XML looks something like the following, which we've excerpted for brevity:

```
<?xml version="1.0" encoding="utf-8" ?>
<rsp stat="ok">
    <photo id="30211741" secret="bbadd69e06" server="21"
```

```
         dateuploaded="1122879388" isfavorite="0" license="2" rotation="0">
          <title>Tiny Sea Cave</title>
          <description>More of a hole worn in the rock, with lots of little
                  seashells washed inside.</description>
              <tags>
               <tag id="100601461" author="59597347@N00"
                 raw="carmel">carmel</tag>
               <tag id="100601464" author="59597347@N00" raw="sand">sand</tag>
                <tag id="100601465" author="59597347@N00"
                  raw="shells">shells</tag>
                <tag id="100601940" author="59597347@N00"
                  raw="geo:lat=36.5443288">geolat365443288</tag>
                <tag id="100602480" author="59597347@N00"
                  raw="geo:lon=-121.933093">geolon121933093</tag>
                <tag id="100602494" author="59597347@N00"
                  raw="geotagged">geotagged</tag>
              </tags>
          </photo>
        </rsp>
```

As you can see, we have all the info we need to locate this photo on a map.
All we need to do is search for photos with the geotagged tag, loop over each
photo, and request the full information from Flickr. Once we have that, we
can use the Google Maps API to generate the map itself and throw down
some markers.

The Catch

It sounds easy, but there is one small catch: you're going to be running your
photo map page on your server, and you want to get the XML from a different server. For security reasons, most modern browsers, particularly Firefox
and Safari, won't allow you to do this. Unless your web page is sitting on
Flickr's web site, you can't load the Flickr XML directly into your JavaScript.

What you can do, however, is run a *proxy* on your own server, which will
call Flicker's API for you and pass the results back to your browser. Since
the domain of your map page and your XML proxy will be the same, you
won't trip any browser's security features. You'll need a web server somewhere that runs some form of server-side code. Within the JavaScript on the
map page, we'll pass the URL of the XML you want to retrieve and the Java-
Script function you want to handle the XML to the proxy script, and then
the proxy will return a bit of executable JavaScript to your calling page.

Here's some PHP, which I put in a file called *passThru.php* on my web
server, that does the trick:

```php
<?php
$page = '';
$fh = fopen($HTTP_GET_VARS['sURL'],'r') or die($php_errormsg);
```

```
while (! feof($fh)) {
    $page .= fread($fh,1048576);
}
fclose($fh);

$page = str_replace("\r\n", ' ', $page);
$page = str_replace("\n\r", ' ', $page);
$page = str_replace("\n", ' ', $page);
$page = str_replace("\r", ' ', $page);
$page = str_replace("'", '&lsquo', $page);
$functionName = $HTTP_GET_VARS['sFunction'];
header('Content-Type: text/JavaScript');
print "thisXML = '$page';";
print "$functionName;";
?>
```

Here's a snippet of JavaScript code that shows how we use the XML proxy to get Flickr metadata into our page:

```
1  var thisXML;
2  var sFlickrAPIKey = "[your API key]";
3  var sFlickrURL = 'http://www.flickr.com/services/rest/?method=flickr.photos.
   search'
4      + '&tag_mode=all&tags=geotagged&per_page=20&api_key=' + sFlickrAPIKey;
5  var sPassThruURL = 'http://www.geobloggers.com/googleMapHacks/passThru.cfm';
6
7  var newJSElement = document.createElement("script");
8  newJSElement.src = sPassThruURL + '?sURL=' + escape(sFlickrURL)
9                                 + '&sFunction=fnHandleFlickr()';
10 newJSElement.type = "text/JavaScript";
11
12 document.getElementsByTagName("head")[0].appendChild(newJSElement);
```

Here's what's going on. In lines 1 through 5, we define thisXML as a global variable, set up our API key, set the URL we actually want the data from, and then set the URL where our XML proxy sits. Line 7 sets up a new HTML script element, and line 8 sets its src attribute, passing the URL we want to get, and the function we want to handle it when it comes back. In line 9, we set the type attribute of the new script element, so that the browser knows it's JavaScript. Line 10 sets everything in motion by attaching our JavaScript to the document's head element, causing the browser to fetch and execute the code via our XML proxy.

The function that gets called needs to convert the string representation of the XML into an actual XML document, so the function starts out like this:

```
function fnHandleFlickr() {
    try {
        var xmlDoc = xmlParser.parseFromString(thisXML, "application/xml");
    } catch(er) {
        alert("Sorry, couldn't parse the XML returned by Flickr!");
    }
}
```

So why are we doing it this way, instead of, say, using XMLHttpRequest( )? The main advantage of getting XML by constructing a new <script> element and then populating it from a proxy is that, by using a standard browser feature, we circumvent the security limitations of better-known ways of fetching XML into a browser.

If you were to use such a proxy to return the XML directly to an XMLHttpRequest( ) call, it would still have to run on the same server as the HTML page. By contrast, with our method, the page on which we are running our Google Maps hack and our XML proxy can be on completely different servers on different domains across the Internet.

> If you decide to set up a proxy script like the one described here, you will *definitely* want to hardcode part of the address that you're getting the XML from in the server script or do some kind of checking on the URL that's passed in, so that you're not setting up an HTTP proxy that's wide open to the entire Internet. You should *not* run the proxy server code as is.

The Code

The code for this hack runs to about 150 lines, so we'll just review the highlights here. You can see it in action at *http://mappinghacks.com/projects/gmaps/flickr.html*. See the code itself by selecting View Source in your browser. In essence, the JavaScript does exactly as we've described above, using the script insertion maneuver to first fetch a list of geocoded photos from Flickr. Next, it takes the first photo found and asks Flickr for its details. The fnHandlePhoto( ) function is called by the JavaScript returned by the proxy, and this function extracts the specific geo:lat and geo:long tags from each image:

```
function fnHandlePhoto( ) {
    var bDidItWork = true;
    var fGeoLat, fGeoLong;

    try {
        var xmlDoc = xmlParser.parseFromString(thisXML, "application/xml");
        // Note, it's possible geo:long could also be called geo:lon,
        // so we'll look for both versions.
        var aTags = xmlDoc.documentElement.getElementsByTagName("tag");
        for (i = 0; i < aTags.length; i++) {
            if (aTags[i].attributes['raw'].value.length > 7) {
                var sTag = aTags[i].attributes['raw'].value;
                if (sTag.substr(0,7).toLowerCase( ) == 'geo:lat')
                    fGeoLat = parseFloat(
                        aTags[i].attributes['raw'].value.split('=')[1] );
                if (sTag.substr(0,7).toLowerCase( ) == 'geo:lon')
                    fGeoLong = parseFloat(
                        aTags[i].attributes['raw'].value.split('=')[1] );
```

```
        }
      }
  } catch(er) {
  }
```

In the above code fragment, which has been edited a bit for readability, the XML stored by the proxy in thisXML is parsed, and then the resulting document object is scanned for tag elements. The highlighted code examines each tag element to see if they are prefixed with geo:lat= or geo:long= and, if so, extracts the coordinates from them as floating point values.

Next, assuming that the coordinates were extracted properly, the fnHandlePhoto( ) function creates a new GMarker object using the Google Maps API, and uses other information from Flickr about the photo to generate an HTML info window that pops up when the marker is clicked. This popup will include a thumbnail of the photo, the title, the owner's screen name, and a link to the photo's Flickr page.

```
if (!isNaN(fGeoLat) && !isNaN(fGeoLong)) {
        var point = new GPoint(fGeoLong,fGeoLat);
        var marker = new GMarker(point);
        var sHTML = "";

        var xmlInfo = xmlDoc.documentElement.
    getElementsByTagName("photo");
        var xmlTitle = xmlDoc.documentElement.getElementsByTagName("title");
        var xmlOwner = xmlDoc.documentElement.getElementsByTagName("owner");

        sHTML += '<strong>'
            + xmlTitle[0].firstChild.nodeValue + '</strong><br />';
          sHTML += xmlOwner[0].attributes['username'].value + '<br />';
       sHTML += '<a href="http://www.flickr.com/photos/'
            + xmlOwner[0].attributes['username'].value + '/'
            + xmlInfo[0].attributes['id'].value + '/" target="_blank">'
            + '<img src="http://photos'
            + xmlInfo[0].attributes['server'].value
            + '.flickr.com/' + xmlInfo[0].attributes['id'].value + '_'
            + xmlInfo[0].attributes['secret'].value
            + '_s.jpg" width="75" height="75" /></a>';

        GEvent.addListener(marker, "click", function( ) {
              marker.openInfoWindowHtml(sHTML);
        });

        map.addOverlay(marker);
```

The highlighted lines above construct the HTML for the image thumbnail, which as you can see is a bit complex. After displaying the marker on the map, the code then continues to see if there are any photos left to be processed from the original query, and, if there are, it picks the next one, and repeats until they're all shown on the map.

This is all well and good, but it *is* quite slow, because the browser has to ask the proxy to look up each and every photo in Flickr one at a time. One advantage of this approach, however, is that you can customize the query using the intersection of multiple tags. Near the top of the JavaScript section in *flickr.html*, you'll see a line that reads as follows:

```
var lstTags = 'geotagged';
```

If you're feeling creative, you can alter this to show geotagged photos of specific things or places:

```
var lstTags = 'geotagged,flower'; //get geotagged flowers
var lstTags = 'geotagged,flower,london'; //get geotagged london flowers
```

Hacking the Hack

In practice, all those API calls to the Flickr server do take up quite a bit of the user's time, waiting for each photo to show up on the map. Using your Flickr API key, you could set up a system to collect the photos you're interested in, and put them into your own data store, from which you can quickly generate the maps you want to see. Alternatively, you can use an *aggregator*, such as Geobloggers (*http://geobloggers.com/*), which polls Flickr periodically for new geocoded photos, and then offers an API to fetch metadata about them based on location. The Geobloggers API is documented at *http://www.geobloggers.com/services/*.

Our Geobloggers API example, which you can find at *http://mappinghacks.com/ projects/gmaps/geobloggers.html*, calls in Flickr image data from Geobloggers, using the bounding area of the map as a guide as to what to load in. One choice bit of code from that file, edited for readability, looks like this:

```
// Get rid of any old pins
map.clearOverlays();

// Get the map's bounding box from the Google Maps API
var sNewBounds = map.getBoundsLatLng();

// Build up the new URL based on the view window we are looking at.
var newGeoBloggersURL =
    'http://www.geobloggers.com/fullscreenBackend/dataFeed.cfm?'
        + 'iMaxRecords=' + iMaxRecords + '&sSearchType=newest'
        + '&minLon=' + sNewBounds.minX + '&maxLon=' + sNewBounds.maxX
        + '&minLat=' + sNewBounds.minY + '&maxLat=' + sNewBounds.maxY;
```

The URL assembed in `newGeoBloggersURL` is then passed to our XML proxy. When it comes back, it's passed to another function that generates the markers:

```
pins = xmlDoc.documentElement.getElementsByTagName("pin");
for (var i = 0; i < pins.length; i++) {
```

```
    var point = new GPoint(
        parseFloat(pins[i].getAttribute("lng")),
        parseFloat(pins[i].getAttribute("lat")));

    var html = '<strong>' + pins[i].getAttribute("title") +
        '</strong><br />';
    html = html + '<img src="' + pins[i].getAttribute("sPhotoURL")
                        + '" width="75" height="75" />';

    var marker = createMarker(point,html,pins[i].getAttribute("icon"));
    map.addOverlay(marker);
    ...
}
```

What's particularly cute about this method is that Geobloggers actually creates small thumbnails of each photo to use as markers on the map, in place of the usual Google Maps markers, as you can see in Figure 5-19.

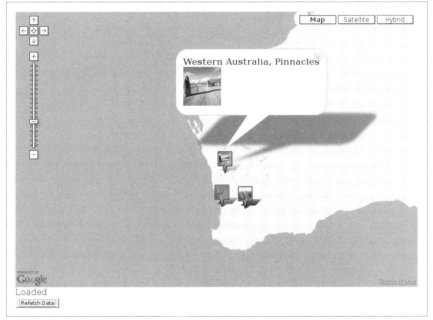

Figure 5-19. A map of local photos from Flickr, via the Geobloggers API

Additionally, since the Geobloggers API is location-centric, when you zoom or re-center the map, a click to the Refetch Data button causes the map to update with new photos, based on the location of the map. Modifying this code to do this automatically, using the GEvent object from the Google Maps API, is left as an exercise for the reader—see "Make Things Happen When the Map Moves" [Hack #60] for more details.

—Dan Catt

Geotag Your Own Photos on Flickr

#47   Maps and pictures go together like a horse and buggy.

Ever since Flickr started cataloguing people's digital photography, many have been clamouring to be able to geolocate photos. The idea of geotags was proposed by Dan Catt. As described in "Browse Photography by Shooting Location" [Hack #46], Dan created a service called Geobloggers (*http://www.geobloggers.com*) to aggregate the geotagged photos.

One of Flickr's key features is that it allows you to add *tags* to your photos. A tag can be a word or group of words, such as "vacation" or "my kids." There are three tags you need to add to photos to be able to geolocate them: geo:lat=*xx.xxxx*, geo.lon=*yy.yyyy*, and geotagged.

The latitude and longitude are expressed in decimal degrees. Latitudes south of the equator and longitudes west of Greenwich are negative. As different latitudes and longitudes appear to be different tags to Flickr, the geotagged tag is necessary to let you search for geotagged photos. There are two ways to geotag photos: manually and using Google Maps.

If you have a GPS, use it to record the latitude and longitude as you take photos by taking a photo of the GPS. You can set the GPS to display in decimal degrees (which may be represented as *hddd.ddddd°* in the GPS settings), however, GPSes often display in degrees and minutes, as shown in Figure 5-20, or degrees, minutes, and seconds.

Figure 5-20. Take a photo of the GPS to make geotagging easy

If you have GPS coordinates in degrees, minutes, and seconds, try the FCC's converter at *http://www.fcc.gov/mb/audio/bickel/DDDMMSS-decimal.html.*

In Flickr, add the three tags to each photo, which is represented by that latitude and longitude. Taking the location in the photo as an example, the tags I would add to the photo are:

```
geo:lat=71.171067
geo:lon=25.783050
geotagged
```

There is, thankfully, an easier way. We can use Google Maps and a nifty Greasemonkey script to do all the heavy lifting for us.

The hard bit is setting up. You need to install Firefox (*http://www.mozilla.org/products/firefox/*), and then Greasemonkey (*http://greasemonkey.mozdev.org/*). Flickr user CK has written a Greasemonkey script called *GmiF*. Version 2.3 of GmiF can be found at *http://www.flickr.com/photos/ckyuan/30014875/*. In Firefox, right-click on the *flickr.gmap.user.js* link, and select "Install user script." Then click OK in the dialog box. Now when you go to a Flickr photo page, there will be an extra icon on the photo toolbar, as shown in Figure 5-21.

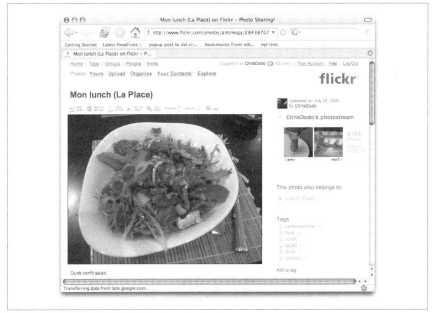

Figure 5-21. A Flickr photo page, with extra GMaps button

Clicking the GMaps button adds a Google Map into the page, along with several choices as shown in Figure 5-22.

Figure 5-22. A map embedded in the photo page

Drag and zoom the map to find the point where the photo was taken. You may have to switch to satellite mode to see where you are at higher zooms. Then click on the map in the exact place where you took the photo, and a red pointer will be displayed, as in Figure 5-23.

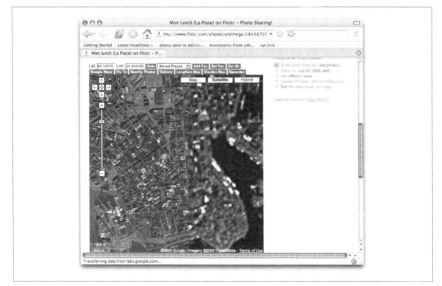

Figure 5-23. A red geolocation pointer appears

Click the red pointer, and a bubble will display a thumbnail of the photo, location, and more actions, as shown in Figure 5-24.

Figure 5-24. A geotagging bubble

Finally, select the "Add geo tags" link. This adds the required tags to the photo, as shown in Figure 5-25.

Figure 5-25. The final set of tags, including geotags

The photo is now geotagged; you can submit it to Geobloggers or wait for them to find it with the automatic search of photos tagged geotagged. Once you've picked up the process, geotags can be added quickly to sets of photos.

—*Chris Heathcote*

HACK
#48

Tell Your Community's Story

Give a guided tour of your community with photos and a Google Map.

We've all been there before; huddled around a computer, looking at photo after photo of a friend or family member standing in front of one tourist attraction after another. I don't know about you, but after the third picture I start to fade fast. It's not that the pictures are necessarily boring (although they very well might be); they're just so repetitive.

The laws of physics require that a photo be a representation of a physical place, but we so rarely display photos within any context of physical location. Google maps provides just such a context, and the effect of placing photos on a map at the location they were taken adds an extra dimension of information to the photo. I'm not suggesting that your slideshow of Hawaii with eight photos of you on the shores of a beautiful beach will become the most enthralling presentation ever, but you might hold people's attention for six photos rather than three.

The Hack

Community Walk (*http://www.communitywalk.com/*) attempts to facilitate the process of placing photos on a map showing where they were taken. The intent of it was, surprisingly enough, not to simply alleviate the boredom of vacation slideshows, but rather to allow people to share their communities. I roughly define a community as a group of things that share some commonality in the mind of some person or group of people. Although a community does not necessarily have to exist in a physical area, it does have to involve something that exists in a physical location, even if that is just the people that are involved in the community.

Many communities may exist in the same physical area as well. It all depends on the perspective of the people involved. A baseball fan may see SBC Park in San Francisco as one of the many ballparks in the United States, as shown in Figure 5-26.

The manager of a hotel may see the ballpark as a highlight of the area around the hotel, as in Figure 5-27.

With Community Walk, I wanted to give people a way to share these different perspectives, providing different ways to organize and display the various things in a community on a map. I also wanted to allow the creator of the map to configure the map to behave exactly as desired. The hotel manager may not want anyone else to be able to edit the map of the hotel or write comments on the various locations on the map, while the ballpark aficionado may want to allow certain people to edit the map and everyone to add comments about the various ballparks and baseball teams that play in those parks. Community Walk allows for all this and then some.

Getting Started

To get started with Community Walk, go to *http://www.communitywalk.com* and enter the street address or latitude and longitude of your location. This will create the initial map and pop up a window to enter in necessary information about the location. If the location is close to where you want it to be, but not

Figure 5-26. A fan's-eye view

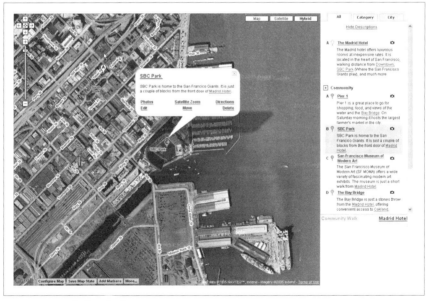

Figure 5-27. The hotelier's perspective

exactly right, you can move it after you save it by clicking Move on the window that pops up when you click Save.

You will initially have the option of choosing from ten categories that describe the location. The default options for the category are Business, Education, Entertainment, General, Hotels, Parks, Residence, Restaurants, Shopping, and Transportation, but these can be changed. In order to change them, though, you'll need to create a user account. You can do this by clicking the Login link under the righthand panel. You can also log in directly from *http://www.communitywalk.com*.

Once logged in you will be able to configure everything about the map, including which categories are available, which tabs are available to organize the locations on the map, who can edit the map, whether or not users can make comments on the locations on the map, and so on. Right after you log in, you will be brought to a page that lists all of your maps, allowing you to configure, view, or edit each map, and if you started creating a map before logging in, that map will be available for configuration automatically. You can also access this screen by clicking Configure Map on the bottom of the map.

Adding Your Own Locations

Now comes the fun part: adding locations to the map. You can do this by clicking Add Markers at the bottom of the map. This presents you with three options: By Click, By Address, and By Lat/Long. Each of these offers a different way to put a location on the map, although my preferred manner is By Click, as it allows me to quickly add locations directly onto the map exactly where I want them to be.

Once a location is added, you will be presented with the same pop-up window that you saw when you first created the map. Now you will be able to choose from the categories you designated when you configured the map, as well as enter the rest of the information for the location. When entering the description, you also have the option of using some special wiki-like commands that allow you to format the text in the description and include links to external web sites as well as links that change the state of the map without leaving it. At the time of this writing, the available commands were as shown in Table 5-1.

Table 5-1. Community Walk's wiki-like commands

Command	Resulting text
`bold("sample text")`	sample text
`italic("sample text")`	*sample text*
`link("http://www.communitywalk.com", "Community Walk")`	CommunityWalk
`internal_link("3wx82-0$j.>23jWKl5%", "Madrid Hotel")`	Madrid Hotel

In the `internal_link` command, the first parameter `3wx82-0$j.>23jWKl5` is a set of directions for the map, telling it where to center, what location to show, what picture to show, and so on. This value can be determined by putting the map in the state, panning and zooming to the view that you want to see, with the pictures you want to see on it, and then selecting all of the text after the # sign in the URL. If the URL in the address bar were *http://www.communitywalk.com/group?id=328#3wx82-0$j.>23jWKl5%*, the `internal_link` state parameter for that view of the map would be `3wx82-0$j.>23jWKl5%`.

At any point you can go back and edit the information for any location by simply selecting that location and clicking Edit in the window that pops up. You can also move the location or delete it by clicking Move or Delete, respectively. These links will not be available when someone is simply viewing the map.

Adding Photos to the Map

Once the location has been created, you can add photos to the location by clicking Add Photos from the window that pops up when you select the location (a user viewing the map will see a link for "No Photos"). This will open a window that will allow you to upload photos. The photos will be automatically resized if they are too big and will be displayed in the order they were uploaded. You can change the order by clicking Reorder after the photos are displayed and dragging them into their new order. For each photo, you can enter a title and short description. The description can also contain the same commands described for the main description.

Personally, I usually don't have my photos named very well on my computer. So I prefer to simply organize the photos that I want to use for a specific location into a folder on my computer, upload all the photos in the folder, disregarding the order, and then reorder the photos and enter the title and description from the resulting view, where I can see which photo I am dealing with.

Each location that has photos uploaded to it will have a small camera icon next to it on the righthand panel. Additionally, if the map is configured to allow comments then the righthand panel will have a comments icon that will change color depending on how long ago a comment was added to the location.

Lastly, in addition to allowing for comments to be left on a map, Community Walk allows people to share each location they create with the community (or keep them private), is fully integrated with *http://del.icio.us/*, and will soon have an API for accessing all of the shared location information.

The goal of Community Walk is really to bring people within a community together in a space that lets them share their experiences. As enabling as the Internet is, it almost seems to be pulling us away from the physical world around us. Hopefully, by adding a dimension of the physical world to the Internet, Community Walk will allow people to better interact with the communities around them, bringing us back into that physical world just a bit.

—Jared Cosulich

Generate Geocoded RSS from Any Google Map
#49   Don't tell anyone, but the Semantic Web really is cool.

One thing that bugs me about Google Maps is that, since the API is entirely JavaScript, the annotation layer in a hack is only available visually and is not machine parseable. It's understandable that Google didn't push any particular geodata file format, as these will emerge, but it's frustrating that right now so much cool data is being created as lone silos, in an inaccessible and un-remixable way.

Yet the data is there, in the JavaScript and Document Object Model objects created by the Google Maps API. It should be possible to muck around in there and rescue that data from its lonely and isolated existence. This hack describes a Firefox JavaScript Bookmarklet that pulls point annotation information from many Google Map hacks and produces geocoded RSS.

The Hack

The first step is to find the GMap object in memory, which is the key to the Google Maps object structure. Every page that shows a Google Map (under the official API) must have a line that looks like this:

```
var map = new GMap(document.getElementById("map"));
```

The bookmarklet assumes the GMap object is a global variable. If the page creates the GMap object within a function, the bookmark will fail. User-created global variables and methods can be accessed by iterating through the global object this. Without a JavaScript function to query an object for its user created class, the bookmarklet calls getCenterLatLng( ) on each global object within a try/catch block. If this call does not generate an error, the GMap object has been found and things can move forward. The other assumption is that overlays are GMarker objects that respond to click events by calling openInfoWindowHtml( ). This is probably the most common way of constructing a Google Map.

Since there is no API method to list overlays, a JavaScript Data Dumper, such as the one at *http://www.mattkruse.com/JavaScript/datadumper/*, can be very useful to investigate the structure of the GMap object and find the overlays, without following through the API's obfuscated code. We can start by creating a basic Google Map with overlays and info windows, according to the documentation. Next, we load in *datadumper.js*, set DumperMaxDepth = 2, and call DumperPopup(map). Setting DumperMaxDepth to a small value is crucial, since the GMaps object has self references and will send the Dumper into an infinite loop. The dump reveals an array within the GMap object called overlays. Calling DumperPopup(map["overlays"]) shows a list of objects, each containing a point property. Each GPoint object has an x and y value, which on inspection are the lat/long location of the overlay. Rockin'!

But what about the overlay content? That HTML exists within an anonymous function passed to the GEvent.addListener method. That function is placed in the _e__click array and is already compiled. The only way to get at that content is to call the function. The trick is to capture the call to openInfoWindowHtml by copying the existing method at GMarker.prototype.openInfoWindowHtml and replacing it with our own function, which captures the HTML argument when requested, and otherwise calls the original backed-up method.

Finally, the RSS is produced by iterating through the overlays array, grabbing the x and y from the point, executing call() on the _e__click function, and wrapping it up within an RSS item element. The geocoded RSS is then written to a new window.

The Code

The HTML below (and online at *http://brainoff.com/gmaps/gmaps.bklet.html*) produces a bookmarklet from this script, which can be copied to your Firefox toolbar. When viewing a Google Map, click the bookmarklet, and if the map has been produced according to the assumptions, RSS will be generated. It's not possible to change the content type of a document from JavaScript, so Firefox will render the RSS as HTML. View the source to see the XML.

```
<html>
<head>
<script language="Javascript">
gmapref = false;

/* Search through Global Objects for the GMap*/
for (objName in this) {
      obj = this[objName];
      try {
            obj.getCenterLatLng();
            gmapref = obj;
            break;
      } catch (e) {}
}

if (gmapref) {

      /* Capture calls to openInfoWindowHtml, and grab the marker html */
```

```
GMarker.prototype._openInfoWindowHtml=GMarker.prototype.
openInfoWindowHtml;
GMarker.prototype.openInfoWindowHtml=function(a){
        if (document.capture) { document.desc = a; }
        else { this._openInfoWindowHtml(a); }
};

/* Generate RSS by iterating through overlays, looking for points, and
capturing info window HTML */
var rss='<?xml version=\'1.0\'?>\n<rss version=\'2.0\' xmlns:geo
    =\'http://www.w3.org/2003/01/geo/wgs84_pos#\'>\n<channel>\n';
var i;
for (i=0; i<map['overlays'].length; i++) {
        try {
        item =  '\t<item>\n\t\t<geo:lat>' + map['overlays'][i]['point'].y
            + '</geo:lat><geo:long>' + map['overlays'][i]['point'].x
            + '</geo:long>\n\t\t<description><![CDATA[';
        document.capture = true;
        document.desc = '';
        map['overlays'][i]['_e__click'][0].call();
        item = item  + document.desc;
        document.capture = false;
        item = item  + ']]></description>\n\t</item>\n';
        rss = rss + item;
        } catch(e) { document.capture = false; }
}
rss = rss + '</channel></rss>';

/* Write out RSS to a new window */
var w = window.open('about:blank');
w.document.open();
w.document.writeln(rss);
w.document.close();
}
void(0);
</script>
<script>
function buildbookmarklet() {
        var s = document.getElementsByTagName("script");
        var script = s[0].innerHTML;
        script = script.replace(/\n/g, "");
        var b = document.getElementById("bookmarklet");
        b.innerHTML = "<a href=\"JavaScript:" + script + "\">GMaps2RSS</a>";
}
</script>
</head>
<body onLoad="buildbookmarklet()">
<div id="bookmarklet">
</div>
</body>
</html>
```

—Mikel Maron

Geoblog with Google Maps in Thingster

HACK
#50

Share your favorite places with friends.

In this hack, I discuss our Thingster Geoblogging service and some of the details of how I integrated Google Maps. We provide Thingster free of charge at *http://www.thingster.org/*, and it is open source and open data licensed as well. You're welcome to log in, create an account, and play with it; you're also welcome to run your own copy or just take any ideas you like and build your own equivalent.

My own interest in place-tagging came from a very simple desire: I wanted to be able to share information about my favorite places with my friends. The fact that there are not 10,000 companies already doing this has always completely mystified me. It seemed like a perfectly logical business plan if you were so minded—certainly better than, say, "pets.com."

It is pretty obvious that the blogging paradigm is the right way to hang Post-It notes in space. People already use blogs in almost exactly this way: you own your own blog, you publish in a formal publishing framework, and blogs export this wonderful RSS format that is machine-readable. Blogs have already been extended to blog pictures, songs, and even video: blogging by location is the next logical step.

The challenge in blogging about places is that our blogging tools or content management systems need to support some kind of satisfying, fast, and compelling map interface. These tools need to be as easy to use as ordinary blogging tools. A clever novice should be able to walk up to a mapping service, create an account, and post her first geotagged post in under a minute.

Enter Thingster

In 2004, Ben Russell and I first conceived Thingster as an "anything tool," where one could blog about any kind of thing. Maps were the first clear interest and my good friends Tom Longson and Brad Degraf quickly jumped on board to help play with the idea. We thought that if community driven maps existed, then we could start to share information about our communities more intelligently, and that this might even change the way we engage and interact as citizens. This is the sort of big *if* that always seems to be a warning of several months of sleepless nights hacking.

Let me point out that those of you who haven't had to suffer in the dark ages before Google Maps simply have no appreciation of how hard it was to build a compelling web mapping service. It was uphill with snowstorms both ways and we had to arrive before we left. We had tried several other mapping solutions that were available in the open source community and I even personally did try to build my own mapserver (which is available at *http://maps.civicactions.net*). The labour, time, and ultimate performance of rolling our own is completely humbling. We recognized just how high the bar is set in what users expect from a web mapping service.

Today Google Maps provides us with that last missing piece, and not only is Thingster finally able to articulate its vision, but several other exciting projects, such as *http://ning.com*, *http://platial.com*, and *http://tagzania.com* are also rapidly beginning to explore the possibilities of easy access to a compelling web mapping service.

Adding Maps to Blogs

In the development of my own approach it became obvious that there are several key things that map-based content management systems should do:

1. They should use tags in a way similar to the notable *http://del.icio.us* project. Organizing place information seems to be so difficult otherwise.

2. "Post to Map" is crucial. People want to interact with a map when they make a post, not try to enter a street address or a longitude/latitude pair by hand.

3. There should be an opportunity to post a comment with regards to a previously placed post. Rather than ending up with a cloud of posts around a restaurant or a swimming hole, it is important to let people use discovery first to prevent clutter.

4. There must be extensive pivots. One should be able to examine a location and see all the comments about that place. Or to then look at an author of a particular comment and see other posts that author might have made about other locations. Mapping seems to often imply relationships to the other people who have that same interest; it makes sense to find ways to create synergy.

5. The mapping service has to be fast and lightweight overall. Google Maps more than delivers on this.

Practice

Connecting Google Maps to a blogging tool requires connecting both an input side and an output side. You want to both capture Google Maps position information for new posts, and you want to plot posts to Google Maps when you are viewing the blog.

On the input side, I connected the Google Maps navigation to the form input box. As you drag Google Maps around, it instantly updates the user input form box so that when the user finally submits the post, the post has

the map location that they have suggested. This code was quite a small bit of
JavaScript, and it looked something like this:

```
var map = null;
map = new GMap(mapdiv);
map.addControl(new GSmallMapControl( ));
map.centerAndZoom(new GPoint(-123,45), 6);

// REGISTER CHANGES INTO FORM IF FORM EXISTS

GEvent.addListener(map, "moveend", function( ) {
  var center = map.getCenterLatLng( );
  var latLngStr = center.y + ' ' + center.x;
  if( parent.document.form && parent.document.form.locationinput ) {
    parent.document.form.locationinput.value = latLngStr;
  }
});
```

On the output side, when I want to plot the points in my content management system to Google Maps, I request an RSS feed of the particular channel that the user wants to plot and simply plot those points. That code is
slightly larger because it has to fetch an XML document from the server (the
RSS feed), walk through it, and post those posts into Google Maps. You can
use the GXmlHttp class from the Google Maps API as a means of fetching this
data on the fly, without having to worry about browser compatibility issues.

Once I have one of my RSS feeds with some geo-data in it, I instruct Google
Maps to plot each of the points:

```
// ITERATE ITEMS - BUILD MAP WHEN NEEDED

var latmin = 0;
var latmax = 0;
var lonmin = 0;
var lonmax = 0;
var visited = 0;

for(var content = data.firstChild; content != null; content =
    content.nextSibling ) {

        if( content.nodeName != 'item' ) {
                continue;
        }

        // get some stuff
        var title = getfield(content,"dc:title");
        var link = getfield(content,"dc:link");
        var description = getfield(content,"dc:description");
        var location = getfield(content,"th:location");
```

```
if(!location || location.length < 2) {
        continue;
}

var strs = location.split(" ");
var a = strs[0];
var b = strs[1];
if( a.indexOf('(')>=0) {
        continue;
}

var lat = 0;
var lon = 0;
try {
        lat = parseFloat( a );
        lon = parseFloat( b );
} catch(e) {
        continue;
}
a = "" + lat;
b = "" + lon;
if( a == 'undefined' || a == "NaN" ) continue;
if( b == 'undefined' || b == "NaN" ) continue;
if( lon == 0 && lat == 0 ) {
        continue;
}
a = 1234;

// bounds builder
if( visited == 0 ) {
        latmin = latmax = lat;
        lonmin = lonmax = lon;
} else {
        if( latmin > lat ) latmin = lat;
        if( latmax < lat ) latmax = lat;
        if( lonmin > lon ) lonmin = lon;
        if( lonmax < lon ) lonmax = lon;
}
var point = new GPoint(lon,lat);
var marker = new GMarker(point);
var html = title;
GEvent.addListener(marker,"click",function( ) {
    marker.openInfoWindowHtml(html);
} );
        map.addOverlay(marker);
        visited++;
}
var latc = latmin + (latmax - latmin) / 2;
var lonc = lonmin + (lonmax - lonmin) / 2;
// should pick zoom better some year
map.centerAndZoom(new GPoint(lonc,latc), 13);
}
```

How Do You Actually Use Thingster?

In Thingster, you first create an account and log in using the register page at *http://thingster.org/register*. Once you are in your home page, you can select "post" to create a new post. The post form allows image upload and has an integrated map, as shown in Figure 5-28.

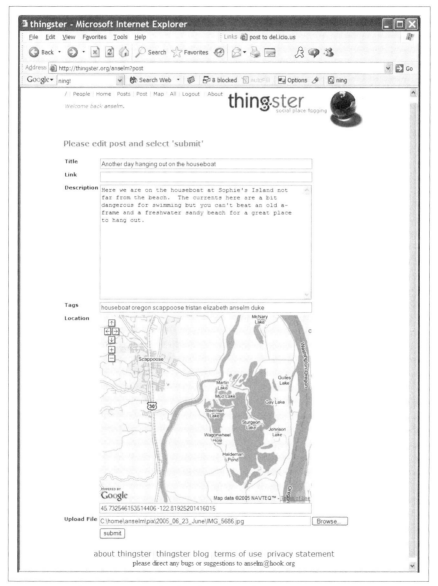

Figure 5-28. Thingster image upload with integrated map

When you are done posting, return to your home page, where you can see a compilation of your posts and pictures on a map, as depicted in Figure 5-29.

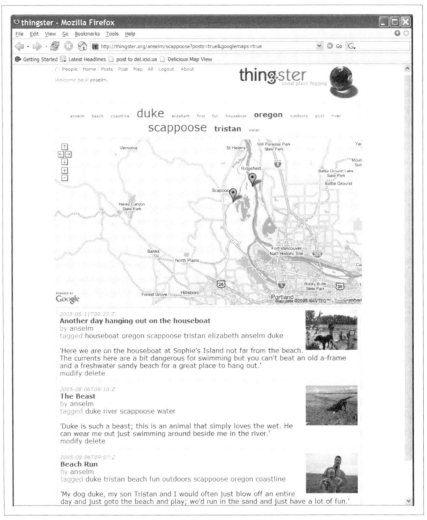

Figure 5-29. Thingster's compilation of your posts and pictures on a map

Having Google Maps in Thingster lets us explore a number of tasty implications we originally thought might exist. Better maps affect what we see, the choices we make, the repercussions of those decisions, and perhaps even the shape of our societies. Our goal in providing this service is to explore such ideas.

—Anselm Hook

## CHAPTER SIX

API Tips and Tricks
Hacks 51–61

The official Google Maps API makes a lot of things easy. Here are some hacks that push the API in new directions and extend the API with external libraries. Tricks such as filling your whole 21-inch flat panel display with a map, customizing your info windows with an embedded map the way the driving directions work, and integrating Flash with your maps.

You can even add custom labels and photographs on top of your Google Maps. Perhaps this technique reaches the height of elegance (absurdity?) when used to compare the size of Burning Man with New York's Central Park.

The chapter ends with several tricks to allow you to use one developer's key for multiple domains and directories. Do you really want to manage multiple keys because you have the domain *http://mydomain.com* and you serve the same pages from it and *http://www.mydomain.com*? I didn't think so!

HACK #51 Make a Fullscreen Map the Right Way
Map too big? Map too small? Flex those pixels into shape!

Imagine you're the proud new owner of a big, shiny 21-inch flat-panel display, and you surf to your favorite Google Maps web site—only to find it still confines you to a tiny little 3-inch-square map. It's an embarrassment, to say the least. Likewise, think about those poor fellows with small monitors who are scrolling until their fingers fall off to get around your gigantic 1600×1200–pixel map. Such sites ought to come with warning labels about claustrophobia.

A good Google Map stretches itself to fit comfortably on your screen. In this hack we'll investigate a simple two-step approach to make your map always take up the whole window, then build on the technique to include a fixed right-side panel, similar to the *maps.google.com* web site. We'll also point out some tricks to help you avoid common pitfalls that unsuspecting web developers stumble into when trying to make auto-sizing maps.

Making a Map Take Up the Full Screen

The first step is to include the following style declaration in the head section of your page. If your map div is named something other than map, you'll need to replace #map with the appropriate name (e.g., #mymap).

```
<style type="text/css">
    html, body, #map {
        width:   100%;
        height: 100%;
    }
    html {
        overflow: hidden;
    }
    body {
        margin:  0px 0px 0px 0px;
        padding: 0px 0px 0px 0px;
    }
</style>
```

The width and height declarations cause the map container to fill the entire document body, and the body to take up all the available window space. Make sure you don't have any inline width or height attributes on your map element that could override these. The overflow:hidden line hides any scrollbars the browser would otherwise display, and the margin and padding lines get rid of the white border that is shown by default around a document. This leaves us with a map container that stretches to fit all the available window space in the browser (minus that reserved for the toolbars, status bar, etc.).

The Google map automatically takes up this whole container when you instantiate it, and most web developers stop here, thinking all is well. However, somewhat less obvious is the fact that the map doesn't detect when its container has been resized—at least, not as of version 1 of the API. Resizing a map that isn't aware when its container size changes can produce some misleading effects, which you can see by going to *http://www.googlemappers.com/articles/fullscreenmap/bad.htm*.

When you enlarge the browser window, you'll see more of the map revealed and might be tempted to *think* it is stretching to fit your window. But what you are actually seeing is the "off-screen" portion of the map—surrounding tiles that have been preloaded, but aren't supposed to be showing on your screen.

If you open the web page in a very small browser window and then enlarge it enough, you'll run out of off-screen tiles and will start to see the gray background shown in Figure 6-1. Additionally, double-clicking the map will make it pan the point you clicked to the *old* center of the window, based on its dimensions at the time it was created.

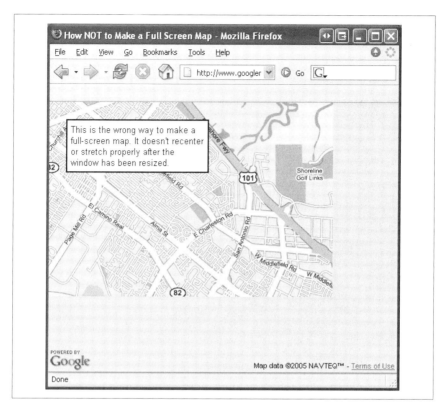

Figure 6-1. A full-screen map done the wrong way

To make your map resize and re-center properly, you need to let it know when its container has resized. To do this, we make use of an undocumented Google Maps API method called `map.onResize()`, calling it whenever the window dimensions change. Include the following JavaScript code, after you create your map object:

```
if (window.attachEvent) {
    window.attachEvent("onresize", function() {this.map.onResize()} );
    window.attachEvent("onload", function() {this.map.onResize()} );
} else if (window.addEventListener) {
    window.addEventListener("resize",
        function() {this.map.onResize()} , false);
    window.addEventListener("load", function() {this.map.onResize()} ,
false);
}
```

This is the final step needed to obtain a properly working fullscreen map. You can see the complete implementation of these two code snippets at *http://www.googlemappers.com/articles/fullscreenmap/default.htm*. You may want to check there for the most up-to-date example of the fullscreen map.

Adding a Side Panel to the Map

It's easy to add a fixed-width panel alongside an auto-sizing map. Here we show the code needed for a fullscreen map with a panel 300 pixels wide docked to the right side of the screen.

Replace the style declaration used in the head section with the following one:

```
<style type="text/css">
    html, body {
        width:  100%;
        height: 100%;
    }
    html {
        overflow: hidden;
    }
    body {
        margin:  0px 0px 0px 0px;
        padding: 0px 0px 0px 0px;
    }
    #map {
        margin-right: 302px;
        height: 100%
    }
    #rightpanel {
        position:  absolute;
        right:             0px;
        top:               0px;
        width:             300px;
        height:            100%;
        overflow:          auto;
        border-left: 2px solid black;
        padding: 0px 5px 0px 10px;
    }
</style>
```

The map's right margin is set to the width of the panel, plus another 2 pixels to account for its left border. The overflow:auto attribute in the right panel causes it to show scrollbars if the content is too big to fit in the panel. The border and padding are added just to make things look cleaner.

It's important that the padding-top and padding-bottom attributes for the right panel be 0px, or the panel's scrollbar will extend underneath the window's status bar, as shown in Figure 6-2. This has to do with a bottom margin the Google Map API internals add below the map, which unintentionally makes the browser think the window content extends slightly below the screen.

Finally, in the body section declare your side panel right after your map div.

```
<div id="rightpanel"></div>
```

Figure 6-2. The unfortunate effects of including top and bottom side panel padding

That's all there is to it! You can fill the side panel with any information you'd like. You can see an up-to-date example at *http://www.googlemappers.com/articles/sidepanel/default.htm*, which is depicted in Figure 6-3.

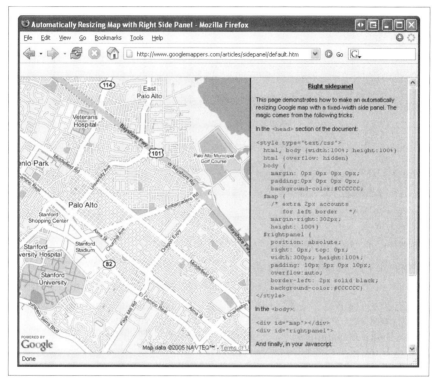

Figure 6-3. A properly configured side panel

—*Richard Kagerer*

Put a Map and HTML into Your Info Windows
HACK #52

Add more context to your info windows by including a map and HTML.

There are times you want to include both a map and some text in the same info window. With a little hackery you can get the sort of effect demoed at *http://mappinghacks.com/projects/gmaps/map_in_box.html* and shown in Figure 6-4.

Figure 6-4. A map and text in the same info window

Within the Google Maps API there is an info window class that enables you to click on a point or overlay and get additional information about whatever it was that you clicked on. According to the API documentation, there are really only two types of methods that create info windows. The first type is those that take some kind of HTML in one of their arguments, namely openInfoWindow( ), openInfoWindowHtml( ), and openInfoWindowXslt( ). The second type is really just a single method that takes no HTML as input and produces a blow-up map of some point inside of the info window, but nothing else. This method is showMapBlowup( ).

There are also times when we need both a map and text in the same window. However, when we look at the full prototype for the showMapBlowup( ) method, namely showMapBlowup(point, zoomLevel?, mapType?, pixelOffset?, onOpenFn?, onCloseFn?), we see there is no way to insert text into a map blowup. How do we get a map and text into an info window?

When we look at the openInfoWindowHtml( ), we see that it has the prototype openInfoWindowHtml(marker, htmlStr, pixelOffset?, onOpenFn?, onCloseFn?), where htmlStr is *any* string of HTML. Well, since we are using a div element to create the main map, why not try putting a div element into the htmlStr? As it turns out, that works almost wonderfully:

```
GEvent.addListener(testmarker, "click", function ( ) {
  var text = '<p style="text-align: left">';
  text += '<div id="minimap" style="width: 200px; height: 200px"></div>';
  text += 'Here is some text.<br>';
  text += 'This is a link to <a href=
              "http://maps.google.com/">Google Maps</a>';
  testmarker.openInfoWindowHtml(text);
  var minimap = new GMap(document.getElementById(minimap));
  minimap.centerAndZoom(pt,1);
  minimap.addControl(new GSmallMapControl( ));
});
map.addOverlay(testmarker);
```

Here pt is a previously defined point, and testmarker is a marker that we have to place somewhere. Note that, if you like, you can add your own controls to the blow-up map and put it into a different mode (satellite or hybrid).

However, there is a problem with all this. If we close the info window and then reopen it, we find that the map is gone! We haven't been able to figure out why this happens, but it turns out that there is a workaround:

```
var count = 0;
GEvent.addListener(testmarker, "click", function ( ) {
  var text = '<p style="text-align: left">';
  var whichmini = "minimap" + count;
  text += '<div id="';
  text += whichmini + '" style="width: 200px; height: 200px"></div>';
  text += 'Here is some text.<br>';
  text += 'This is a link to <a href=
              "http://maps.google.com/">Google Maps</a>
<br>';
  text += 'The current value of the infoWindow map counter is ' + count + '.';
  testmarker.openInfoWindowHtml(text);
  var minimap = new GMap(document.getElementById(whichmini));
  minimap.centerAndZoom(pt,1);
  minimap.addControl(new GSmallMapControl( ));
  count++;
});
map.addOverlay(testmarker);
```

What we have done here is add in a counter. Each time we open the info window, the counter is incremented by one. So if we put this counter into the id for the div element, then each time that we open the infoWindow, we will be opening a new div element. Note that we need to reference this new name in the constructor for the mini-map as well.

See Also

- Part of the credit for this should go to *april@syclo.com*, who came up with the idea of putting a div element inside of the HTML in an info window. I came up with the code that added the counter and made it work more than once. See the thread at *http://groups-beta.google.com/group/Google-Maps-API/browse_frm/thread/ab3075a8e91f8ecf/* for more details.

—John T. Guthrie

Add Flash Applets to Your Google Maps

#53   Spice up your Google Map info windows with Macromedia Flash animation, and even Java applets.

Integrating Macromedia Flash with a Google Map is a snazzy way to enhance the multimedia experience of your web page. Although the examples given here are toys, no doubt the intrepid reader can find Useful Uses for this sort of integration in the real world.

Flash in the Info Window

As a first step, we'll embed a small Flash animation I've created called *FlashBit.swf* into the pop-up window of a marker. The animation is just some text with a blue ball that bounces across it when clicked, as seen in Figure 6-5.

We're going to use the openInfoWindowHtml( ) method of the GMarker class to add the required HTML to our document. The string we'll be passing is stored in a variable called flashHtml.

```
flashHtml = '<object classid="clsid:d27cdb6e-ae6d-'
    + '11cf-96b8-444553540000" '
    + 'codebase="http://fpdownload.macromedia.com/pub/'
    + 'shockwave/cabs/flash/swflash.cab#version=7,0,0,0" '
    + 'width="128" height="53" id="FlashBit" align="middle">'
    + '<param name="allowScriptAccess" value="sameDomain" />'
    + '<param name="movie" value="FlashBit.swf" />'
    + '<param name="quality" value="high" />'
    + '<param name="bgcolor" value="#ffffff" />'
    + '<param name="wmode" value="transparent" />'
    + '<embed src="FlashBit.swf" quality="high" '
    +   'bgcolor="#ffffff" width="128" height="53" '
    +   'name="FlashBit" align="middle" '
    +   'allowScriptAccess="sameDomain" '
    +   'type="application/x-shockwave-flash" '
    +   'wmode="transparent" '
    +   'pluginspage="http://www.macromedia.com/go'
    +   '/getflashplayer" />'
```

Figure 6-5. Flash animation in a Google Maps info window

```
+ '</object></center>';
```

Although the code above may look a little convoluted, it's really nothing more than a typical Flash object declaration. The object tag is used by Internet Explorer on Windows platforms, while Netscape and Internet Explorer for the Mac both use the embed tag instead. More information on why you need both tags can be found in Macromedia's knowledge base at *http://www.macromedia.com/cfusion/knowledgebase/index.cfm?id=tn_4150*.

The most important parameters are movie and src, which should both point to the Flash SWF file. It's also important to set the wmode parameter to transparent in both the object and embed tags. Otherwise, the Flash object will overlap the map controls when the user scrolls the info window under them, as seen in Figure 6-6.

The following straightforward code creates our map. A marker called flashMarker is added to the map and, when clicked, it will call the onFlashMarkerClick( ) function:

```
var map = new GMap(document.getElementById("map"));
map.addControl(new GSmallMapControl( ));
map.addControl(new GMapTypeControl( ));
map.centerAndZoom(new GPoint(-122.07, 37.44), 4);

var flashMarker = new GMarker(new GPoint(-122.07, 37.433));
map.addOverlay(flashMarker)
GEvent.addListener(flashMarker,'click', onFlashMarkerClick);
```

Figure 6-6. Overlap caused by not including the wmode parameter

Unfortunately, there's a slight bug in that the Flash applet can "jump" out of the window after being clicked if it is inside the very first info window that is opened. You can see the problem by going to *http://www.googlemappers.com/articles/embedapplets/default.htm* and clicking "Show me the bug."

However, I've found that if the map has to be scrolled to show the info window, the bug doesn't occur. So in the onFlashMarkerClick( ) handler, I've put in a small hack that scrolls the map away from the marker the first time openInfoWindowHtml( ) is called. This way, the Google Map API internals will scroll the map back to the marker before opening the info window, and the bug won't occur.

```
var flashFixed = false;

function onFlashMarkerClick( ) {

    html = '<center><div style="width:200px; font-size:10pt">'
        + '<br/>Click below to poke the Flash object.</div>';
    html = html + flashHtml;

    if (!flashFixed) {
        flashFixed = true;     // only need to do this once
        map.centerAndZoom(new GPoint(-122.07, 37.43), 4);
    }

    // Now open the real one on top
    flashMarker.openInfoWindowHtml(html);

}
```

Communication Between Flash and Your Google Map

Integrating Flash and Google Maps becomes much more interesting when you get the two talking to each other. You can make use of the Flash fscommand( ) method to invoke any JavaScript function on the page, and use the

SetVariable( ) method in your JavaScript code to pass data back into your Flash applet. A complete tutorial is available in a Flash TechNote at *http://www.macromedia.com/cfusion/knowledgebase/index.cfm?id=tn_15683#jtfc*.

You can also take a look at my scuba-diving log at *http://www.leapbeyond.com/ric/scuba/* to see an example of an application that tightly integrates a Flash web site with a Google Map. Just go into the logbook a few pages and hit one of the map icons to get started.

Beyond Flash

The technique described can work with other types of objects in addition to Flash files. For example, you can embed a Java applet into the info window. Figure 6-7 shows how I used Robert Jeppesen's Durius Java applet (available at *http://www.durius.com/*) to embed a Google logo that ripples with a watery effect when you pass the mouse over it.

Figure 6-7. A Java applet embedded in a Google Map info window

The second marker is added after creating your map:

```
var appletMarker = new GMarker(new GPoint(-122.082667, 37.423269));
map.addOverlay(appletMarker);
GEvent.addListener(appletMarker,'click', onAppletMarkerClick);
```

Here's the click handler:

```
function onAppletMarkerClick( ) {
```

```
html = '<center><div style="width:200px; font-size:10pt">'
    + '<br/>Move your mouse around the image below '
    + 'to poke the Java applet.</div>'
    + '<div style="width:200px; font-size:8pt"><br/>'
    + '<em>Note: Clicking it will leave this page</em></div>';

// In the html string, create a div containing the applet
html = html +
    '<div id="applet" style="width:128px; height:53px;">' +
    '    <applet archive="DuriusWaterPic.jar" ' +
    '    width="128px" height="53px" align="bottom" ' +
    '    code="DuriusWaterPic.class">' +
    '        <param name="cabbase" value="DuriusWaterPic.cab" />' +
    '        <param name="image" value="GoogleLogo.gif" />' +
    '        <param name="dotsize" value="3" />' +
    '        <param name="dim" value="2" />' +
    '        <param name="noise" value="0" />' +
    '        <param name="mouse" value="1" />' +
    '        <param name="delay" value="10" />' +
    '        <param name="orientation" value="v" />' +
    '        <param name="bg" value="233423" />' +
    '        <param name="reg" value="43752326" />' +
    '    </applet>' +
    '</div></center>';

appletMarker.openInfoWindowHtml(html);
}
```

You can see all of these examples at *http://www.googlemappers.com/articles/ embedapplets/default.htm.*

—Richard Kagerer

Add a Nicer Info Window to Your Map with TLabel

HACK #54

Callouts, info windows—anything that can fit on a web page—can fit on a map.

The early Google Maps hacks share a similar affliction: they suffer from red pushpin syndrome. Sometimes the pushpins are green. You can create custom icons, but they are a bit of a challenge, and then you just get a different little symbol.

What you (might) want is the ability to customize the map with unique info windows, images, callouts, and anything else that strikes your fancy. Tom Mangan created the TLabel extension to allow you to embed any DOM object (anything that can appear on a web page) on a Google Map. Figure 6-8 shows Tom's canonical example from the TLabel page at *http:// gmaps.tommangan.us/tlabel.html*, with a Google satellite image of two U.S.

Air Force SR-71 Blackbirds and a U-2 spy plane at the Blackbird Air Park, in Palmdale, CA. (For the curious, this is at 34.602975 N, 118.085926 W.)

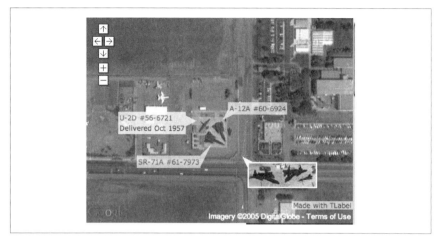

Figure 6-8. SR-71s at the Blackbird Air Park, with TLabel annotations

Callouts identify each plane. The numbers are links to sites that have more information on each plane. There is also a thumbnail image that was taken from ground level. The image has a tool tip that reads "Click for larger." Surprisingly, clicking on that link leads to a larger image of that thumbnail.

Using TLabel

The TLabel page is at *http://gmaps.tommangan.us/tlabel.html*. There is a link to a JavaScript file, currently *http://gmaps.tommangan.us/tlabel.19.js*, but check for the current version. Copy that file onto your own server and include it after you include the Google Maps API.

```
<script src="http://maps.google.com/maps?file=api&v=1&key
   =AOJVHiMoLlyAv...x3sA" type="text/javascript"></script>
<script src="tlabel.10.js" type="text/javascript"></script>
```

Now, create some objects! You control the TLabel object by creating a new object and then setting the properties. There is a demo of some TLabel tricks at *http://mappinghacks.com/projects/gmaps/brc_tlabel.html*. Here is code to create a label, as shown in Figure 6-9:

```
var label = new TLabel( );
label.id = 'mail_box';
label.anchorLatLng = new GPoint (-119.226396, 40.768080);
label.anchorPoint = 'bottomLeft';
label.content = 'Mail Box';
label.percentOpacity = 85;
map.addTLabel(label);
```

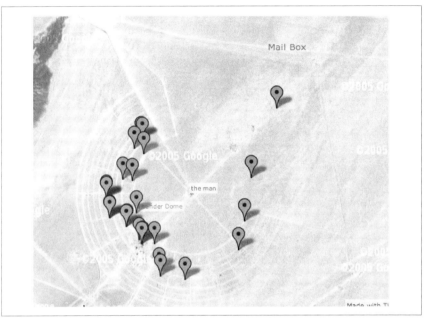

Figure 6-9. Black Rock City, annotated with TLabels

First, the code declares the variable named label to hold the newly created TLabel object. Next, we set the id of the TLabel. The id is vital! It must be unique. It is easy, and catastrophic, to end up with a duplicate label (where *catastrophic* means it doesn't work). The anchorLatLng is a GPoint object, i.e., the location where this object is anchored to the earth. The anchorPoint defines which part of the content will touch the anchor lat and long.

In this case, bottomLeft means that the bottom-left corner of our marker hits the point in the anchorLatLng. The choices are topLeft, topCenter, topRight, midRight, bottomRight, bottomCenter, bottomLeft, midLeft, or center. The default is topLeft. The content can be anything that can fit on a web page! In this case, we use the words "Mail Box." Table 6-1 summarizes these properties.

Once you have created the TLabel object and set the properties, there are four useful methods: add the object to your map with map.addTLabel(label), remove it with map.removeTLabel(label), move it around with label. setPosition(GPoint), or change its opacity (100% means you can't see through it at all) with label.setOpacity(percentage).

Table 6-1. Useful properties of the TLabel object

Property	Description
id	Specifies an ID for the label object. This ID is required and must be unique for each label you embed. The ID is exposed to the DOM, so you can dynamically adjust the label's style if you choose.
anchorLatLng	The longitude and latitude where the anchorPoint will be pinned to the map. Takes a GPoint object.
anchorPoint	The point on your embedded object that will be pinned to anchorLatLng. anchorPoint accepts the following values: topLeft, topCenter, topRight, midRight, bottomRight, bottomCenter, bottomLeft, midLeft, and center. The default is topLeft.
content	The XHTML code defining the element you wish to embed.
percentOpacity	A number between 0 and 100 inclusive, determining the opacity of the image. Default is 100, i.e., completely opaque.

You can replace the content with something more elaborate. This implements an onMouseOver event; so moving the mouse over the image pops up more information (i.e., a tool tip).

```
label.content  = '<img src="images/blank.png" alt=""
    style="width: 12px; height: 20px;" onmouseover="showFloat(\'sInfo\');"
onmousemove="floatCoords(\'sInfo\',event);"
    onmouseout="hideFloat(\'sInfo\');" />';
```

It is all a question of controlling what is in the content variable. You can put the whole thing into one string or split it across lines. If you split it, you need to remember to terminate each line of a multiline section with a quote or you'll get an "unterminated string literal" message.

Check out Tom's site at *http://gmaps.tommangan.us/* for more nifty hacks.

—written with assistance from Tom Mangan

Put Photographs on Your Google Maps

Treat photographs as map layers and add them to your Google maps.

While figuring out how to lay my own images into the Google Maps interface, I ended up with some pretty useful JavaScript, so I bundled it up as a tightly integrated extension to the official API. The result is TPhoto. TPhoto allows you to embed alternate aerial photographs inside your Google Maps. The added photos pan and zoom along with the main map view, without interfering with any clicks on the map. Figure 6-10 shows an example of an aerial photo of Groom Lake from 1959 overlaid over the Google Satellite imagery.

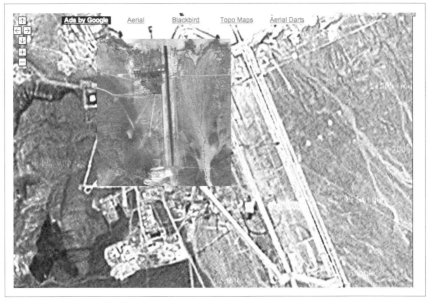

Figure 6-10. Groom Lake, 1959

Groom Lake. Dreamland Resort. Watertown. The Ranch. For such a secretive place, people certainly know it by a lot of names! The image in Figure 6-10 comes from my Area 51 page at *http://gmaps.tommangan.us/groom_lake.html.* Figure 6-11 shows a 1968 image over the Google Satellite imagery.

You can add the ability to overlay photos onto your own Google Maps by installing the TPhoto extension.

Download the TPhoto library from *http://gmaps.tommangan.us/tphoto.html/.* The current version is *tphoto.16.js*, available at *http://gmaps.tommangan.us/ tphoto.16.js.* Place it on your server and include it after you include the Google Maps API in your JavaScript. You could include it directly from the *tommangan.us* server, but it is on very rare occasions not available, so I recommend you download the file to your own server and link it as shown here:

```
<script src="http://maps.google.com/maps?file=api&v=1&key=ApAU1_iS-dEaDI.RA"
    type="text/javascript"></script>
<script src="tphoto.16.js" type="text/javascript"></script>
```

There are two ways to use TPhoto. In the first method, you supply the lat/long of the top left and bottom right corners of your image. In the second method, you supply a single lat/long anchor point, the base zoom level, and the dimensions of your image. The first method looks like:

```
var groom1959 = new TPhoto();
groom1959.id = 'groom1959';
groom1959.src = 'images/groom1959.jpg';
```

Figure 6-11. Area 51 in 1968, over Google Satellite imagery

```
photo.percentOpacity = 50;
groom1959.anchorTopLeft = new GPoint(-115.823107,37.248368);
groom1959.anchorBottomRight = new GPoint(-115.801649,37.230123);

map.addTPhoto(photo);
```

Here is one way to create a button that will show and hide the overlaid image. This would appear in an HTML form button.

```
<input type="button" value="show 1959" id="show1959" onClick="showImage(); ">
```

The button calls the showImage() Javascript method. The variable show serves as a toggle. It starts at 0 (i.e., don't show the image) and flips state each time the button is clicked. Either the addTPhoto method or the removeTphoto method will be called depending on the value of show. The text displayed on the button is also toggled from "show 1959" to "hide 1959."

```
var show = 0;
function showImage( ) {
        show = 1-show;
        if (show == 1) {
                map.addTPhoto(groom1959);
                document.getElementById('show1959').value = 'hide 1959';
        } else {
                map.removeTPhoto(groom1959);
                document.getElementById('show1959').value = 'show 1959';
        }
}
```

The second approach takes different parameters:

```
photo = new TPhoto( );
photo.id = '[id]';
photo.src = '[src]';
photo.size = new GSize(width,height);
photo.baseZoom = [zoomLevel];
photo.percentOpacity = [percent];
photo.anchorPx = new GPoint(x,y);
photo.anchorLatLng = new GPoint(lng,lat);

map.addTPhoto(photo);
```

There are only a few methods you need to use with TPhoto.

TPhoto( )
> The constructor, which creates a new photo instance. Takes no parameters.

The extension adds two methods to the GMap object:

addTPhoto(*photo*)
> Adds the given photo to the map.

removeTPhoto(*photo*)
> Removes the given photo from the map.

setOpacity(*percentOpacity*)
> Defines the desired opacity of the embedded image. *percentOpacity* is a number from 0 to 100, inclusive.

Setting opacity allows you to see through the overlaid image to the base layer. It allows you to do things like compare then and now imagery as shown in Figures 6-12 and 6-13. These are aerial views comparing the overlaid 1994 USGS photo over the Google aerial imagery. The first image shows the Google Aerial base layer view with the 1994 photo overlaying it and set to 20% opacity. You can see through the older image to how things are now (where *now* is when the image was taken).

The right view is at 100% opacity. In the left image you can see buildings that didn't exist in 1994. The two Blackbirds are a constant.

Figure 6-13 is an image of the Blackbird Airpark in Palmdale, California from the Blackbird Sighting page at *http://gmaps.tommangan.us/blackbirds.html*. The Blackbirds map was my first Google Maps project. Soon after the API was released, I found myself in need of a project that would enable me to go about breaking maps. As it happened, I had just read about Robb Magley's search for the crash site of one of the Blackbirds and thought it would be fun to find out where all of them are now. This is the kind of application that Google Maps has made possible!

—*Tom Mangan*

Figure 6-12. Blackbirds at 20% opacity

 ## Pin Your Own Maps to Google Maps with TPhoto
Georeference your own maps and then pin them anywhere.

The first time I visited New York City from the Bay Area, I was excited to see everything, all at once. I figured that Manhatten is small, about 10 1/2 miles from tip to tip, and the boroughs are just a bit larger. How long could it take to go 10 miles?

A temporary New Yorker friend told me, "You can think of Manhattan as being the whole Bay Area. Sure you can drive from Palo Alto to San Francisco, across to Oakland and down the East Bay to San Jose, but would you? Manhattan is physically smaller, but in terms of travel times it is similar."

We can use TPhoto [Hack #55] to take an image of one place and center it in another. At *http://www.mappinghacks.com/projects/gmaps/brc_ref.html* you see the Google aerial photo of the site of the Burning Man festival in the Black Rock desert of Nevada. If you click "show plan," you'll get the 2005 Burning Man city plan overlaid on the Google Map as shown in Figure 6-14.

Figure 6-13. Blackbirds at 100% opacity

But you don't have to overlay the city plan on the Google Map in the proper place! You can scroll the map to another area and then click on a point to overlay the city map on that point. Figure 6-15 shows a hypothetical Burning Apple festival centered on 79th Street in the middle of Central Park.

It is interesting that Manhattan is oriented nearly the same way as the Playa, from southwest to northeast, and the Festival covers about two-thirds of the width of Manhattan. The Metropolitan Museum of Art ends up more or less by the Large Scale Sound installations.

The distance from Center Camp to the perimeter fence is about 27 city blocks—from 72nd Street to 99th Street. And moving out a few zoom levels leaves us in awe at how tremendously big and dense an experience it is to be in New York.

Taking it home, way home to Sebastopol, and centering on O'Reilly, gives us the results in Figure 6-16.

This was produced with the single-point method of TPhoto [Hack #55]. This makes TPhoto work as a simple georeferencing tool. Georeferencing is the

Figure 6-14. Black Rock City in its proper place

act of mapping the pixel space of an image to a coordinate system that is pegged to the earth's surface.

You need to provide the image size, zoom level, and a single point. But we can change the properties of a TImage object dynamically. As an example, let's geo-reference the Black Rock City 2005 Plan. You can download the 65KB PDF image from *http://www.burningman.com/preparation/maps/05_maps/*. First convert the PDF to a JPEG. You can do this in any image-processing tool. If you have ImageMagick installed, this command works:

```
convert brc_2005.pdf brc_2005.jpg
```

Next, you need to find the pixel coordinates of a recognizable point. I used the GIMP to edit the image. Photoshop would also work. Open the image, then zoom in and place the cursor right over the Man. I get x=917, y=963. Also note the height and width of the image: 1833×2274.

Finally, you need to rotate the image so that North is up. I used the rotate tool to align the grids with the North arrow. It was a -37 degree rotation.

This is the core code that overlays the image:

```
var brc = new TPhoto( );
brc.id = 'brc';
brc.src = 'images/brc_2005_rotate.jpg';
```

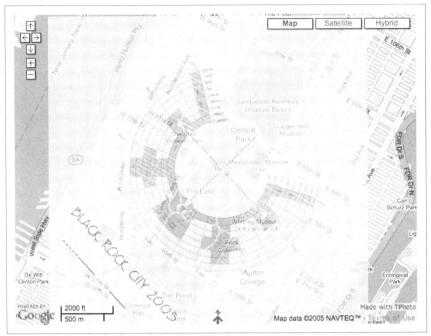

Figure 6-15. Black Rock City centered on Central Park

```
brc.size = new GSize(2032, 2432);
brc.baseZoom = 1;
brc.percentOpacity = 40;
brc.anchorPx = new GPoint(1110, 948);
brc.anchorLatLng = new GPoint(-119.23616409301758,40.754279292683094);
```

This loads the image *images/brc_2005_rotate.jpg* and centers it so that the x,y pixel coordinate maps to the passed lat/long. You can adjust the Gsize (specified in pixels) and baseZoom so that the displayed image takes up the right amount of space. This happens automatically with the two-point use of TPhoto.

You can change the opacity of the overlaid image [Hack #55]. This HTML defines two buttons that increase and decrease the photo opacity when they are clicked:

```
<input type="button" value="opacity +" id="opacityup"
onClick="changeOpacity(10);">

<input type="button" value="opacity -" id="opacitydown"
onClick="changeOpacity(-10);">
```

When the buttons are clicked, either +10 or –10 is passed to the changeOpacity method:

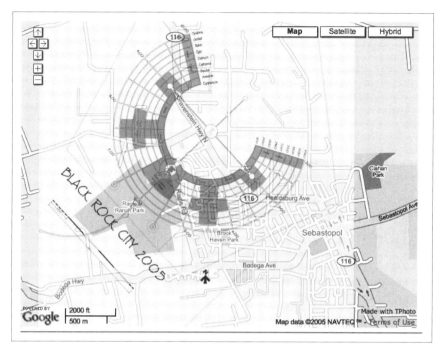

Figure 6-16. Black Rock City centered on O'Reilly Media

```
function changeOpacity (z) {
        var temp = brc.percentOpacity;
        temp += z;
        if (temp > 100) {
                temp = 100;
        }
        if (temp < 0) {
                temp = 0;
        }
        map.removeTPhoto(brc);
        brc.percentOpacity = temp;
        map.addTPhoto(brc);
        document.getElementById('opacity').value = brc.percentOpacity;
}
```

This routine attempts to increase or decrease the opacity by the passed +10 or -10 and then checks that the opacity is not greater than 100 or less than 0. Assuming it is within range, it removes the photo from the active map, sets the opacity to the new value, and then redisplays the image and updates the displayed opacity.

The showImage method is called when the user clicks "show plan," and is even more simple:

```
function showImage( ) {
```

```
        show = 1-show;
        if (show == 1) {
                map.addTPhoto(brc);
                document.getElementById('showplan').value = 'hide Plan';
        } else {
                map.removeTPhoto(brc);
                document.getElementById('showplan').value = 'show Plan';
        }
}
```

The variable show serves as a toggle. It is initially set to 0, and then the line show = 1-show toggles it between 1 and 0. When it is 1 the photo is displayed and when it is 0 the photo is hidden.

Do a Local Zoom with GxMagnifier

Context is key: GxMagnifier lets you choose the appropriate context.

The zoom feature on Google Maps is nice, except when you want to see a zoomed out view so that you have some context and yet still see detail. The normal cartographic answer to that conundrum would be that you are out of luck. Lucky for us, this is no ordinary cartographic environment!

The Hack

GxMagnifier is a free add-in control for Google Maps that creates a moveable, magnified window on top of your map. Figure 6-17 shows GxMagnifier in action.

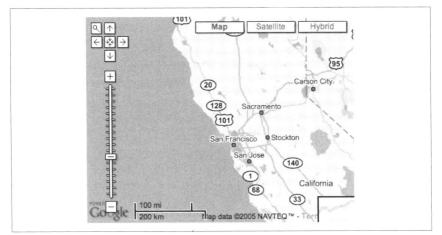

Figure 6-17. GxMagnifier's "Hello World"

Does this look like an ordinary Google Map to you? Click the magnifier icon in the top-left corner of the map. Now, wherever you go on the map, you get a magnified view. This feature can be used with a mere two lines of code. Like a lot of JavaScript libraries, you first load it:

```
<script src="GxMagnifier.1.js" type="text/javascript"></script>
```

Then, add the control in your code:

```
map.addControl(new GxMagnifierControl());
```

Note that we're passing a custom control object to the standard map. addControl API call. This is all you need to do to get the basic magnifier control. This is only the most basic example of what GxMagnifier can do! The full documentation, with complete reference to the API can be found here: *http://www.googlemappers.com/libraries/gxmagnifier/docs/default.htm.*

Doing More with GxMagnifier

In our simple example we instantiated the GxMagnifierControl object within our map.addControl() call:

```
map.addControl(new GxMagnifierControl());
```

This is a dead simple approach, but it doesn't allow us to control the GxMagnifierControl later on. GxMagnifier can do more for us! The next examples will start with this basic framework, with the crucial lines highlighted. Of course, you'll need to use your own developer's key.

```
<!DOCTYPE html PUBLIC "-//W3C//DTD XHTML 1.0 Strict//EN" "http://www.w3.org/
TR/xhtml1/DTD/xhtml1-strict.dtd">
<html xmlns="http://www.w3.org/1999/xhtml">
<head>
    <title>GxMagnifier Example Framework</title>
    <script src="http://maps.google.com/
maps?file=api&v=1&key=ilovemykidsmandms" type="text/javascript"></script>
    <script src="GxMagnifier.1.js" type="text/javascript"></script>
</head>

<body>
    <div id="map" style="width: 300px; height: 300px"></div>
    <script type="text/javascript">
    //<![CDATA[

    if (GBrowserIsCompatible()) {
      var map = new GMap(document.getElementById("map"));
      map.centerAndZoom(new GPoint(-122.4618, 37.7902), 4);

      // Create the magnifier
      var magControl = new GxMagnifierControl();
      map.addControl(magControl);
```

```
        // Get reference to the associated GxMagnifier for use in the examples
        var mag = magControl.GxMagnifier;

        // ...rest of the example goes here...

    }

    //]]>
    </script>
  </body>
</html>
```

That looks like a long example, but it is similar to the Google Maps "Hello World" example, with the addition of these lines:

```
var magControl = new GxMagnifierControl();
map.addControl(magControl);
var mag = magControl.GxMagnifier;
```

This defines the variable `magControl`, which we can use to set attributes, and then adds the control to the map. The `GxMagnifierControl` class is just a wrapper, as most of the time we'll be accessing its related `GxMagnifier` object by reading the `GxMagnifierControl.GxMagnifier` property into the variable mag.

What can you do with `magControl` now that you have it? Many things!

Zooming. GxMagnifier automatically adjusts its zoom level as your main map is zoomed. Here we make it magnify by 3 zoom levels, instead of the default 2.

```
mag.setMagnification(3);
```

You can also set a negative zoom level, which is useful in conjunction with *docking*, as described below.

Resizing. By default, the magnified viewport is one third the size of your main map. You can change its dimensions.

```
mag.setSize(new GSize(150, 80));
```

Capturing the click. You may not want your magnifier to zoom in on the map when the user clicks it. Here we override the click event to tell us where we clicked and then close the magnifier window. You can use `GEvent.bind()` for more sophisticated handling.

```
mag.disableDefaultClickHandler();
GEvent.addListener(mag, "click",
  function(point){
    alert("You clicked " + point.toString());
    this.hide(); // note, "this" is the GxMagnifier instance
  });
```

Moving the button. Here we place the magnifying glass button 10 pixels from the top right corner. Note that GxMagnifierControl.setDefaultPosition() has to be called before adding the control to the map.

```
var magControl = new GxMagnifierControl();
magControl.setDefaultPosition(new GxControlPositionHack(1, 10, 10));
map.addControl(magControl);
```

Automatically panning. The magnifier can scroll the map when it gets moved near an edge. Note the panning region extends inward from the edges of the main map by half the size of the magnifier window.

```
mag.enableAutoPan();
```

Docking. You can free the magnifier from the map's container and put it anywhere on the page. We do this by creating a GxMagnifier instance directly and telling it to use our own HTML div element. Here's a fullscreen map, with the magnifier docked to the bottom right corner. The example deviates a bit from our typical ones.

Inside the head element, we define some custom CSS styles for the page, the map, and our magnifier display:

```
<!-- Set up the containers, and make a "fullscreen" window -->
<style type="text/css">
  html, body {width: 100%; height: 100%}
  body {margin-top: 0px; margin-right: 0px; margin-left: 0px; margin-bottom:
0px}
  #map {position:absolute; width:100%; height:100%}
  #magnifier {position:absolute; right:0px; bottom:0px; width:200px; height:
200px;
  border:2px solid; border-bottom-style:outset}
</style>
```

In the body, we add HTML div elements for the map and the magnifier:

```
<div id="map"></div>
<div id="magnifier"></div>
```

And, finally, here's the JavaScript:

```
// Create the magnifier
var div = document.getElementById("magnifier");
div.style.zIndex = 10; // make it stay on top
var mag = new GxMagnifier(map, null, div);
mag.map.setMapType(G_SATELLITE_TYPE)

// Monitor the window resize event and let the map know when it occurs
// This isn't required for GxMagnifier, but it is required to accomplish
// a correct fullscreen Google Map.
if (window.attachEvent) {
  window.attachEvent("onresize", function() {this.map.onResize()} );
```

```
  } else {
    window.addEventListener("resize", function( ) {this.map.onResize( )} ,
    false);
  }
```

Note the line:

```
mag.map.setMapType(G_SATELLITE_TYPE)
```

The docked map in the corner shows the satellite imagery that corresponds
to the point of the mouse, as shown in Figure 6-18. You can find out more
about this feature at *http://www.googlemappers.com/libraries/gxmagnifier/
docs/examples/docking.htm.*

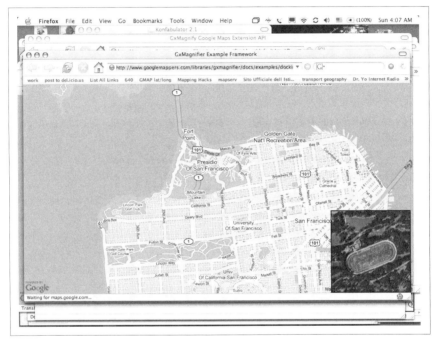

Figure 6-18. Magnifier docked with a satellite view

Multiple magnifiers and negative zoom. You can include multiple GxMagnifi-
ers on your map. Figure 6-19 expands on the previous example on docking,
and uses a negative magnification factor to create a docked "birds eye view" of
where you are on the map. See it in action at *http://www.googlemappers.com/
libraries/gxmagnifier/docs/examples/multiple.htm.*

In case you're curious, I got the idea of trying to make a magnifier control for
Google Maps after watching a concept video that shows a similar feature in
mapping technology demonstrated under Windows Longhorn (a.k.a. Vista).

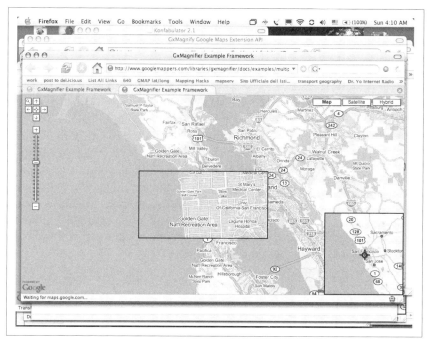

Figure 6-19. An orientation map and a magnified map

See Also

- GxMagnifier is not supported by Google or part of its official API, and it is beta software, so there may be some bugs. If you run into anything, report it in the Google-Maps-API forum. I try to keep an eye on messages there, but chances are one of the other members will be able to respond with a fix faster than I can.

- The GxMagnifier documentation page has much more detail and lives at *http://www.googlemappers.com/libraries/gxmagnifier/docs/default.htm.*

- The Google Mappers community is a good place to find out more about custom Google Maps API extensions: *http://www.googlemappers.com/.*

—Richard Kagerer

HACK #58 Find the Right Zoom Level

You've got some points to show on a map. How do you pick the right zoom level to show them all at once?

The Google Maps API is powerful but, as tends to be the case for such toolkits, has some omissions and inconveniences. For example, in many real-world mapping problems, it's common to have a set of points or lines that

we wish to display on a map. Typically, we choose the outer four corners, or
extents, of the map to match the *bounding box* of the data, which is given by
the minimum and maximum *x* and *y* coordinates in our data set. By selecting the map extents to match the bounding box of the data, we can guarantee that everything we want to show should be visible in the map display.

The bounding box of a data set is usually very easy to calculate. One way to
do so is to simply iterate through the data set, looking for the largest and
smallest coordinates in both dimensions. The problem is that the Google
Maps API doesn't give us any way to set the map extents based on a bounding box. Instead, the API exports a centerAndZoom( ) method that accepts a
center point of the map, expressed as a latitude and longitude pair, and a
zoom level. Google documents the zoom level as an integer, and the examples in their documentation all use 4 as the zoom level, but no definition of
the zoom levels themselves is given. Experimentation shows that they corre-
spond with the ticks on the zoom level control.

Our question is then very simple: given a bounding box, how does one
determine an appropriate center and zoom level, so that our data is guaranteed to appear on the screen, regardless of screen geometry?

The Brute Force Method

One approach is to look at the current map geometry and see if the screen
will hold the bounding box and keep zooming in or out as needed. The
zoom levels are approximately powers of two, so it's practical to use a sort
of brute-force method, and just multiply or divide the current level by two,
and see if it still fits. The following JavaScript does just that:

```
function computeZoom(minX, minY, maxX, maxY) {
  var zl;
  var bounds = map.getBoundsLatLng( );
  var cz = map.getZoomLevel( );
  var mapWidth = Math.abs(bounds.maxX - bounds.minX);
  var mapHeight = Math.abs(bounds.maxY - bounds.minY);
  var myWidth = Math.abs(maxX - minX);
  var myHeight = Math.abs(maxY - minY);
  var changeZoom = myWidth > mapWidth ? 1 : -1;
  // Just rip through until we find the lowest that will hold our span.
  // For certain geometries (around hemisphere boundaries), this won't work
  for (zl = map.getZoomLeve( ) ; zl > 2 && zl < 17 ; zl += changeZoom) {
    width = width * Math.pow(2, changeZoom);
    height = height * Math.pow(2, changeZoom);
    if ((width < lon) || (height < lat))
      return zl - 1;
  }
  return zl;
}
```

This makes setting that center point and zoom level very simple:

```
centerLat = (minLat + maxLat) / 2;
centerLon = (minLon + maxLon) / 2;
var zl = computeZoom(minLon, minLat, maxLon, maxLat);
map.centerAndZoom(new GPoint(centerLon, centerLat), zl);
```

The Analytic Method

However, we can simplify this approach even further. Empirically, we note that at zoom level 17, the resolution of the map is 1.46025 degrees of longitude per pixel. Similarly, we can observe that this resolution halves for each subsequent zoom level, and that this seems to be invariant for the *x* axis of the map. For the *y* axis of the map, this property applies to lower zoom levels of the map, but not the higher zoom levels, because instead of wrapping the map, blank space is shown above and below the poles.

Nevertheless, as a first approximation, we can calculate what the resolution of our map ought to be, given the display geometry of the map in pixels and a bounding box, to get a map that covers the whole box. We can exploit this relationship by taking the logarithm of the ratio of 1.46025 to our desired resolution to the base 2, and then subtracting this value from 17. The following JavaScript performs this operation:

```
function calculateZoom2 (minX, maxX, minY, maxY) {
    var mapElement = document.getElementById("map");
    var degLonPerPixel = Math.abs(maxX - minX) / parseInt(mapElement.style.
width);
    var degLatPerPixel = Math.abs(maxY - minY) / parseInt(mapElement.style.
height);
    var resolution = Math.max( degLonPerPixel, degLatPerPixel );
    return Math.ceil( 17 - Math.log(1.46025 / resolution) / Math.log(2) );
}
```

Since the JavaScript Math.log( ) returns the logarithm to the base *e*, we use the mathematical relationship $log_a(x) = log_b(x) / log_b(a)$ in the code example above to obtain the logarithm to the base 2. Similarly, we use Math.ceil( ) to find the smallest integer greater than or equal to the result, to ensure that the resulting map is at least as large as our bounding box. As for the difference in resolutions between the *x* and *y* axes for the higher zoom level, we observe empirically that the maximum resolution for the *y* axis at any zoom level is smaller than the resolution of the *x* axis at zoom level 15. At zoom level 15, the entire world is still shown north to south, so this won't be a problem either.

The main advantage of this method is that, unlike the brute force method, it can be applied on the server side as well as the client side. The corresponding bit of Perl code from a CGI script might look like this:

```
my $zoom = int( 17 - log(1.46025 / $resolution) / log(2) ) + 1;
```

This approach requires a little bit less code than the brute-force method, and it feels a lot more elegant. The disadvantage, of course, is that it relies on hardcoded constants that could break if Google decides to change the semantics of its zoom levels without warning, though this seems unlikely at the moment.

The Undocumented API Method

Of course, Google probably needs its own method to determine the right zoom level right? As it happens, the 1.0 version of Google Maps API does provide such a method, albeit an undocumented one. The following code makes use of this undocumented method:

```
var center = new GPoint( (minX + maxX) / 2, (minY + maxY) / 2 );
var span = new GSize( maxX - minX, minX - minY );
var zoom = map.spec.getLowestZoomLevel(center, span, map.viewSize);
map.centerAndZoom(center, zoom);
```

This method may be the simplest of all, but it relies on two presently undocumented features of the Google Maps API: the map.spec.getLowestZoomLevel( ) method and the map.viewSize property. Using them runs an even higher risk than the other two methods that your code will break at some point, should Google alter its API. However, we won't be at all surprised if Google decides to document this method, or methods like it in future releases. Read more about this issue on the Google Groups thread at *http://xrl.us/getLowestZoomLevel*.

One final thought: all these methods try to find the optimal match between the supplied bounding box and a corresponding zoom level. If your bounding box area should happen to match a zoom level exactly, this might not be what you want, because the outliers of your data set will be displayed at the very edge of the map. For this reason, it might be smart to expand the width and height of your bounding box by, say, 10%, to ensure that not only is everything displayed on the map, but everything is displayed well within the map.

—Robert Lipe

HACK #59 Show Lots of Stuff—Quickly

Lots of Google Maps overlays means lots of time spent waiting for them to draw on the map—unless you're smart.

When dealing with nontrivial numbers of overlays to draw on a Google Map—as in more than a hundred or so markers or vertices in a polyline— the drawing time required for a GMap object becomes really noticeable. The inclination is to want to show markers as quickly as possible, so that the user gets immediate feedback on what's going on, but it's been discovered that if you buffer the objects and then manually trigger the redraw, it is much faster.

The Code

We can accomplish this buffering by adding a custom method of our own to the Google Maps API, which we'll call addOverlays( ). By assigning it to the GMap class prototype, it becomes available on any GMap objects we create. The code looks like this:

```
// This is a bit of a trick for the 1.0 API. The 'addoverlay' method
// is agonizingly slow, so we buffer up the markers in the 'overlays'
// array and then deliver them to GMAP in one shot.

GMap.prototype.addOverlays=function(a) {
        var b=this;
        for (i=0;i<a.length;i++) {
                try {
                        this.overlays.push(a[i]);
                        a[i].initialize(this);
                        a[i].redraw(true);
                } catch(ex) {
                        alert('err: ' + i + ', ' + ex.toString( ));
                }
        }
        this.reOrderOverlays( );
}
```

The addOverlays( ) method can be used directly in your code or included via a script element in your HTML, after you include the Google Maps library.

Using this technique is really easy—instead of calling map.addOverlay( ) for each marker or polyline we create, we'll push each overlay onto an array, and then pass the array to map.addOverlays( ). Here's a fragment of a simple GPX reader that displays waypoint data using this idea:

```
var wpts = GPX.documentElement.getElementsByTagName("wpt");
var markers = [];
for (var k = 0; k < wpts.length; k++) {
        var point = new GPoint(trkPts[k].getAttribute("lon"),
                               trkPts[k].getAttribute("lat")));
        var marker = new Gmarker(point);
        // ... we could do things with the marker here,
        // like set a custom icon or configure an info window ...
        markers.push( marker );
}
        // Now let gmap have the waypoints all in one chunk.
map.addOverlays(points);
```

In a similar fashion, if you have multiple contiguous lines to draw, it's smarter to compress them all into a single polyline, rather than ask the GMap object to render each one separately:

```
// Coalesce each GPX trk/trkseg/trkpts section into a single object.
// Each trkseg is a different object so that the lines don't get all
// glommed together.
var tracks = GPX.documentElement.getElementsByTagName("trk");
var trkpts = [], polylines = [];
for (var i = 0; i < tracks.length; i++) {
  var trkSeg = tracks[i].getElementsByTagName("trkseg");
  for (var j = 0; j < trkSeg.length; j++) {
    var trkPts = trkSeg[j].getElementsByTagName("trkpt");
    for (var k = 0; k < trkPts.length; k++) {
      trkpts.push(new GPoint(trkPts[k].getAttribute("lon"),
                             trkPts[k].getAttribute("lat")));
    }
    polylines.push(new GPolyline(trkpts, trkcolor, 5));
    trkpts = [];
  }
}
map.addOverlays(polylines);
```

In testing one GPX file with 1,700 trackpoints, using this technique reduced the time required to display from 48 seconds to 6 seconds.

 Be careful not to get carried away with this idea, as lines will be drawn between every point in a single GPolyline. If your intent is to preserve breaks in the drawn line, be sure to preserve them as multiple GPolyline objects.

Additional optimizations are possible. For example, are all those track-points really necessary? Tools such as GPSBabel's *arc* filter can simplify the polyline, while retaining its basic shape. Different GPolyline objects with different amounts of detail could be chosen based on the current zoom level. As a rule, the less data Google Maps is obliged to work with, the faster it will perform.

See Also

- GPSBabel lives at *http://www.gpsbabel.org/*.
- "View Your GPS Tracklogs in Google Maps" [Hack #37] implements a line simplification algorithm in Ruby and in JavaScript.
- "How Big Is That, Exactly?" [Hack #28] also uses a line simplification algorithm to speed up the drawing of state and country shapes.

—Robert Lipe

Make Things Happen When the Map Moves

HACK #60

You can make your maps more interactive by responding to user-initiated events.

Balancing what to show and what not to show on a Google Map can be tricky. On one hand, for performanc reasons, you want to restrict the overlays displayed on the map to just the ones that would appear within the current view. On the other, if the user should pan or zoom the map, you might want the map's contents to change in response. Fortunately, the Google Maps API offers a way to make this happen automatically.

The Hack

Poor Clio's Side-by-Side Google Maps at *http://jamesedmunds.com/poorclio/ googlemap11.cfm* offers a terrific example of how Google Maps hacks can respond to user actions. The site, built by James Edmunds, shows two Google Maps of the same location side by side. On the left, the regular map mode is shown, while the map on the right shows the same map in satellite mode. Figure 6-20 shows the side-by-side view of the area around 30th Street Station in Philadelphia, with the rail yards extending away to the north.

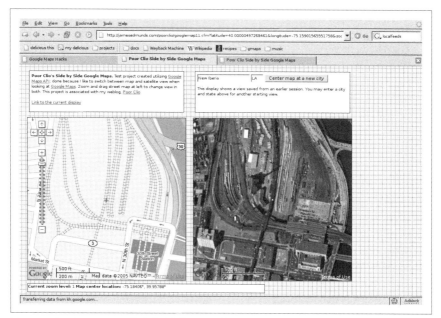

Figure 6-20. Two views of Philadelphia's 30th Street Station, side by side

What's novel about this site is that if you drag the map on the left with your mouse, double-click to recenter it, or zoom in or out, the satellite view on the right recenters and zooms to match. Until Google introduced hybrid mode maps, this was effectively one of the only ways to compare the satellite and map views. The secret to how it works lies in the Google Maps Event API.

The Code

If you've written or looked at JavaScript code that uses the Google Maps API to cause info windows to pop up when the user clicks on a marker, then you've probably seen a method call that looks like this:

```
GEvent.addListener(marker, "click", function( ) {
    marker.openInfoWindowHtml(html);
});
```

This method uses the GEvent class to register a click event on a marker object. When the marker is clicked, the anonymous function gets called, and the info window is opened. As it happens, the Google Maps API offers several other events for tracking and responding to user interactions.

Here's a snippet of code from the Poor Clio's Side-by-Side page:

```
function onMapMove( ) {
    smap.centerAndZoom(map.getCenterLatLng( ), smap.getZoomLevel( ));
    updateStatus( );
}

function onMapZoom(oldZoom, newZoom) {
    smap.centerAndZoom(map.getCenterLatLng( ), newZoom);
    updateStatus( );
}

GEvent.addListener(map, 'move', onMapMove);
GEvent.addListener(map, 'zoom', onMapZoom);
updateStatus( );
```

These dozen or so lines of JavaScript code handle virtually all of the user interactions needed to keep the two maps in sync. The first thing to note about this code is that, unlike most Google Maps API examples, you'll see *two* GMap objects in this code, one called map in the JavaScript, and the other called smap. Well, why not?

The first of the two functions shown above, onMapMove( ), takes the GPoint object representing the latitude and longitude of the center of the regular map, and the integer representing the current zoom level of the regular map, and passes them to the centerAndZoom( ) method of the satellite map. When this happens, the satellite map automatically zooms and recenters to match the center point and zoom level of the regular map. The onMapZoom( ) function does basically the same thing, but it takes two arguments, representing the old and new zoom levels of the regular map, and uses the new zoom level of the regular map as the new zoom level of the satellite map. The two calls to GEvent.addListener( ) hook these functions into the move and zoom events on the regular map, respectively, so that when the user changes the view of the regular map, the satellite map follows.

The calls to updateStatus( ) interspersed through the code above cause the latitude, longitude, and zoom level display below the two maps to keep in sync as well. The code looks like this:

```
function updateStatus( )
{
    var point = map.getCenterLatLng( );
    var status =
        "<b>Current zoom level:</b>  " + map.getZoomLevel( ) +
        " <b>Map center location:</b> " +
        Math.round(point.x * 100000) / 100000 + "&deg;, " +
        Math.round(point.y * 100000) / 100000 + "&deg;";
    document.getElementById("status").innerHTML = status;
}
```

The use of Math.round( ), coupled with multiplication and division by a constant power of ten, is a standard trick for rounding a floating-point number to a given number of decimal places. The call to document.getElementById( ) fetches the HTML Document Object Model element containing the status message, and the assignment to the innerHTML property updates the HTML inside with the latest center point and zoom.

This same kind of technique can hypothetically be used to have a "Link to this View" URL track the current view, although Poor Clio's doesn't do it that way. Assuming that you had an HTML <a> element with an id attribute set to linkHere, you could do something like the following to update the URL in the href attribute:

```
document.getElementById("linkHere").setAttribute( "href",
    "http://some.server.net/gmaps?ll
        =" + point.x + "+" + point.y + "&z=" + zoom );
```

There's one other trick that the Poor Clio's site uses to keep the maps in sync. Because the satellite half of this page doesn't have zoom and pan controls, the only way to move the satellite map independently is to drag it with the mouse. The site uses this line of JavaScript to keep such a thing from happening.

```
smap.disableDragging( );
```

The other way to solve the problem of the maps potentially getting out of sync, of course, would be to make the event handlers a bit more generic and then add two more calls to `addEventListener( )` to make the regular map follow movements on the satellite map as well.

The GEvent API

The key thing to note about the GEvent API is that all its methods are static, which is to say that they're called on the class itself, and not on an instance of the class. This means you say:

```
GEvent.addListener( ... );    // RIGHT
```

...as opposed to the following, which you should definitely *not* use:

```
var event = new GEvent( );    // WRONG
event.addListener( ... );    // WRONG
```

We mention this because it may run contrary to your expectations, as most of the other classes in the Google Maps API require you to instantiate an object of that class before calling methods on it.

The GEvent API shouldn't be mistaken for the JavaScript event API, which works rather similarly, with its `onClick`, `onMouseOver`, `onChange` methods, and so on. In general, you'll want to use GEvent handlers for Google Maps API objects, and continue to use JavaScript event handlers for everything else. In particular, as of this writing, there isn't anything like an `onMouseOver` event for Google Maps marker objects, and more's the pity. Perhaps Google will fix this in a future version of its API.

Hacking the Hack

Most Google Maps hacks out there rely on an Update Map button (or the equivalent) to update the overlays on a map after the user zooms or pans. This definitely works, but it's not the most elegant solution for refreshing the map's contents, because it relies on the user to do something that could be done automatically in JavaScript.

However, before you run out and add event handlers to your Google Map, consider the following: the Google Maps API doesn't guarantee exactly *when* the registered event handlers will be called, just that they will be called at some point. If you try dragging the regular map around on the Poor Clio's site, you'll notice that there's sometimes a bit of lag, but (assuming you don't drag too quickly) the satellite map otherwise follows along pretty faithfully. This means that the move event on the regular map is getting triggered every so many seconds or milliseconds throughout the drag.

If your intention is to have one map track another, this is definitely what you want to have happen. On the other hand, if you're using the event handler to trigger a download of fresh data off the network, you probably don't want to have multiple overlapping data requests slowing everything down while the user is still trying to drag the map.

First, this means you want to use the moveend event with the GMap object, and not the move event. However, if you really want to be on the safe side, you might do well to combine this with a semaphore and a delay, in case the user does a bit of fine adjustment to recenter or zoom the map to exactly what they want to see. Here's what the code might look like:

```
var updateRequested = 0;

GEvent.addListener( map, "moveend", function( ) {
    updateRequested++;
    window.setTimeout( beginUpdate, 2500 )
});

function beginUpdate ( ) {
    if (--updateRequested > 0) return;
    // *now* check map.getCenterLatLng( ) etc.
    // then launch a new GXmlHttp request
    // and do the update handling when the request is complete
}
```

The use of the global updateRequested variable acts as a semaphore to keep multiple events from triggering multiple network updates that would then stomp all over each other. When a moveend event is triggered, updateRequested is incremented from zero to one, and the network update is scheduled to begin 2,500 milliseconds (i.e., 2.5 seconds) later. In the meantime, further moveend events will increment updateRequested by 1 each time. When beginUpdate( ) gets called 2.5 seconds after the first moveend event, it will decrement updateRequested by 1, and then check to see if the semaphore is still greater than zero. If it is, then subsequent movements of the map must have occurred in the meantime, and the update is therefore deferred.

Finally, the last beginUpdate( ) will trigger 2.5 seconds after last moveend event, at which point the user has stopped moving the map around, the updateRequested semaphore will be decremented back to zero and, then and only then, the update will occur. Choosing the right delay so that network updates are smooth and non-overlapping, but so that the user experience isn't too terribly degraded, is probably a matter that merits some experimentation.

HACK   Use the Right Developer's Key Automatically
#61   What to do when your web site lives at two domains that resolve to the same server.

Adding a Google Map to our web page [Hack #10] solved all our problems. Right? Not quite. The map works perfectly when we use *http://geocoder.us*, but the DNS for the Geocoder site, like that of many sites, is configured to treat *http://www.geocoder.us/* as a synonym for *http://geocoder.us/*. The two domains resolve to the same server, which means that the same page will be served up to people asking for either domain. This works fine, until you put the Google Maps API key into the mix.

When you have the same Google Maps hack on two different URLs, even though they point to the same place, you get the message "The Google Maps API key used on this web site was registered for a different web site. You can generate a new key for this web site at *http://www.google.com/apis/maps/*." One can be forgiven the odd chuckle at the irony of *http://maps.google.com/apis/maps/*, as shown in Figure 6-21.

Figure 6-21. Getting the developer key right is a tricky thing

How does Google know what server and directory your request is coming from?

For Google Maps to work you need to include the Google Maps JavaScript library into your page as shown in this example:

```
<script
    src="http://maps.google.com/maps?file=api&v=1&key=yourkeyhere"
```

```
    type="text/javascript">
</script>
```

A user will load your page by fetching it from your server. His web browser will then look through that page and identify images, scripts, plug-ins, and anything else that was not in the page and so needs to be loaded.

When the browser sees the script element, it attempts to load the script specified in the URL listed in the src attribute. When a browser asks for information from a web server, it also sends information, including the name of the server and the page that referred the user to get the script. Google Maps is probably using the HTTP referer that is automatically sent to the server by your browser.

There are two general ways to solve this problem. Either you maintain more than one developer key and somehow pick the right one to use when you load the Google Maps library, or you force people to always use the URL that is associated with your developer key by silently fixing bad URLs.

Pick the Right Key in Perl

If you generate the page from a script, such as with PHP, Python, or Perl, you can maintain a list of server names and directories and the matching developer keys and then dynamically generate the script element to load the Google Maps library. This is a Perl example that sets the correct developer's key based on the HTTP_HOST that was used to call the script. I've shortened the developer's keys and replaced the actual domain names with placeholders.

```perl
#!/usr/bin/perl

# These are the keys for www.testingrange.com/pix, www.chilidog.com/pix,
#    and www.journalsonline.com/pix
my $key_tr = "ABQIAAAAJhHGNa8WG19AE1v8pOOkZxQpjl...4EDQ";
my $key_jo = "ABQIAAAAJhHGNa8WG19AE1v8pOOkZxSB9G...nOFw";
my $key_cd = "ABQIAAAAJhHGNa8WG19AE1v8pOOkZxQCuE...rtNA";

# which server are we?
my $http_host = $ENV{HTTP_HOST};

my $key = '';

# set the key to match the host
$key = $key_tr if ($http_host =~ /first-domain/);
$key = $key_jo if ($http_host =~ /second-domain/);
$key = $key_cd if ($http_host =~ /third-domain/);

print "Content-type: text/html\n\n";
print qq(
<!DOCTYPE html PUBLIC "-//W3C//DTD XHTML 1.0 Strict//EN"
    "http://www.w3.org/TR/xhtml1/DTD/xhtml1-strict.dtd">
```

```
<html xmlns="http://www.w3.org/1999/xhtml">
  <head>
    <script src="http://maps.google.com/maps?file=api&v=1&key=$key"
      type="text/javascript"></script><!---->
  </head>
  <body>
    <div id="map" style="width: 500px; height: 400px"></div>

    <script type="text/javascript">
    //<![CDATA[
    var map = new GMap(document.getElementById("map"));
    map.addControl(new GSmallMapControl( )
    map.centerAndZoom(new GPoint(-122.8288, 38.4025), 3);
    //]]>
    </script>
  </body>
</html>
);
```

This script sets variables for the developer keys for each of our domains, then sets the variable $key to one of those values depending on the host-name that was used to call this script. If we have *first-domain.com*, *second-domain.com*, and *third-domain.com* all pointing to the same web page, then this script will set the correct developer's key.

In real life, I would use a template. In this example, the Hello World map is in the script and is printed out with the print qq( ) command. The qq( ) operator in Perl automatically does variable interpolation, which means the variable $key will be replaced with the correct developer's key.

```
<script src="http://maps.google.com/maps?file=api&v=1&key=$key"
  type="text/javascript"></script><!---->
```

This example assumes completely different server names. The more common case is to have *http://www.mydomain.com* and *http://mydomain.com* both work. Assuming you've set the keys correctly, these lines will do that.

```
$key = $key_plain if ($http_host !~ /^www/);
$key = $key_www if ($http_host =~ /www/);
```

These lines say to use the value of $key_plain if the HTTP_HOST does *not* start with www, and use the value of $key_www if the host *does* start with www. The important point is to use the right key. If you have scripts in different directories, you'll want to take a look at the variables $ENV{SCRIPT_NAME} and $ENV{REQUEST_URI}. These variables contain the full path and page. You'll need to strip off the page name so you can compare the host and directory. There is more than one way to do it!

Use JavaScript to Accomplish the Same Goal

You can get the same effect dynamically with JavaScript. This is the Hello
World map with a bit of JavaScript that looks to its own href to determine
which URL it was loaded as, and then loads the map library by dynamically
selecting the right developer's key. In this example, I've shortened the full
developer's keys because you can't use my keys, and they are just too ugly to
be printed in a book.

```
<!DOCTYPE html PUBLIC "-//W3C//DTD XHTML 1.0 Strict//EN"
    "http://www.w3.org/TR/xhtml1/DTD/xhtml1-strict.dtd">
<html xmlns="http://www.w3.org/1999/xhtml">
  <head>
        <script type="text/javascript">

        // These are the keys for the servers
        var key_tr = "ABQI...";
        var key_jo = "ABQI...";
        var key_cd = "ABQI...";

        // Three nearly identical code blocks.
        // First define a regular expression that will match my server
        var reg_tr = new RegExp("testingrange");

        // Test the regular expression against the url for the  current
        // page, which is available in  window.location.href
        // if it contains our pattern then use it to load the script.

        if( reg_tr.test(window.location.href) ) {
            loadScript(key_tr);
        }

        //same as above for next server
        var reg_jo = new RegExp("journalsonline");
        if( reg_jo.test(window.location.href) ) {
            loadScript(key_jo);
        }

        //same as above for yet another server
        var reg_cd = new RegExp("chilidog");
        if( reg_cd.test(window.location.href) ) {
            loadScript(key_cd);
        }

        // build the script tag in the variable src and then
        // write it into the document
        function loadScript(key) {
            var src ='<' + 'script src=' + '"' +
            'http://maps.google.com/maps?file=api&v=1&key='+key+'"'+
            ' type="text/javascript"><'+'/script>';
            document.write(src);
        }
```

```
        //]]>
      </script>
  </head>
  <body>
    Which server is this?
    <div id="map" style="width: 500px; height: 400px"></div>

    <script type="text/javascript">
    //<![CDATA[

    var map = new GMap(document.getElementById("map"));
    map.addControl(new GSmallMapControl());
    map.centerAndZoom(new GPoint(-122.8288, 38.4025), 3);

    //]]>
    </script>
  </body>
</html>
```

The difference from the original Hello World is the script block in the
header. It defines variables for the different developer's keys, and then picks
the right key based on the current URL, which is available to JavaScript in
the variable window.location.href. There is a lot in common between the
JavaScript and Perl approaches. They both pick from a set of developer's
keys. The next approach lets you use a single key, but it changes the URL
that the user sees.

Using Apache's mod_rewrite to Share Keys

If you are using the Apache web server you may be able to use the mod_
rewrite module to quietly fix your URLs so that they match your developer
key. In this example, we will use mod_rewrite to silently add www. to the front
of any calls to *http://mappinghacks.com*. This technique assumes that your
Apache is set up to allow *.htaccess* to override the FileInfo setting.

Apache has a lot of options, including options that can be set on per directory basis. The most common way to set them is the Apache configuration
file (often */etc/httpd/conf/httpd.conf*) or in a file called *.htaccess* in the directory where you keep your web pages.

The *.htaccess* file will only work if the Apache configuration file is set up to
allow it to work. In your *httpd.conf* file, there will be at least one <Directory>
section. Note that Apache configuration is Byzantine in its complexity, so
forgive my simplifications. There needs to be a line in the <Directory> section that starts with AllowOverride and specifies either All, which means the
.htaccess file can control all aspects of Apache's access to that directory, or
FileInfo, which allows the *.htaccess* file to control file things, including use
of the mod_rewrite module.

Edit .htaccess to Rewrite Requests

I generated a key for *http://www.mappinghacks.com/projects/gmaps*. But I'd like people to be able to use *http://mappinghacks.com/projects/gmaps* as well. Here is an example of a mod_rewrite rule that will redirect requests from *http://mappinghacks.com/projects/gmaps* to *http://www.mappinghacks.com/projects/gmaps*. Create a new *.htaccess* file, or edit the existing one, to add these three lines.

```
RewriteEngine on
RewriteCond "%{HTTP_HOST}"    "!^www"      [NC]
RewriteRule "(.*)"            "http://www.%{HTTP_HOST}%{REQUEST_URI}"
```

The first line turns on mod_rewrite. The second line looks at the HTTP_HOST field, which should be the server name from the URI, mappinghacks.com or www.mappinghacks.com. It does a regular expression match against the pattern !^www. Bang (!) means negation, or not, the caret (^) means to match at the start of the string, and [NC] says to ignore case (i.e., No Case). The RewriteRule tells Apache what to do if the Rewrite Condition is met. So this says "if the HTTP host doesn't start with *www* replace the whole URI with *http://www.* plus the HTTP host, plus the filename, and any parameters that were originally passed." To make it simpler, it just says "make sure the URL starts with *www.*"

See Also

- Apache URL Rewriting Guides:

  - Apache Version 1.3: *http://httpd.apache.org/docs/1.3/misc/rewriteguide.html*

  - Apache Version 2.0: *http://httpd.apache.org/docs/2.0/misc/rewriteguide.html*

  These are almost conversational guides to mod_rewrite. From the 2.0 version: "With mod_rewrite you either shoot yourself in the foot the first time and never use it again or love it for the rest of your life because of its power."

## CHAPTER SEVEN

Extreme Google Maps Hacks
Hacks 62–70

So far, we've seen the power and ease with which Google Maps can show nearly anything on a map, from your vacation photos to a hypothetical nuclear explosion. Now it's time for us to take Google Maps hacks to the next level by adding whole new feature sets and APIs. In this chapter, we'll supplement the missing features of Google Maps in various ways, by turning street addresses into map coordinates, generating dynamic icons using Google's polyline service, adding new controls to bring in background imagery from around the 'Net, and even creating our own custom background tiles! These hacks go far above and beyond anything that even Google could have imagined or intended for Google Maps—that's why we call them "Extreme Google Maps Hacks."

HACK #62 Find the Latitude and Longitude of a Street Address

The Google Maps API won't do it for you, but there are other ways to find the coordinates of a given street address.

As we've seen all through this book, Google Maps makes it easy to make custom maps of anything for which you have a latitude and a longitude. However, people don't tend to think of places in terms of geographic coordinates; more often, people commonly know and refer to places by a street or mailing address. In order to find and show these places on a map, we need to be able to turn a given address into the corresponding latitude/longitude coordinates. The process of turning addresses into map coordinates is generally referred to as *geocoding*.

Unfortunately, for all the great things that the Google Maps API offers, the very common task of geocoding street addresses simply isn't among them. Although the Google Maps web UI will show you the location of an address, often with great accuracy, the problem is that Google doesn't own this data and has been unable to negotiate permission with its data providers to offer address lookups as a service in the API. Furthermore, screen-scraping the Google Maps results page is strictly a no-no, according to the Terms of Use. If you want to stay legit—and not risk angry takedown letters from you-know-who—how can you get the lat/long coordinates for a given street address?

The Hack

Fortunately, within the United States, the Census Bureau collects street address information as part of its constitutionally assigned duties of enumerating the populace of the country every ten years. What's more, the Census Bureau publishes this information in the public domain, in the form of the TIGER/Line data set. This data is freely available from the Census Bureau web site at *http://www.census.gov/geo/www/tiger/*. As of 2004, updated versions are published twice a year.

The problem is that the TIGER/Line data set is composed of 3,233 separate ZIP files, one for each county in the entire United States. The entire data set is 4.3 GB compressed and runs to almost 16 GB uncompressed. That's a lot of data to struggle with if you just want to look up a few lousy addresses. This is where *Geocoder.us* comes in.

Geocoder.us offers a web service (*http://geocoder.us/*) for geocoding U.S. street addresses from TIGER/Line data. Actually, several styles of web service are offered, including SOAP, XML-RPC, and REST. All of these services have but one goal, which is to take a street address or intersection in the U.S. and turn it into latitude and longitude coordinates that can be displayed on a map.

Figure 7-1 shows the working demo application of the Geocoder.us service at *http://geocoder.us/demo.cgi*. The latitude and longitude returned from the lookup can be trivially turned into a marker on a map, using the Google Maps API. You can use this URL to test out the service manually, but if you want to do address lookups in your program, you should *definitely* use the web service interfaces instead.

The Code

XML-RPC. The easiest way we know for accessing the Geocoder.us web service is to use the XML-RPC interface from within Perl. The outline of the code looks like this:

```
use XMLRPC::Lite;

my $result = XMLRPC::Lite
  -> proxy( 'http://rpc.geocoder.us/service/xmlrpc' )
  -> geocode( '1005 Gravenstein Hwy, Sebastopol, CA 95472' )
  -> result;
```

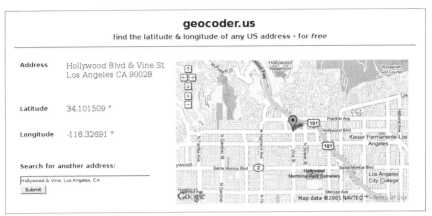

Figure 7-1. The geocoder.us site at work

Either a properly formatted U.S. street address or an intersection of the form "Hollywood Blvd & Vine St, Hollywood, CA" will be accepted by the web service. You must supply *either* a city and state *or* a ZIP Code, though providing both doesn't usually hurt.

If the lookup succeeds, then the $result variable will contain a reference to an array. Each item in the array is a hash, or associative array, that contains key/value pairs describing the results of the lookup. The following outlines the structure of the data returned by the XML-RPC request:

```
$result = [
    {
            'number' => '1005',
            'prefix' => ''
            'street' => 'Gravenstein',
            'type' => 'Hwy',
            'suffix' => 'N',
            'city' => 'Sebastopol',
            'state' => 'CA',
            'zip' => '95472',
            'lat' => '38.411908',
            'long' => '-122.842232',
    }
];
```

As you can see, the Geocoder.us web service attempts to break an address into its components and then normalizes those components before doing the lookup, and then returns the normalized components along with the coordinates. Here's a bit of code that prints the latitude/longitude pairs returned:

```
if ($result) {
    for my $address (@$result) {
        if ($address->{lat}) {
            print "Address found: $address->{lat} $address->{long}\n";
```

```
        } else {
            print "Couldn't locate the address!\n";
        }
    }
} else {
    print "Couldn't parse the address!\n";
}
```

The $result variable should be tested for truth before accessing its contents, because the service will return an undefined value if the address can't be parsed. If the address *can* be parsed, but no match is found in the database, the result will be an array containing a single hash, with an empty string in place of the latitude and longitude values. Finally, if the address given matches multiple addresses in the database, the array will contain a separate hash for each match found.

> The XMLRPC::Lite Perl module is part of the SOAP::Lite distribution. If you don't have either module installed on your system, download them from the CPAN at *http://search.cpan.org/* or use the CPAN shell to install them as follows:
>
> # **perl -MCPAN -e 'install XMLRPC::Lite'**
>
> XML-RPC client libraries are also available for virtually every programming language out there, so you shouldn't have too much trouble finding one for your language of choice.

REST. If, for whatever reason, you prefer not to use XML-RPC, you can always use the Geocoder.us REST service, by sending an HTTP GET request to http://rpc.geocoder.us/service/rest/geocode?address=*[your address here]*. (Don't forget to URI-escape the address—e.g., turn whitespace to %20—before passing it to your HTTP client, if your client library doesn't do it for you. The URI::Escape module from the CPAN can help with this.)

The REST interface returns an RDF/XML document with geo:Point elements for each address match. Here's an example:

```
<rdf:RDF
  xmlns:dc="http://purl.org/dc/elements/1.1/"
  xmlns:geo="http://www.w3.org/2003/01/geo/wgs84_pos#"
  xmlns:rdf="http://www.w3.org/1999/02/22-rdf-syntax-ns#">

<geo:Point rdf:nodeID="aid34279220">
    <dc:description>1005 Gravenstein Hwy N, Sebastopol CA 95472</dc:
description>
    <geo:long>-122.842232</geo:long>
    <geo:lat>38.411908</geo:lat>
</geo:Point>
</rdf:RDF>
```

Multiple geo:Point elements will be returned in the document if multiple matches for the requested address are found.

Here's a bit of Perl code that makes use of the REST service. You will need the XML::Simple, LWP::Simple, and URI::Escape modules from the CPAN.

```perl
use XML::Simple;
use LWP::Simple;
use URI::Escape;
use strict;

sub geocode_rest {
    my $xml = get( "http://rpc.geocoder.us/service/rest/geocode" .
                    uri_escape( $address );
    if ($xml) {
        my $result = eval { XMLin( $xml, ForceArray => ['geo:Point'] ) };
        if ($result) {
            my $points = $result->{'geo:Point'};
            for my $point (@$points) {
                my $lat = $point->{'geo:lat'};
                my $lon = $point->{'geo:long'};
                if ($lat and $lon) {
                    ### Success! Do something with the coordinates.
                } else {
                    ### Couldn't find a match for the address.
                }
            }
        } else {
            ### Couldn't parse the XML, so the service spit
            ### out an error message, meaning it couldn't parse the address.
        }
    } else {
        ### The HTTP GET failed, indicating a network error.
    }
}
```

SOAP. The SOAP interface to the Geocoder.us web service is probably the most difficult to use, entirely owing to the subtle complexities of SOAP itself. However, if you're a Java or C# user, it might actually be easier for you to use SOAP than the other web service interfaces, because you can usually autogenerate result classes from the WSDL description. Accordingly, you may be pleased to know that a WSDL file exists for the Geocoder.us SOAP interface at *http://geocoder.us/dist/eg/clients/GeoCoder.wsdl*.

The Caveats

In principle, you should be able to access the Geocoder.us web services directly from the browser by using JavaScript, but in practice, the browser security model of the better web browsers out there will prevent you from using JavaScript to access Internet domains aside from the one that your page originates from. One way around this, which many sites are currently using, is to set up a server-side script that accesses the Geocoder.us site, as shown above. You can then use the GXmlHttp class from the Google Maps API to request address lookups via your site's geocoding proxy, and get the results back in JavaScript as either XML or plain text, depending on your preferences.

One caveat you should be aware of is that the TIGER/Line data set is less complete and/or less accurate in some areas than the commercial data sources that Google Maps uses to locate addresses. The flip side, of course, is that TIGER/Line is freely available. It's a trade-off! In general, residential addresses are more likely to be accurate than addresses in industrial areas or commercial office parks.

Also, you *need* to examine the terms and conditions of service for Geocoder. us at *http://geocoder.us/terms.shtml*, before using their service. In particular, use of the free web services for for-profit commercial ends is strictly prohibited. If you are a commercial user, you will need to subscribe to the commercial service instead.

The final caveat is that the Geocoder.us web services are throttled by IP address, to keep the service from being hammered by a single user. As of this writing, a delay of 15 seconds between requests is in place, but Locative Technologies, the maintainers of the Geocoder.us service, reserves the right to adjust this upwards or downwards as necessary. If the service seems unduly slow, it's probably because your requests aren't spaced more than 15 seconds apart. Of course, commercial account users don't suffer this restriction.

If the throttling or the expense are a problem for you, you can always set up your own local Geocoder.us database, by downloading the Geo::Coder::US module and its prerequisites from the CPAN. The documentation for the Geo::Coder::US::Import module, which comes with the distribution, contains all the instructions you need for getting the TIGER/Line data from the Census Bureau, and using it to build your own local database. Although the Geocoder.us database for the whole country runs to almost 800 MB, you can simplify things for yourself by constructing a database composed only of the counties you're interested in.

Geocoding Addresses Outside the U.S.

Geocoding street addresses outside the U.S. for free is considerably harder, because the data sets simply aren't freely available. (Denmark is one notable exception.) In Canada, you may be able to use the Geocoder.ca web site at *http://geocoder.ca/*, but that service is based on government data that itself is not freely available. For Europe, Japan, and the rest of the world, you may have to purchase access to a commercial data set in order to geocode addresses in your country. The alternative is to petition your government's legislators to change its geospatial data access policies, so that citizens in your country can access information whose collection has already been subsidized with your tax money!

See Also

- If you plan to use the Geocoder.us web services, you should definitely read the developer documentation at *http://geocoder.us/help/*, as well as the terms and conditions of service at *http://geocoder.us/terms.shtml*.

- If you want to set up your own U.S. address geocoder, you can start by getting the Geo::Coder::US backend code from *http://search.cpan.org/ ~sderle/Geo-Coder-US/*, or by using the CPAN shell to install the module and its prerequisites automatically. Be sure to read the documentation for the Geo::Coder::US::Import module.

- The Geo::StreetAddress::US module contains all of the rules for how street addresses are parsed. We always welcome patches to this module, to help improve our hit rate!

- The Census Bureau's TIGER/Line data set lives on the Web at *http:// www.census.gov/geo/www/tiger/*.

HACK #63 Read and Write Markers from a MySQL Database

Keep track of almost anything with Google Maps and a relational database.

Adding a map of something new to Google Maps is good fun, but there is a lot of data already in SQL databases that is just begging to be mapped. This tutorial describes the way the Subfinder application, at *http://www.map-server. com/googlemaps/subfinder.php*, is integrated with a MySQL database using PHP. The Subfinder is itself an extension of the Who Locations site at *http:// www.map-server.com/googlemaps/wholocations2.php*, which is described in a tutorial at *http://www.map-server.com/googlemaps/tutorial.html*. Figure 7-2 shows a map of the sites that any fan of The Who must know about.

There are easier ways to get points on a Google Map, but to integrate with a MySQL database you will need:

1. An Apache web server running PHP and MySQL. (Other web server software with PHP and MySQL will probably do as well.)

2. A table in your database with lat, long, and description columns.

3. Some basic HTML and PHP knowledge.

We are going to use PHP to dynamically create an HTML document with the appropriate Google Maps JavaScript code. One of the functions shown in this sample is the option for users to add their own locations, with addi-

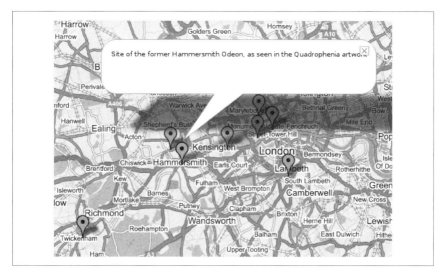

Figure 7-2. A map for Who fans

tional attributes, into the database. The value of one of the attribute determines the type of marker placed.

Structuring Your Database

The database can be recreated with this snippet of SQL:

```
CREATE TABLE subfinder (
    id int(11) NOT NULL auto_increment,
    lat decimal(10,6) NOT NULL default '0.000000',
    lon decimal(10,6) NOT NULL default '0.000000',
    desc varchar(255) NOT NULL default '',
    url varchar(255) NOT NULL default '',
    marker char(1) NOT NULL default '',
    PRIMARY KEY  (id)
) TYPE=MyISAM;
```

If you save this into the file *create_subfinder.sql*, you can create a new database and this table with the following commands:

```
$ mysqladmin create sub_db
$ mysql sub_db < create_subfinder.sql
```

As you can see, there are fields for the latitude and longitude values, a description, URL (which will of course be displayed as a link), and a marker field. The value of the marker field will determine the type of marker placed. This application, which lists submarines visible on the Google Maps photos, makes a distinction between submarines that are in active duty (*A*), museum ships (*M*), places where submarines have sunk (*S*), and places where important events have taken place (*E*). The appropriate letter is displayed in the marker.

The Code

This system uses two PHP files to do its work. The main file, *subfinder.php*, is used to read the data from the database and display it on the map. The second file, *subfinder_load_db.php*, is called by the first to write data into the database. A standard HTML form is used for this.

The *subfinder.php* file imports the Google Maps API, and sets up the map in the usual way. The following bit of JavaScript creates the custom markers:

```
subfinder.php: setting up the custom markers
<script type="text/javascript">
//<![CDATA[

var baseIcon = new GIcon();
baseIcon.shadow = "http://www.map-server.com/img/shadow50.png";
baseIcon.iconSize = new GSize(20, 34);
baseIcon.shadowSize = new GSize(37, 34);
baseIcon.iconAnchor = new GPoint(9, 34);
baseIcon.infoWindowAnchor = new GPoint(9, 2);
baseIcon.infoShadowAnchor = new GPoint(18, 25);

// Creates a marker whose info window displays the given number
function createMarker(point, text, markerstyle)
{
  var icon = new GIcon(baseIcon);
  icon.image = "http://www.map-server.com/img/marker" + markerstyle + ".png";
  var marker = new GMarker(point, icon);
  // Show this markers index in the info window when it is clicked
  var html = text;
  GEvent.addListener(marker, "click", function() {
    marker.openInfoWindowHtml(html);
  });
  return marker;
}
```

In the code above, I've copied the PNG image used by the official Google sample to my own server for this. I then made four different PNG files, one for each letter used (A, E, M, S). This letter is being passed on through the markerstyle variable.

Next, the map is defined, some controls are added, and the initial map view is set through the map.centerAndZoom function. A relatively new addition to the Google Maps API (undocumented at the time of this writing) is the GScaleControl class, which adds a scale bar in the lower-left corner:

```
var map = new GMap(document.getElementById("map"));
map.addControl(new GLargeMapControl());
map.addControl(new GMapTypeControl());
map.addControl(new GScaleControl());
map.centerAndZoom(new GPoint(0, 0), 16);
```

Next, we use some PHP code to read the information from the database, parse it, and write it into the document. I've used an external configuration file (*conf.php*) to declare the variables that hold the server, username, and password for my database connection. A link to the database is set up and a query is passed to it.

```php
<?php

include_once("conf.php");
$link = mysql_connect($dbserver, $username, $password)
    or die("Could not connect: " . mysql_error());
mysql_select_db("dbmapserver",$link)
    or die ("Can\'t use dbmapserver : " . mysql_error());

$result = mysql_query("SELECT * FROM subfinder",$link);
if (!$result)
{
  echo "no results";
}
```

The result of this query is then put into an array. For every element in the array, the function createMarker (which was defined above) is called with the lat, long, and description of that point. Note that this will generate the code for the browser to interpret. If you look at the source code of the page in your browser, you'll see the result of this PHP code.

```php
while($row = mysql_fetch_array($result))
{
  if ($row['marker'] == 'A') $marker_type = 'Active';
  if ($row['marker'] == 'M') $marker_type = 'Museum';
  if ($row['marker'] == 'S') $marker_type = 'Sunk';
  if ($row['marker'] == 'E') $marker_type = 'Event';
  $info_text = "<b>" . $marker_type . "</b><br>" .
          $row['desc'] . "<br><br><a    href=" . $row[url] .
          " target=_blank>Link</a>";
  echo "var point = new GPoint(" . $row['lon'] . ","
                     . $row['lat'] . ");\n";
  echo "var marker = createMarker(point, '" . $info_text
                     . "','" . $row['marker'] . "');\n";
  echo "map.addOverlay(marker);\n";
  echo "\n";
}

mysql_close($link);
?>
```

The next piece of code from *subfinder.php* sets up the HTML form to add new information to the database:

```javascript
GEvent.addListener(map, 'click', function(overlay, point) {
  if (overlay) {
    //map.removeOverlay(overlay);
```

```
  } else if (point) {
    var form;
    form  = '<form name="form1" method="post" action="subfinder_load_db.php">';
    form += '<table border="0"><tr><td>Lat:</td>';
    form += '<td align="left"><input name="new_lat" type=text id=new_lat
value="
          + point.y + '"></td>';
    form += '<td rowspan="4">';
    form += '<input name="new_marker" type="radio"
       value="A" checked="1"> Active';
    form += '<br><input name="new_marker" type="radio" value="M">Museum';
    form += '<br><input name="new_marker" type="radio" value="S">Sunk';
    form += '<br><input name="new_marker" type="radio"
       value="E">Event</td></tr>';
    form += '<tr><td>Lon:</td>';
    form += '<td align="left">';
    form += '<input name="new_lon" type="text" id="new_lon" value="
       + point.x + '"></td></tr>';
    form += '<tr><td>Text:</td>';
    form += '<td align="left">';
    form += '<input name="new_desc" type="text" id="new_desc" size="60">';
    form += '</td></tr>';
    form += '<tr><td>URL:</td><td align="left">';
    form += '<input name="new_url" type="text" id="new_url" size="60">';
    form += '</td></tr>';
    form += '<tr></td><td align="left">';
    form += '<input type="submit" name="Submit" value="Submit"></td></tr>';
    form += '</table></form>';
    output.innerHTML = form;

    if (map.getZoomLevel() >= zoomToLevel) {
      map.centerAndZoom(point, zoomToLevel);
    }
    map.addOverlay(new GMarker(point));
  }
});
//]]>
</script>
<div id="output"></div>
```

The block that contains all the HTML is generated when the user clicks
somewhere on the map to add a location, which sets up a form to allow the
user to add more information. This form is stored in output.innerHTML. The
point.x and point.y variables are being supplied by the listener.

The PHP file that gets called by the form in *subfinder.php* is a lot simpler.
The code, stored in *subfinder_load_db.php*, is just your basic "take the
parameters and stuff them in the database" code:

```
<?php

include_once("conf.php");
```

```
echo "<html><head><link href=\"/style/hans.css\" rel=\"stylesheet\" type=\
"text/css\">";
echo "</head><body>";
echo "Lat: " . $new_lat . "<br>";
echo "Lon: " . $new_lon . "<br>";
echo "Text: " . $new_desc . "<br>";
echo "URL: " . $new_url . "<br>";
echo "Marker: " . $new_marker . "<br>";
echo "Will now be added to the database...";

$new_desc = addslashes($new_desc);
$link = mysql_connect($dbserver, $username, $password)
    or die("Could not connect: " . mysql_error());
mysql_select_db("dbmapserver",$link)
    or die ("Can\'t use dbmapserver : " . mysql_error());
$sql = "INSERT INTO subfinder ";
$sql = $sql . "VALUES('','"
    .$new_lat."','"."$new_lon."','"."$new_desc."','"."$new_url."','"
    .$new_marker ."')";
$result = mysql_query($sql ,$link);
if (!$result)
{
  echo "<p>Due to an error (" . mysql_error() . ")<br>, your entry could "
  . "not be loaded into the database. Please return to "
  . "<a href=\"subfinder.php\">Subfinder</a>.";
} else {
  echo "<p>Your entry has been loaded into the database. "
  . "Please return to <a href=\"subfinder.php\">SubFinder</a>.";
}

echo "</body></html>";
?>
```

Once again, the *conf.php* with the access variables is read. One important
thing to note here is the addslashes( ) function. As we mentioned earlier,
JavaScript can be quite fussy about quotes and special characters. If there
are any of those characters in the texts you want to display in the info windows, it may result in either the map not being drawn at all, or just your
markers not being drawn. The addslashes( ) function properly escapes those
characters before putting the text into the database so that your users don't
have to worry about that themselves.

See Also

• Red Geographics Map-Server page: *http://www.map-server.com/*

—Hans van der Maarel

Build Custom Icons on the Fly

HACK #64

Using libraries that extend the Google Maps API in various ways, you can quickly achieve powerful results.

The XMaps library is a set of extensions to the Google Maps API. As of this writing, the library builds on the Google Maps API to add many capabilities that the API itself does not provide. As of this writing, the additional features provided by XMaps include filled polygons, text along polylines, and custom icons and markers. For this hack, we will see how to easily create new icons by making use of the XIcon and XMarker classes from XMaps. The XMaps library lives on the Web at *http://xmaps.busmonster.com/*.

The Hack

The XIcon class is similar to Google's GIcon class, but it automates some of the steps necessary to create icons, making it simpler to make new icons on the fly. You could do the same thing that the XIcon class does by using a server-side script, but here we are using something that does not require any extra server horsepower or bandwidth from you. XIcon objects are limited in that they are a filled concave polygon (e.g., the outline of a car, lion, or circle), but you have the advantage of being able to specify the color, size, opacity, and any text on it on the fly.

The GIcon class makes use of a set of pre-rendered PNG images stored on a server somewhere. The default GIcon uses three images from Google Ride Finder to create its resulting image: the reddish-orange marker image, a nearly transparent version of that same image (for click detection on IE), and a mostly transparent shadow image. Figure 7-3 shows the parts of this pre-rendered icon.

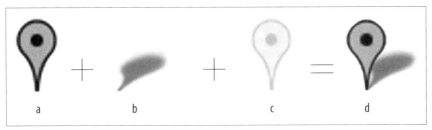

Figure 7-3. Google Maps pushpin icon parts: (a) the pushpin image, (b) the shadow, (c) the click target for IE, and (d) the resulting icon

Instead of using pre-rendered images, an XIcon's images are created on the fly by using the existing (but unofficial) service that Google Maps already uses to draw polylines. Using this service, we can actually draw images of any color and opacity. By specifying the outline of the icon shape, the XIcon class can create the necessary images for you (including the shadow image). For example, if we wanted to create a rounded box icon, we could come up with a list of points for the outline, give them to XIcon, and get the set of images shown in Figure 7-4 for the icon.

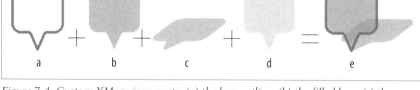

Figure 7-4. Custom XMaps icon parts: (a) the box outline, (b) the filled box, (c) the shadow, (d) the click target, and (e) the final rounded box icon

Because we are creating an additional image in the set of images used for the icon, we cannot use the existing GMarker class in the Google Maps API, which can only use the images in a GIcon. Instead, we use the XMarker class, which can handle either GIcon or XIcon objects. XMarker gives us an additional ability that GMarker does not provide, namely the ability to place text or other HTML on top of the icon. When we create our icon, we will specify the bounds of any content that might be displayed on top of the icon, and an XMarker will use these bounds to place text or a generic HTML DOM element on top of the icon.

The Code

Suppose, for example, that we wanted to create a web site all about the Bermuda Triangle. What better icon to use for our map than a custom-made triangle pointing at our map! I'll assume you are familiar with the general layout of a Google Maps page. The fragments of code here require that there is an existing GMap object already created and assigned to a JavaScript variable called map.

The first thing we'll have to do is include the XMaps library along with the Google Maps API JavaScript files. Here's the code that should appear at the beginning of our page. Note that you will want to replace the API key with one for your site, and you will want to make sure you are using the most recent version of the XMaps library from *http://xmaps.busmonster.com/*.

```
<script src="http://maps.google.com/maps?file=api&v=1&key=abcdefg"
    type="text/javascript"></script>
<script src="http://xmaps.busmonster.com/script/xmaps.1b.js"
    type="text/javascript"></script>
```

Next, let's define the icon's shape. Here I've specified a triangle approximately 30 pixels to a side.

```
var triShape = {
    iconAnchor: new GPoint(15, 26),
    infoWindowAnchor: new GPoint(15, 0),
    shadow: true,
    contentAnchor: new GPoint(0, 0),
    contentSize: new GSize(31, 20),
    points: [0,0, 15,26, 30,0]
};
```

As you'll see, we can scale this later, so the initial size does not matter too much. The shape description is contained in a simple associative array, with the following properties:

iconAnchor

This is the pixel of the icon's image, which should be tied to the point on the map. In this case, it is the bottom middle pixel (the triangle's bottom point).

infoWindowAnchor

This is the pixel on the icon's image, which should be tied to the bottom point of the info window.

shadow

This determines if the icon will have a shadow or not (the shadow is created for us automatically).

contentAnchor T

This is the top left pixel on the icon's image that should be used for any HTML content on top of the icon (e.g., text).

contentSize

This is the size, in pixels, of the box in which HTML content is allowed.

points

This is an array of x/y pairs that define the shape of the icon. In this case, we have the corners of an upside-down triangle.

You can see the purpose of some of these properties in Figure 7-5.

Now we are ready to give our shape a name. We do this so that XMaps can cache the URLs that are used to generate these shapes for better performance.

```
XIcon.shapes['triangle'] = triShape;
```

Our shape is now registered with the Xmaps API, and we are ready to use it. When we create an XIcon, we have a number of style properties we can specify. Each of these has defaults, so you will not always have to specify all of them, but I will do so here to show you an example of each property:

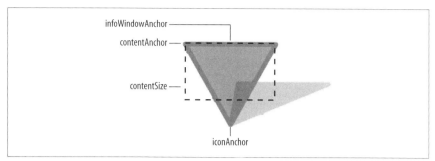

Figure 7-5. Triangle icon properties

```
var triStyle = {
    scale: 1.5,
    outlineColor: '#ffffff',
    outlineWeight: 2,
    fillColor: '#7f00ff',
    fillOpacity: 0.5
};
```

Once again, the icon's style is defined with a simple associative array. Here's what each property does:

scale

Specifies how big we want our icon. Since I specified 1.5, we will end up with a triangle with approximately 30 * 1.5 = 45 pixels per side.

outlineColor

Specifies the color for the outline of the icon. Here, we are using a white outline.

outlineWeight

Specifies the width, in pixels, of the icon's outline.

fillColor

Specifies the color of the interior of the icon.

fillOpacity

Specifies the opacity of the interior of the icon; must be in the range 0 to 1.

We are ready to create our icon. The call to the constructor looks like this:

```
var triIcon = new XIcon('triangle', triStyle);
```

Now we have an icon we can use with any XMarker. Here, we'll plot one:

```
var bermudaTriangle = new GPoint(-70.532227, 25.878994);
var iconText = "?";
var hoverText = "The Bermuda Triangle";
var triMarker = new XMarker(bermudaTriangle, triIcon, iconText, hoverText);
map.addOverlay(triMarker);
```

The XMarker constructor takes a point and a few optional arguments. We pass the icon we created as well as some text to be displayed on the icon and when the mouse hovers over the icon. The XMaps API allows us to pass the XMarker object directly to map.addOverlay( ), just as if it were an ordinary GMarker.

And we're done! With a minimum of effort, we have a new marker with a custom icon that has its own shadow, is scaled and colored like we want, and has the clickable region specified by the icon outline. To see the results, browse over to *http://xmaps.busmonster.com/triangle.html* and check it out.

We can follow these same steps to create lots of reusable icons. To give you a head start, XMaps comes with a few handy premade icons, including the rounded box you saw in Figure 7-4. You can play around with the web pages listed below to see more examples of custom icons with XMaps.

See Also

- The XMaps Library at *http://xmaps.busmonster.com/* has links to the newest version of the library, full documentation, and many examples.

- The Bermuda Triangle example at *http://xmaps.busmonster.com/triangle.html* shows a completed version of our code fragments from above.

- The Icon Color Shades example at *http://xmaps.busmonster.com/shades.html* shows different icons of different colors.

- The Bermuda Triangle entry at *http://en.wikipedia.org/wiki/Bermuda_triangle* in Wikipedia has plenty of information about how and where to get lost at sea!

—*Chris Smoak*

Add More Imagery with a WMS Interface

#65   What's a pretty face like you doing on the geospatial web?

The Google Maps service is cool, the user interface is wonderful, the API is a joy, and the maps are pretty, but there is more to the world of mapping than what fits on one company's massive server farm.

The Hack

The Open Geospatial Consortium (OGC) has defined a number of interoperability standards for web mapping applications. The simplest to understand is the Web Mapping Service (WMS) specification. In Google Maps terms, you would ask a WMS server for a tile that contains something like a Google Map or Satellite image. The key is that the WMS is not limited to the data that

Google Maps maintains. There are WMS servers with things from Landsat imagery to topographic (elevation) data to habitat data. WMS requests are normally made by programs, but you can assemble a request by hand.

If you put this URL into your browser:

```
http://wms.jpl.nasa.gov/wms.cgi?request=GetMap&layers
    =global_mosaic_base&srs=EPSG:4326&bbox=-87.90,24.38,-76.65,30.01
    &FORMAT=image/png&width=600&height=400&styles=pseudo
```

you will get the image of Florida shown in Figure 7-6.

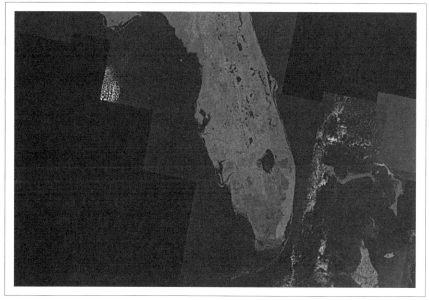

Figure 7-6. Florida as shown by a WMS request

This looks a lot like a Google Maps tile. Even without understanding the format of a WMS request, you can look at that URL and get some information. For example, it has a bbox (or *bounding box*) that covers the area from 87.9 W to 76.65 W and 24.38 N to 30.01 N, which happens to be most of Florida.

You can make a request to a WMS server for a map that covers a certain area. But what is a map? WMS returns a raster (an image) for the selected area and for selected features. WMS Servers report what their capabilities are, what sorts of information they contain, and WMS clients can then select the layers they want to show.

David Knight has written a JavaScript extension library that you can insert into your own Google Maps page to let you browse through tiles from a WMS server using the Google Maps user interface. For an example of this, visit the Global Coordinate page at *http://globalcoordinate.com/*. Figure 7-7 shows Landsat imagery of South Florida within a Google Maps interface. The Global Coordinate page also demonstrates near real-time updating of the map from RSS feeds.

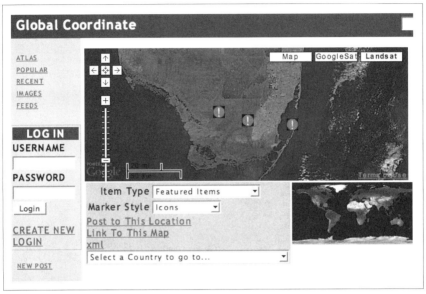

Figure 7-7. Florida from a WMS Server

The Code

We've created a simple example of a WMS-enabled Google Map at *http://mappinghacks.com/projects/gmaps/wms.html*. Sure you have the standard map and satellite views, but it includes a little extra kick in the data layer department. It also includes Landsat and VMAP0 data for the whole world and elevation and landcover layers for the United States. It will produce a display like Figure 7-8.

Assuming you have created the Hello World map [Hack #10], you can add these WMS layers with this code:

```
<script src="http://www.globalcoordinate.com/jscript/WMSTiles.js"
    type="text/javascript"></script>
```

This includes David's library. You can look at it by pointing your browser to this URL: *http://www.globalcoordinate.com/jscript/WMSTiles.js*.

Using the WMS tiles library is fairly straightforward. In the following Java-Script example, the mapSpecs variable holds an array of objects that is used to load parameters needed for the WMS fetch and display.

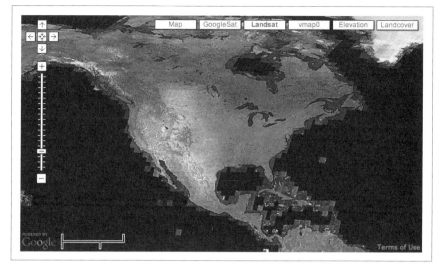

Figure 7-8. WMS layers on a Google Map

```
var mapSpecs = [];
createMapSpecs( );

_SATELLITE_TYPE.getLinkText = function( ) {
    return "GoogleSat";
}

mapSpecs.push(_GOOGLE_MAP_TYPE);
mapSpecs.push(_SATELLITE_TYPE);
```

First, we create a new WMS map specification and then push it onto mapSpecs. To create a layer, pass the base WMS URL and the name that you want displayed on your map. There are four layers here: Landsat, VMAP0, National Elevation Dataset (NED), and National Landcover Dataset. These four layers come from three different servers. The Geospatial web is alive, and with a few lines of code you can add more, different, and sometimes better layers to your Google Maps applications!

```
wmsSpec =new _WMSMapSpec ("http://wms.jpl.nasa.gov/wms.cgi?request
    =GetMap&layers=global_mosaic_base&srs=EPSG:4326","Landsat");
mapSpecs.push(wmsSpec);

wmsSpec =new _WMSMapSpec ("http://geocoder.us/surfer/wms.cgi?service\
    =wms\&version\=1.1.1\&request=GetMap&layers=vmap0&srs
    =EPSG:4326", "vmap0");
mapSpecs.push(wmsSpec);

wmsSpec =new _WMSMapSpec
    ("http://gisdata.usgs.net/servlet/com.esri.wms.Esrimap?servicename
    =USGS_WMS_NED&request=GetMap&layers=US_NED_Shaded_Relief&srs
    =EPSG:4326","Elevation NED");
mapSpecs.push(wmsSpec);
```

```
wmsSpec =new _WMSMapSpec
   ("http://gisdata.usgs.net/servlet/com.esri.wms.Esrimap?servicename
   =USGS_WMS_NLCD&request=GetMap&layers=US_NLCD&srs=EPSG:4326","Landcover");
mapSpecs.push(wmsSpec);
```

Next, we pass the array of mapSpecs to the GMap constructor and set normal attributes with the API calls.

```
var map = new GMap(document.getElementById("map"),mapSpecs);

map.setMapType( _SATELLITE_TYPE );
map.addControl(new GLargeMapControl());
map.addControl(new GScaleControl());
```

This puts the map layer choices on the map. Without this, the only way to select between Map, Satellite, Landsat, VMAP0, NED, and Landcover would be with custom navigation—say a button that triggers JavaScript to set the appropriate map type. (Map "type" is Google-speak for "raster layer".)

```
map.addControl(new GMapTypeControl());
map.centerAndZoom(new GPoint(-120, 38), 4);
```

The Virtues of Additional Map Layers

Different layers make more sense for different uses, and at different zoom levels. The San Francisco Bay area looks sort of patchy in the Google Satellite image in Figure 7-9.

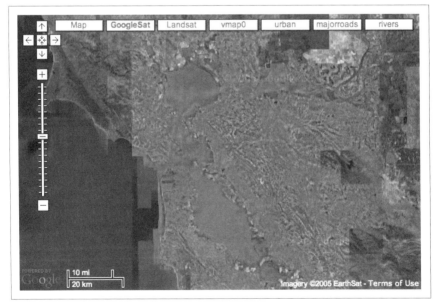

Figure 7-9. Google Satellite image of the Bay Area—pretty choppy

In Figure 7-10, the Landsat imagery is smoother and more informative at this scale.

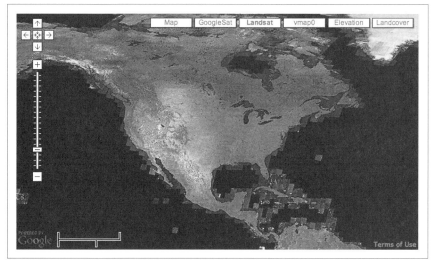

Figure 7-10. The Landsat image looks nice at this scale

The National Elevation Dataset covering the Bay Area, shown in Figure 7-11 is just beautiful.

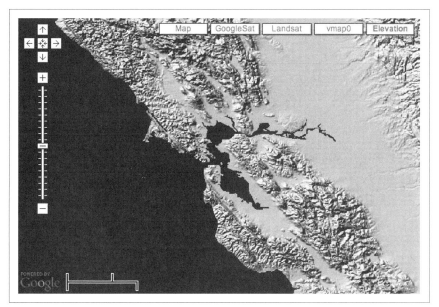

Figure 7-11. The National Elevation Dataset for the Bay Area

At a larger level, the NED and Landcover images are useful in understanding the natural history of the United States, as shown in Figures 7-12 and 7-13, respectively.

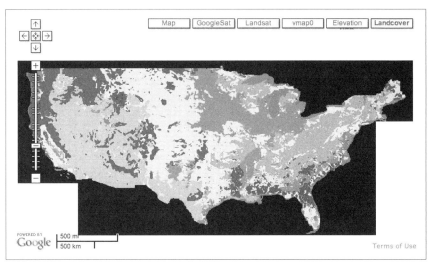

Figure 7-12. U.S. Landcover

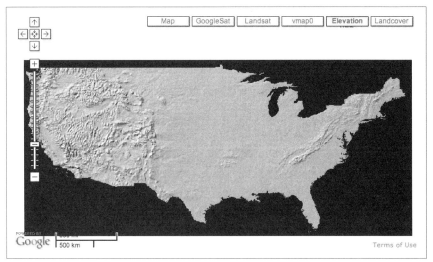

Figure 7-13. U.S. National Elevation Dataset

Finding and Using Other WMS Servers

We can find WMS servers that have a lot of different data! And all those WMS servers are kind enough to tell us what information they have available. Ionic

Software provides the AskTheSpider service at *http://askthespider.com/* to serve as a central search engine for the Geospatial Web. Each result from Ask-TheSpider includes the links to the GetCapabilities page for each server. You can also search for "WMS Servers" on Google and be provided with a lot of choices.

To see which layers a WMS server has available, issue a GetCapabilities request. This is an HTTP GET call to a URL, probably a script, on the WMS server. For example, ask the WMS server at the Jet Propulsion Laboratory (JPL) what it can deliver. Load *http://wms.jpl.nasa.gov/wms.cgi?request=GetCapabilities* into your browser, and an XML file is returned. Depending on your browser, the capabilities will be displayed, or you may be given the opportunity to save the page to your local drive. Technically, a proper capabilities request needs the service and version parameters; for example:

```
http://wms.jpl.nasa.gov/wms.cgi?request=GetCapabilities&service
   =WMS&version=1.0.0
```

However, many WMS servers are forgiving about this.

The capabilities document from the JPL WMS server is a 1,696-line XML document that includes lots of detail to specify what is available. The capabilities document will contain one or more Layer elements. Here is part of one of the shorter Layer sections from the JPL capability document:

```
<Layer queryable="0">
     <Name>us_colordem</Name>
     <Title>Digital Elevation Map of the United States, DTED dataset, 3
second resolution, hue mapped</Title>
     <Abstract>
        The DTED Level 3 US elevation, mapped to a color image using the
full spectrum.
        This result is not achievable by using SLD, so it is presented as a
different layer.
     </Abstract>
     <LatLonBoundingBox minx="-127" miny="23" maxx="-66" maxy="50"/>
     <Style>
       <Name>default</Name>
    <Title>Default Color Elevation</Title>
     </Style>
     <ScaleHint min="45" max="5000" />
     <MinScaleDenominator>20000</MinScaleDenominator>
   </Layer>
```

Even with no more documentation on WMS, you can guess that this is the Digital Elevation Map of the United States, and you know that it has data for latitudes from 23 N to 50 N, and 127 W to 66 W—i.e., the continental United States.

The original long request that generated an image of Florida starts to make more sense when you look at the full XML GetCapabilities document. Every element in the URL is defined by the Capabilities document.

```
http://wms.jpl.nasa.gov/wms.cgi?request=GetMap&layers
    =global_mosaic_base&srs=EPSG:4326&bbox=
    -87.90,24.38,76.65,30.01&FORMAT=image/png&width=600&height=400&styles=pseudo
```

The base URL is defined in the OnlineResource element. The available layers are in the Layer elements. The *spatial reference system*, or SRS, corresponds to the exact cartographic projection of the layer and is often defined by European Petroleum Survey Group, or EPSG, codes (there is a long story behind this). These codes are sometimes referred to as *spatial reference identifiers*, or SRIDs. An SRID defines the specific assumptions that are being made about the shape of the earth, how you mark location, and where zero is. In this case, EPSG 4326 refers to the latitude/longitude geographic coordinate system, referenced to the WGS-84 standard ellipsoid and datum.

If you have the PROJ.4 cartographic projections library (*http://proj.maptools.org*), you can examine the list of EPSG codes stored in */usr/share/proj/epsg*. If you have PostGIS (*http://postgis.refractions.net/*) installed you can see what SRID 4326 means by looking in the spatial_ref_sys system table. If you don't have Post-GIS—or don't want to bother—you can mostly assume that everything uses EPSG code 4326. This isn't always true, but it is true often enough to be a useful simplifying assumption.

```
=> select * from spatial_ref_sys where srid=4326;

GEOGCS["GCS_WGS_1984",DATUM["D_WGS_1984",SPHEROID["WGS_1984",6378137,298.
257223563]],PRIMEM["Greenwich",0],UNIT["Degree",0.017453292519943295]] |
+proj=longlat +ellps=WGS84 +datum=WGS84
```

The bounding box used in the bbox parameter defines the minimum and maximum latitude and longitude that will be included in the returned map. The format parameter is the image format to use (PNG, JPG, PNG, PDF), the height and width are the number of pixels in the returned image, and the styles parameter is defined in the Layers section and means whatever that particular server says that it means.

With this knowledge, we can make almost any WMS server a source for imagery that will appear in a Google Maps interface on our own maps. We need to figure out the base URL to generate maps from a particular WMS server. Here is the GetCapabilities line for the JPL WMS server compared with the _WMSMapSpec that is needed by David's JavaScript:

```
http://wms.jpl.nasa.gov/wms.cgi?request=GetCapabilities
http://wms.jpl.nasa.gov/wms.cgi?request=GetMap&layers=global_mosaic_
base&srs=EPSG:4326
```

To get a map you replace GetCapabilities with GetMap. Then you must specify the name of one or more layers. These are from the Name element within the Layers section of the document returned by the GetCapabilities request. You also need to specify the Spatial Reference System, which is in the SRS element within the Layer element.

See Also

- Open Geospatial Consortium's Directory of Services at *http://www. ogcnetwork.org/*. Includes links to the WMS Cookbook at *http://www. opengeospatial.org/resources/?page=cookbooks*, as well as other documents, links to sample applications, and support mailing lists.

- Another WMS Cookbook maintained by Allan Doyle, the Kevin Bacon of the Open Geospatial world: *http://www.intl-interfaces.com/cookbook/ WMS/*.

HACK #66 Add Your Own Custom Map

This time, it's personal.

Well, as everyone else has written in this book, those Google Maps sure are pretty. Then again, there is always room for improvement right? And sometimes Google's maps just don't highlight the right information. To really spice things up, you may want to add your own map...a map that looks the way you want it to look. This off-API hack shows you how to add your own custom map. In "Serve Custom Map Imagery" [Hack #67], you'll get a script to serve custom map tiles, and finally in "Automatically Cut and Name Custom Map Tiles" [Hack #68], there is a script to quickly make the thousands of little images you will need to display your map.

There are plenty of cool reasons to add your own map images. In creating the NYC Subway Google Map hack (*http://www.onnyturf.com/subwaymap.php*), I felt that Google's polylines were not elegant enough, and they were hard to see on top of Google's orange/green default map. To make the subway lines easier to see against the streetscape and to make the lines look nicer, I decided to add a custom map type that I illustrated, as you can see from Figure 7-14.

Another great use of adding your own map is using it as a semi-transparent overlay on the other map images. Figure 7-15 shows the street map layered on top of the satellite map, with a semi-transparent setting allowing you to see the relationship between the two. You can do this sort of thing with your own custom map too.

Creating this transparency effect is outside the scope of this tutorial. You can learn how to add transparency by looking at the source of the example above,

Figure 7-14. Custom map for NYC subway map hack

which can be found at *http://www.kokogiak.com/gmaps-transparencies.html*. You will need to know these basics on adding a custom map in order to add transparency in that way.

Four Steps to Add a Custom Map

There are four simple things you will need to do to add your own map.

- Create a new map type.
- Tell the map where it can find the images for your new type.
- Customize your map's type button.
- Add your new map control to Google Maps' list of map types.

Create a New Map Type

The Google Map comes with three default maps, which you are probably already familiar with, namely, map, satellite, and hybrid. These are known

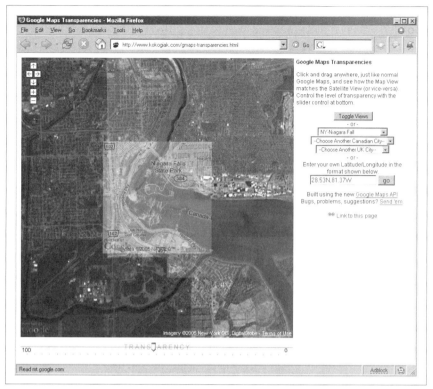

Figure 7-15. Transparent road map overlaying the satellite map

in Google Maps as *map types*, and they are accessed from an array called mapTypes, which is a property of our GMap object. To add your own map, we need to create a new map type and then add it to this array.

Each map type Google provides has many properties. We need to make our custom map type just like these. But we really don't want to have to build a whole map type from scratch, setting all the properties anew. We can save a lot of time by duplicating an existing map type and switching just a few of the values to suit our needs.

For the NYC Subway Google Map hack, I made my map type match Google's default map type. This default map is the first map stored in the mapTypes array. So we are just going to copy that first map type and store it in a variable temporarily for editing (here it is named yourMapType, but you can name this variable what ever you like). There is one special thing we need to be aware of here; since JavaScript assigns object values by reference, we can't just dupe the map type object like this:

```
yourMapType = map.mapTypes[0];
```

We need to make sure we copy all the properties of the map type object, so we have a special little function we are going to include and call to copy all the properties of the default map type:

```
function copy_obj(o) {
    var c = new Object( );
    for (var e in o)
        c[e] = o[e];
    return c;
}
```

Using our copy_obj function, we can now duplicate the default map type:

```
yourMapType = copy_obj(map.mapTypes[0]);
```

Now we change a few of the properties to customize our map type.

Set the Path to Your Map Images

Each Google map type is made up of thousands of image tiles. When you see a Google map in a window, you are really seeing about 12 tiles at a time, depending on your screen size, as suggested by Figure 7-16.

As you drag the map around in the window, your browser downloads the tiles it needs in order to show more of the map. This happens in the background and is one of the more innovative features of Google Maps. Each map type has a path to its associated image tiles. This property is called baseURL. The default maps point to Google's server. To load our own image tiles, we need this path to point at our own server. We actually don't point right at a directory of images. The map sends values to the server and asks for an image in return. So we use a PHP script to serve up the tiles based on the values the map sends (this image serving script is discussed in more detail later in "Serve Custom Map Imagery" [Hack #67]). We set the baseURL to point at this script.

```
yourMapType.baseUrl = "http://www.yoursite.com/googlemap/images/index.php?";
```

You'll notice we include a ? at the end of our path. The Google Maps application adds CGI parameters at the end of the path when requesting images, so the ? is necessary for posting those values. With that path configured, our images will load when our custom map type is selected.

Customize Your Map's Button Name

Although the Google Map API does not automatically add the map types buttons that appear in the upper-right corner of their map, most people add them using the API addControl method. If you call this method in your map, a button will automatically be generated for your map type too, as you can see on the Subway map shown in Figure 7-17.

Figure 7-16. Google Maps tile grid

However, that button did not just magically get the name "Subway." We set the name of our map type's button by setting the getLinkText property. The Google Map application calls it as a function, so we want to return the name we want to give it, like so:

```
yourMapType.getLinkText = function( ) { return 'SUBWAY'; }
```

You'll note that getLinkText is set to a function. This means you can have that function return different values depending on external conditions.

Nice and simple eh? So that's all we have to do to make a custom map type. Now we add it to the array mapTypes.

Add Your Map to the List of Map Types

We will add our map to the end of the mapTypes array, and then, because we love our map more than any other map in the world, we set it to be the default map when our map page first loads. To add our custom map to the list, we just add the map type object that we have been working on to the

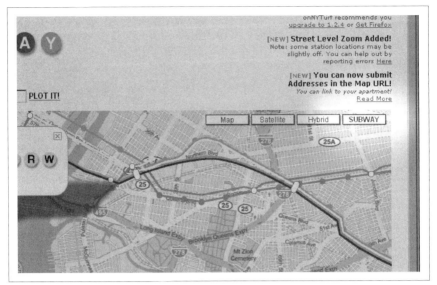

Figure 7-17. Subway map type button

end of the array. We use the API's setMapType( ) method to make our custom map type load first.

```
map.mapTypes[map.mapTypes.length] = yourMapType;
map.setMapType(map.mapTypes[map.mapTypes.length-1]);
```

Finally let's put it all in the context of the rest of our typical map initializing function. This function is called from onLoad attribute of the body element in our HTML:

```
function onLoad( ) {

    //Create a new map and load it to the map at the html object id="map"
    map = new GMap(document.getElementById('map'));

    // Copy Object Function
    function copy_obj(o) {var c = new Object( ); for (var e in o) { c[e] =
o[e]; } return c;}

    //Copy mapType
    yourMapType = copy_obj(map.mapTypes[0]);

    // Set Path to Our Custom Map Image Tiles
    yourMapType.baseUrl = "http://www.yoursite.com/googlemap/images/index.
php?";
    // Map Display name in the auto-generated maplink in the top right
corner.
    yourMapType.getLinkText = function( ) { return 'SUBWAY'; }

    // Register the new mapType with the running google map.
```

```
    map.mapTypes[map.mapTypes.length] = yourMapType;

    //Set the onload view to our new map
    map.setMapType(map.mapTypes[map.mapTypes.length-1]);

    //Add Map Type buttons in the upper right corner
    map.addControl(new GMapTypeControl());

    //Add Small zoom controls
    map.addControl(new GSmallZoomControl());
}
```

Even though we added our map to the list of map types, we still need to serve up the images when requested [Hack #67].

See Also

- "Add More Imagery with a WMS Interface" [Hack #65]
- "Serve Custom Map Imagery" [Hack #67]
- "Automatically Cut and Name Custom Map Tiles" [Hack #68]

—Will James

Serve Custom Map Imagery

HACK #67

You can serve your own custom tiles to Google Maps with a simple script.

If you've created a custom map layer [Hack #66], you need a way to serve requests for tiles. This hack describes a PHP script to serve Google Maps compatible imagery.

Every time you drag the map around in the window, the Google Map application requests whatever tiles it needs in order to show more of the map. It does this by passing three values to the server for each tile it needs: an X coordinate value, a Y coordinate value, and a Zoom value. For each tile it needs, the map application sends a set of these three values.

Our image serving script uses the three values sent by the Google Map application to dynamically create paths to the appropriate image required to fill in a space in the map window. Our script is kept in a file named *index.php*. It assumes that tiles have been created and named by the naming standards described in "Automatically Cut and Name Custom Map Tiles" [Hack #68].

With a little fancy footwork we can also use our script to send generic filler tiles to the map when we don't have custom tiles for a requested area. In the most common case, you will probably want to create a custom map that covers a small area, and not the whole globe. Therefore you will probably need to use some filler tiles where your map does not cover an area or zoom level. We can use our image serving script to determine when we don't have an appropriate custom tile and need to send a filler tile.

 If you decide that you *do* need to make tiles for the whole planet, be sure to read "How Big Is the World?" [Hack #16] first!

To understand this script, we'll start with the whole thing and then break it down. Here is the full script that goes in our file *index.php*:

```php
<?php
    define("NO_DATA", "./no_data.gif");
    define("ZOOM_IN", "./zoom_in.gif");
    define("ZOOM_OUT", "./zoom_out.gif");

    $x = $_GET["x"];
    $y = $_GET["y"];
    $z = $_GET["zoom"];

    $filename = "./nycmaps/${x}_${y}_${z}.gif";
    if ( $z < 2 ) {
        $content = file_get_contents( ZOOM_OUT );
    }else if ( $z > 5 ){
        $content = file_get_contents( ZOOM_IN );
    }else if ( is_numeric($x) && is_numeric($y) && is_numeric($z)
        && file_exists( $filename ) ){
        $content = file_get_contents( $filename );
    }else{
        $content = file_get_contents( NO_DATA );
    }
    header("Content-type: image/gif");
    echo $content;
?>
```

OK, there it is. Now let's break it down.

The first three lines define our filler tiles. We have one for each of three conditions. If we are in an area for which we have data, but not at the current zoom level, we use the *zoom_in.gif* and *zoom_out.gif* images. If we have no data, we send the *no_data.gif* image.

```php
<?php

    define("ZOOM_IN", "./maptiles/zoom_in.gif");
    define("ZOOM_OUT", "./maptiles/zoom_out.gif");
    define("NO_DATA", "./maptiles/no_data.gif");
```

You'll notice that above we also set the path to these tiles to a directory called *maptiles/*. This is where we will put all our image tiles. This directory sits inside the *images/* folder, where this script also resides, as established in "Add Your Own Custom Map" [Hack #66].

Next we get the *x*, *y*, and zoom values from the map and store them in similarly named variables.

```
$x = $_GET["x"];
$y = $_GET["y"];
$z = $_GET["zoom"];
```

Using these three values, we create a path to a tile file, here a GIF, and we store it in the variable $filename. You'll note that the *x*, *y*, and zoom (*z*) values are part of the tile name. This is the basic structure we use to name all our tiles. This is how we differentiate the hundreds or thousands of custom tiles we likely end up with when creating a custom map. Now that's a lot of custom names, but don't worry about it too much, because later we'll automate the cutting and naming of your tiles.

```
$filename = "./maptiles/${x}_${y}_${z}.gif";
```

Now we have a path appropriate to the data sent, but that does not mean the tile actually exists. $filename, whatever its value, is just a fourth image option, in addition to NO_DATA, ZOOM_IN, and ZOOM_OUT. Before we send any image back to the browser, we want to check if the request is within our zoom range and map area. This next chunk of the script uses several if/else statements to filter though the possibilities and determine the appropriate image. The winner will be stored in variable $content. The specific checks we make are explained by the in-line comments:

```
// if the zoom level requested is too close, we send images that
// say zoom out
if ( $z < 2 ) {
    $content = file_get_contents( ZOOM_OUT );

// if the zoom level requested is too far out, we send images that
// say zoom in
} else if ( $z > 5 ){
    $content = file_get_contents( ZOOM_IN );

// here we make sure values were sent for x, y, and zoom, and that
// the image tile actually exists. if it all checks out we send
// the file we defined in $filename
} else if ( is_numeric($x) && is_numeric($y) && is_numeric($z)
            && file_exists( $filename ) ){
    $content = file_get_contents( $filename );

// otherwise, if one of the values was not sent, or the tile does
// not exist we send a NO_DATA image
} else {
    $content = file_get_contents( NO_DATA );
}
```

Now that we know which image we are sending back, we are ready to do so. The reason we didn't just send it previously is that we first need to tell the browser that we are sending an image. We tell it this by sending it some header information:

```
header("Content-type: image/gif");
```

Now we can pass it the image path with a simple echo of $content.

```
echo $content;
?>
```

Conclusion

That's all there is to it! Save it as *index.php* and upload it to your image folder.

There are two things I really like about this script that make it a lifesaver. The first is the NO_DATA condition. For the subway map, I made only tiles that covered the greater NYC area. Outside that, there are no custom tiles. Without the NO_DATA image, in these places where I don't have tiles to match Google's, we would normally see broken image links or the grey background of the map window. But thanks to the NO_DATA image, I can create one blue tile that matches my border and extends infinitely anywhere I don't have custom tiles for a location. Figures 7-18, 7-19, and 7-20 show what my zoom-in, zoom-out, and no-data files look like.

Zoom In

Figure 7-18. Zoom-in image

Zoom Out

Figure 7-19. Zoom-out image

Figure 7-20. No-data image

Alternatively for those more advanced, you could extend this script to relay the *x*, *y*, and zoom values back to Google; then you could request their tiles for places where you do not have any.

The other thing I like about this script is that you can quickly adjust which zoom levels are available. You just set min and max thresholds in those if/else statements and you get alternative tiles sent to the map for anything outside your zoom range. In creating the NYC Subway Map, I tweaked the map art at each level. This is a bit time consuming, but gives me better-looking maps. So I incrementally add new zoom levels as I complete the art. Every time I add a new one all I have to do is go into this script and change the min or max value to make it available.

See Also

- "Add Your Own Custom Map" [Hack #66]
- "Automatically Cut and Name Custom Map Tiles" [Hack #68]

—*Will James*

HACK #68 Automatically Cut and Name Custom Map Tiles

Make time to really enjoy a cup of coffee.

Google Maps are made of dozens to thousands of tile images, depending on the zoom level. At the distant zoom levels you only need a few images to cover a large area. For example, the NYC Subway Map uses 49 images to cover the greater metropolitan area at zoom level 5. But at the closer zoom levels, thousands of images are required. It takes more than 3500 images to cover the NYC metropolitan area at zoom level 2. "How Big Is the World?" [Hack #16] discusses the amount of disk space needed to tile the entire planet. Figure 7-21 shows a custom tile at zoom level 5, while Figure 7-22 shows part of the same area at zoom level 2.

Creating and then uniquely naming each of these images for even a small part of our world would be a daunting task if you had to do it by hand. That's why we use a script to do this. The following hack will show you how to configure a batch processing script to use with Photoshop 7 or CS that will carve all the tiles you need from one big image into hundreds of smaller GIFs and name them exactly as you need them named.

The Google Map Tile Structure

Before we set up and use our script we need to know a few things about Google's tiles. As we learned in "Serve Custom Map Imagery" [Hack #67], each

Figure 7-21. A custom tile at zoom level 5

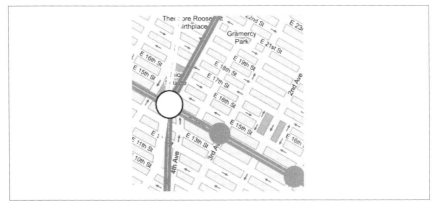

Figure 7-22. A custom tile at zoom level 2

256×256–pixel tile has a longitude, a latitude, and a zoom value. These are represented in the URL by the x, y, and zoom values.

Here is what a tile path from Google looks like:

```
http://mt.google.com/mt?v=w2.4&x=1206&y=1539&zoom=5
```

Figuring Out the Values for Your Tiles

So how do you get the *x*, *y*, and zoom values? Fortunately you don't have to get *all* the x, y, and z values for all your images. We only need to get a set of values for one tile and from there we can derive all the other values we need.

We start with a limited area for our map because we assume you don't want to remap the whole world, but just a small corner of it. All we need then is to get the x, y, and z value of the upper-left corner tile of our map area and know how many tiles wide and high our map area is. For simplicity, our example map is square so that the area width and height are the same, but you could tweak this script to work with rectangular areas. Once we know the upper-left corner tile values, our batch processing script will calculate the rest for us.

Unfortunately getting just these corner tile values is not easy on our own. Fortunately again there is a web site that will help do this for us. The site at *http://www.onnyturf.com/google/latlontotile.html* has a set of tools that will help us figure out this information for the upper-left corner tile values. Figure 7-23 illustrates the process of converting lat/long to tile row and column.

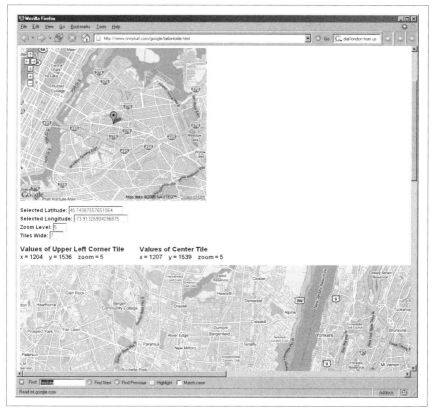

Figure 7-23. Converting latitude and longitude to tile row and column

Using the map on the right side of this page you can find the center of your map area. When you click there the web page will get the latitude and longitude for the center of your map. You can also set the zoom level and tile width here. When you press submit, the web site will return Google's tiles that make up your requested map area. For our batch processing script, you will want to do this for your furthest zoom level. You'll probably have to experiment a little until you get the right values that match your map area. For my NYC Subway map, the furthest zoom level is 5 and my tile width is 7, as shown in Figure 7-24. Your maximum zoom level will probably be somewhere between 5 and 8.

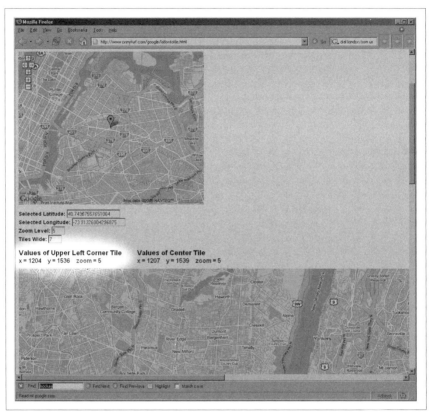

Figure 7-24. Finding the upper-left corner for a given latitude/longitude

To get the values for the upper-left corner tile, we now just right-click on that tile and select View Image. This will load the image into the browser window, and now we can see our x, y, and zoom values in the image URL:

```
http://mt.google.com/mt?v=w2.4&x=1206&y=1539&zoom=5
```

Whew. So there it is. Now we know our start values for this example are:

```
x = 1206
y = 1539
zoom = 5
tile width = 7
```

Configuring the Script

The batch processing script provided is too long to go through in detail here. This hack focuses on showing you how to configure it for your map area so you can make your tiles.

To use the script provided you must enter some custom values, including the ones we just got for our upper-lefthand tile. The values you must customize come at the beginning of the script.

ZoomLevel. Last things first. The first variable you encounter sets the Zoom Level you want to generate tiles for. To create your custom map you will probably want tiles at various levels. For each level you want to create tiles for, you must change this value and rerun the batch processing script on your master art. Here it is set to 3, but you will change this every time you want to run this script for another level.

```
var ZoomLevel = 3;
```

The rest of the variables you must customize you will only customize *once* for your map area. Let's go through them one by one.

FolderPath. This next one sets the path to where your tiles will be saved. This path is for use on a PC. The path on the Mac will be slightly different. This sample path uses a separate folder for each zoom level, and those folders are in a folder *GoogleMap* that sits on the user desktop. You will have to precreate your zoom folders, but the path to those folders is dynamically generated in this example.

```
var FolderPath = "~/Desktop/GoogleMap/Zoom"+ZoomLevel+"Maps/";
```

Furthest zoom upper-left corner values. Lastly, we put our upper-left corner values to work. These are the originating values, off of which the batch processing script will figure out the values for all the tiles you are creating.

```
var OrgX = 1204;    //<-- the X value
var OrgY = 1536;    //<-- the Y value
var OrgZoomLevel = 5;    //<-- the zoom level
var OrgTileWidth = 7;     //<-- the number of tiles wide your full map area is
var OrgTileHeight = 7;    //<-- the number of tiles high your full map area is
```

That's all you have to configure! Here is how the whole thing looks with our customized values at the top:

```
/*  Tile Carver for Photoshop 7 and CS
    Created by Will James
    http://onNYTurf.com
*/
```

```
//**** CUSTOMIZE THE FOLLOWING VARIABLES FOR YOUR MAP AREA ****
var ZoomLevel = 3;

var FolderPath = "~/Desktop/GoogleMap/Zoom"+ZoomLevel+"Maps/";
var OrgX = 1204;
var OrgY = 1536;
var OrgZoomLevel = 5;
var OrgTileWidth = 6;
var OrgTileHeight = 6;


//**** EVERYTHING BEYOND THIS POINT SHOULD NOT BE TOUCHED
//**** UNLESS YOU KNOW WHAT YOU ARE DOING!!! ****

var StartX = OrgX * (OrgZoomLevel - MakeZoomLevel) * 2;
var StartY = OrgY * (OrgZoomLevel - MakeZoomLevel) * 2;

var xTiles = OrgTileWidth * (OrgZoomLevel - MakeZoomLevel) * 2;
var yTiles = OrgTileHeight * (OrgZoomLevel - MakeZoomLevel) * 2;

var PixelWidth = 256;
var PixelHeight = 256;

var TotalTiles = (xTiles)*(yTiles);

preferences.rulerUnits = Units.PIXELS;

var xm = 0;
var ym = 0;

var TileX = StartX;
var TileY = StartY;


for (n=1; n<TotalTiles+1; n++) {

    if (ym == yTiles){
        xm += 1;
        ym = 0;
        TileX += 1;
        TileY = StartY;
        };

    MyXO = xm*(PixelWidth);
    MyXL = xm*(PixelWidth)+(PixelWidth);
    MyYO = ym*(PixelHeight);
    MyYL = ym*(PixelHeight)+(PixelHeight);

    var srcDoc = activeDocument;

    srcDoc.selection.select(Array (Array(MyXO, MyYO), Array(MyXL, MyYO),
      Array(MyXL, MyYL), Array(MyXO, MyYL)), SelectionType.REPLACE, 0, false);
    srcDoc.selection.copy( );
```

```
    var pasteDoc = documents.add(PixelWidth, PixelHeight, srcDoc.resolution,
"Paste Target");
    pasteDoc.paste();
    pasteDoc = null;

    var saveMe = activeDocument;

    saveMe.flatten();

      saveFile = new File(FolderPath + TileX+ "_" + TileY+ "_" + ZoomLevel
        + ".gif");

    gifSaveOptions = new GIFSaveOptions();
    gifSaveOptions.colors = 64;
    gifSaveOptions.dither = Dither.NONE;
    gifSaveOptions.matte = MatteType.NONE;
    gifSaveOptions.preserveExactColors = 0;
    gifSaveOptions.transparency = 0;
    gifSaveOptions.interlaced = 0;

    saveMe.saveAs(saveFile, gifSaveOptions, true,Extension.LOWERCASE);
    saveMe.close(SaveOptions.DONOTSAVECHANGES);
    ym += 1;

    TileY += 1;

}
```

At *http://mapki.com/index.php?title=Automatic_Tile_Cutter*, you can get copies of this script. Save your script as *TileCutterNamer.js*, as it is a JavaScript file. Put the script somewhere easy to find, because next you are going to open it from Photoshop.

Running Our Script in Photoshop

We are going to cut our tiles from one big image. For the NYC Subway map, I created my map art in Adobe Illustrator and then imported it into Photoshop. As you create your custom map, an important thing to keep in mind is to know how wide and high to make your map art. I started in Illustrator with the dimensions for the furthest zoom level; then, when I open the art in Photoshop, I tell Photoshop to create a bitmap to match whichever zoom level I am working on.

We can figure out how wide and high our art must be by multiplying the total number of tiles across and down by the individual tile width of 256 pixels. For my furthest zoom, the width and height of the subway map ends up being 1,792 pixels: 7 tiles wide by 256 pixels. But in our example batch processing script, we are making tiles for zoom level 3; 1,792×1,792 pixels is going to be too small an image to carve all our tiles from.

So how do we get the right width and height for other zoom levels? Every zoom level is twice the height and width of its previous zoom level. So, if our first zoom level was 1,792 pixels wide, we end up with a matrix like Table 7-1.

Table 7-1. Zoom level versus pre-tiled map width

Zoom level	Pixel width
5	1,792
4	3,584
3	7,168
2	14,336

To batch process tiles for zoom level 3 then, I start with a file 7,168 pixels wide. By the way, this is 28 tiles across. We know that because 7,168 pixels divided by 256 pixels is 28. For a square map area 28 pixels wide by 28 pixels high, we are then making 784 tiles! Thank goodness this script also names these tiles for us!

Getting back to our batch processor, I open my Illustrator art into Photoshop at 7,168×7,168 pixels, as shown in Figure 7-25.

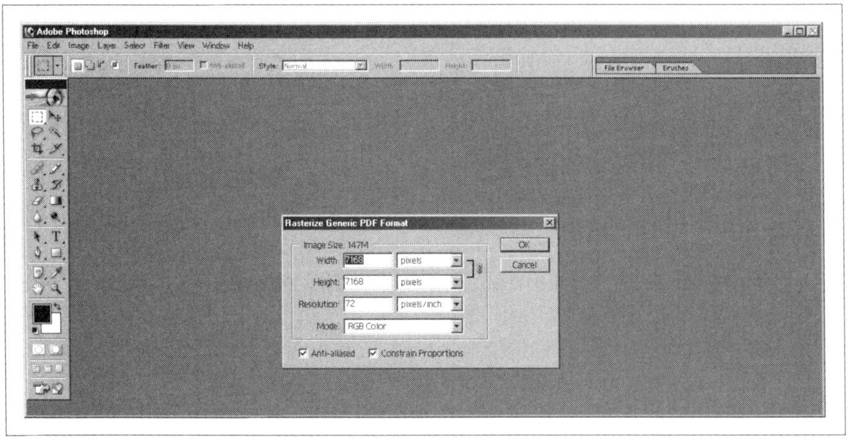

Figure 7-25. Photoshop's File Import dialog

Once the file is rasterized, we run the JavaScript by going to File → Automate → Scripts. In Photoshop 7, this will pop up a small dialogue box. Choose Browse and then find the *TileCutterNamer.js* file and click Open. Off it goes! As the script runs, you can watch Photoshop make new tiles and save them. Fun, I know. If you are cutting a small number of tiles—less than 60, say—the process will take only about a minute. For something like 700 tiles, it will take 10 minutes or more. Level 3 of my subway map is made of more than 3,500 tiles. If you are cutting that many, you might want to make some other plans for the next hour. This might be the time to enjoy that cup of coffee.

When the script has finished cutting the last tile, you will have a folder full of images, as shown in Figure 7-26.

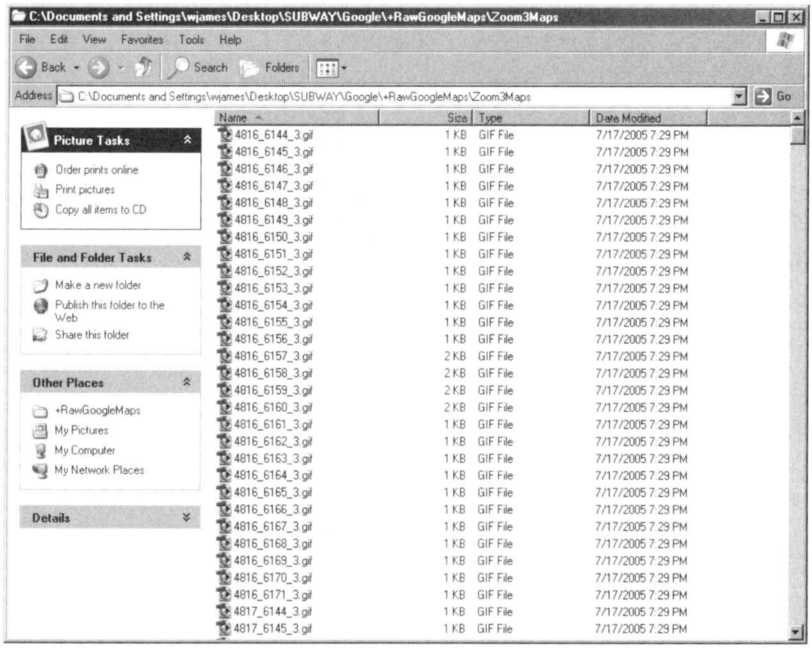

Figure 7-26. The list of completed custom map tiles

The only thing left to do then is upload your new zoom level to your *maptiles/* folder on your server and then go and check out your new map in your web page!

Hacking the Hack

This batch processing script is written to produce GIFs. It could also be written to produce JPGs or PNGs. You will have to customize the settings in this part of the script:

```
//Set path to file and file name
saveFile = new File(FolderPath + TileX+ "_"
    + TileY+ "_" + ZoomLevel + ".gif");

//Set save options
gifSaveOptions = new GIFSaveOptions();
```

```
gifSaveOptions.colors = 64;
gifSaveOptions.dither = Dither.NONE;
gifSaveOptions.matte = MatteType.NONE;
gifSaveOptions.preserveExactColors = 0;
gifSaveOptions.transparency = 0;
gifSaveOptions.interlaced = 0;
```

See Also

- "Add Your Own Custom Map" [Hack #66]
- "Serve Custom Map Imagery" [Hack #67]

—*Will James*

HACK #69 Cluster Markers at High Zoom Levels

When necessary, avoid cramming a map too full of markers by clustering them together.

Two major problems can occur when you try to put too many markers on a Google Map at once. First, the large quantity of markers can take a long time to render, consume a lot of memory in the browser, and pretty much slow things to a crawl. We address this particular problem to some degree in "Show Lots of Stuff—Quickly" [Hack #59]. The other, equally serious problem is a more general matter of good digital cartography, in that too many markers placed too close together can make the markers difficult to click and the map difficult to interpret. Both problems can be fairly effectively solved by first applying a clustering algorithm to a large data set of points, and then by tailoring the display of the point clusters, such that they become readily identifiable and easy to interact with.

The Hack

To experiment with this idea, we took over 600 waypoints from Rich Gibson's GPS receiver, representing the highlights of several years' worth of travels. Since Rich lives in northern California, most of the points are centered around the western United States, while the remainder are scattered from Mexico to Massachusetts to Venice, Italy. We figured that about 600 points would qualify as too many to show on a map at once, but not so many as to make experimentation difficult.

The solution that we eventually hit upon for visualizing all of Rich's travels at once can be seen at *http://mappinghacks.com/projects/gmaps/cluster.html*, as shown in Figure 7-27. The standard Google Maps marker is used to represent a cluster of points, roughly bounded by the red box around the marker. Clicking on a marker pans and zooms the map to the area covered by that cluster. As you get closer in, more localized clusters appear, eventually resolving into the small Google Ridefinder markers, which represent Rich's individual waypoints. Clicking on one of these smaller markers opens a small info window, showing the name and coordinates of the waypoint, as shown in Figure 7-28 .

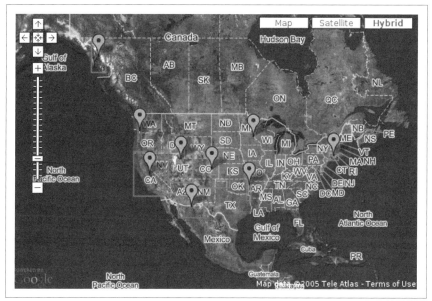

Figure 7-27. Clusters of points show the general outlines of Rich's travels

Although this demo has some obvious deficiencies, we think that, to some degree, it does succeed at summarizing the data at high zoom levels, while still allowing exploration of the individual data points. Coming up with a lightweight and reasonably fast solution to this problem took a lot of trial and error! Before we take a look at the code, let's peer down the blind alleys we followed before finally settling on our current implementation.

Choosing the Right Clustering Algorithm

Stepping away from the map for a moment, let's restate the problem: we have a large number of points in a two-dimensional coordinate system, which we want to assign to a much smaller number of clusters, based in some way on their relative proximity to each other. This is a fairly common problem in computational statistics, and several well-documented algorithms already exist.

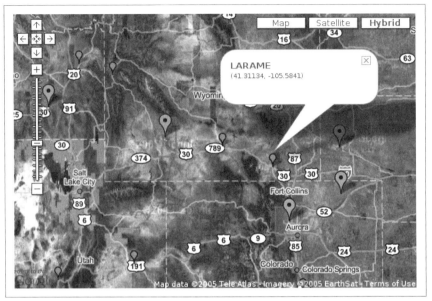

Figure 7-28. Zooming in causes the clusters to resolve as individual waypoints

***k*-means clustering.** The first one we tried was the *k-means clustering* algo-rithm, which is one of the most popular clustering algorithms in the litera-ture, on account of its relative simplicity:

1. Select a center point for each of *k* clusters, where *k* is a small integer.

2. Assign each data point to the cluster whose center point is closest.

3. After all the data points are assigned, move each cluster's center point to the arithmetic mean of the coordinates of all the points in that cluster, treating each dimension separately.

4. Repeat from Step 2, until the center points stop moving.

The other advantage to *k*-means clustering, aside from its ease of implemen-tation, is that it is relatively quick, usually completing in less than $O(n^2)$ time. The most obvious disadvantage of *k*-means is that you have to some-how select the value of *k* ahead of time, but we could try to make an edu-cated guess about that. The primary disadvantage of *k*-means derives from the ambiguity of Step 1: how, exactly, does one select the initial center points? We found that selecting random points in space led to some clusters never acquiring points at all, while randomly selecting points from the data set as initial centers led to the clusters themselves clumping up, which is something we were trying to avoid. Any attempt to choose *k* or the initial centers based on the data itself only complicated matters, in a sort of recur-sive fashion. Also, to top it all off, *k*-means apparently offers not only no guarantee that a globally optimum clustering will result, but not even any guarantee that a "locally" optimum clustering will result. It looked like we were back to the drawing board.

Hierarchical clustering. The next approach we tried was a series of variations on *hierarchical clustering* algorithms. Instead of iteratively building clusters from the top down, as *k*-means does, hierarchical algorithms attempt to cluster the data from the bottom up, instead. A typical hierarchical clustering algorithm works as follows:

1. Assign each point to its own cluster.
2. Calculate the distance from each cluster to every other cluster, either from their respective mean centers, or from the two nearest points from each cluster.
3. Take the two closest clusters and combine them into one cluster.
4. Repeat from Step 2, until you have the right number of clusters, or the clusters are some minimum distance apart from each other, or until you have one big cluster.

By now, you can probably guess that hierarchical clustering presents at least one of the same problems as *k*-means—namely, that you have to know somehow when you have enough clusters. Also, though hierarchical clustering can be shown to produce globally optimal results, optimality comes with a cost: hierarchical clustering algorithms are frequently known to run to $O(n^3)$ time in the worst case. Although this can be mitigated somewhat by clever use of data structures, such as using a *heap* to store the list of cluster distances, we found that our best attempt at implementing hierarchical algorithms provided reliable results, but it was, quite frankly, too slow. Polynomial-time algorithms are absolutely fine when *n* is small, but we wanted an approach that could potentially scale to thousands of points and be able to run dynamically in a reasonable time for an HTTP request. The hierarchical approach apparently just wasn't it for us.

Naïve grid-based clustering. We realized, of course, that we were looking at the problem the wrong way: we didn't need optimal clustering, or mathematically precise clustering, or anything like that. What we were after was some way of consolidating points on a map such that: (a) the markers we display don't wind up overlapping, and (b) we don't show too many markers at once. We can solve requirement (a) by drawing a grid on the map, as shown in Figure 7-29, such that each "cell" in the grid is guaranteed to be at least as large as our marker image when the map is displayed. Next, we take all of the points within any one grid cell and call them a single cluster. For added measure, we can also check each cluster formed this way and see if there are any clusters in the immediately adjacent cells. If there are, we combine them them into a single larger cluster.

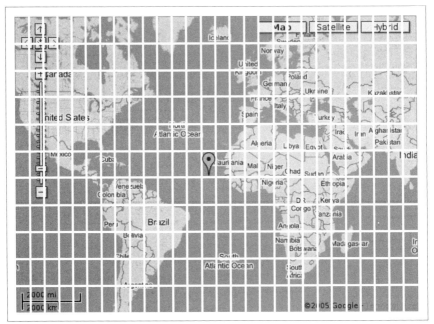

Figure 7-29. Assignment of points to clusters based on grid cell membership

By definition, this approach is guaranteed to solve requirement (a), but how likely is it to solve requirement (b)? Initially, we note that the number of clusters we wind up with isn't sensitive to the number of points being clustered, just to their distribution. Let us assume the worst case, where there is at least one point in every potential cell. Let us suppose that a Google Map of the entire world could be as large as 1,024 pixels wide and 768 pixels high, thereby taking up all of an ordinary desktop screen. If the default Google Maps icon is 20×34 pixels, then we get a worst case of $(1,024 \div 20) \times (768 \div 34)$ = about 1,156 cells or, at most, 1,196 cells if we round up both sides of the product.

However, since every nine cells will be combined into a supercluster, we wind up with an absolute worst-case maximum of under 150 clusters, which, although not great, isn't horrifying, either. Let's just say that if you have a data set that covers the entire surface of the planet, you might think about using something other than Google Maps to illustrate it. Also, you can see that the algorithm is more sensitive to the size of the grid cells than anything else. At the very least, even if our naïve grid-based algorithm isn't perfect, it can be shown to run in $O(n)$ time, which is an improvement over our earlier experiments.

The Code

The code we developed to test the grid-based clustering algorithm has two parts: first, a CGI script written in Perl runs on the server side, which filters a file of waypoints for those points within a given bounding box, clusters those points as described above, and then spits out an XML file describing the clusters; and second, an HTML page on our server contains client-side JavaScript that uses the Google Maps API to fetch the cluster description for the current map view and plot the clusters on the map.

The server-side CGI script. The CGI script itself is only 120 lines of Perl, but we'll just show the highlights here. If you're interested in looking at the full source, you can find it at *http://mappinghacks.com/projects/gmaps/cluster-grid.txt*.

Much like the Google Maps interface, our script expects a lat/long center point for the map, and a map span, measured in degrees latitude and longitude. Additionally, because the map geometry matters to our calculations, we also expect a width and height for the intended map in pixels. The following Perl code takes care of that:

```perl
my $q      = CGI->new;
my %var    = $q->Vars;

if ($var{ll} and $var{spn}) {
    my ($lon, $lat) = split( " ", $var{ll} );
    my ($width, $height) = split( " ", $var{spn} );
    $bbox = [ $lon - $width/2, $lat - $height/2,
              $lon + $width/2, $lat + $height/2 ];
}

if ($var{size}) {
    my ($width, $height) = split( " ", $var{size} );
    $size = [ $width, $height ];
}
```

The result is that the $bbox variable contains a reference to an array listing the minimum longitude and latitude, and the maximum longitude and latitude for our map, in that order. The $size variable similarly stores the width and height of the map in pixels. We then pass $bbox to a function that loads the waypoints from a comma-delimited file, keeping only the ones that fit within our bounding box:

```perl
while (<FH>) {
    chomp;
    my ($lat, $lon, $name) = split /,\s+/, $_;
    push @data, [$lon, $lat, $name]
        if $lon >= $bbox->[0] and $lon <= $bbox->[2]
        and $lat >= $bbox->[1] and $lat <= $bbox->[3];
}
```

This hack would be more elegant if we parsed the waypoints from a GPX file instead, but we were aiming to simplify the problem as much as possible, from a technical standpoint. The points themselves are returned as a reference to an array of arrays. We then estimate the grid size in degrees, starting with a hard-coded icon size in pixels, as follows:

```
my $icon_size = [ 20, 34 ];
my $grid_x = $icon_size->[0] / $map_size->[0] * ($bbox->[2] - $bbox->[0]);
my $grid_y = $icon_size->[1] / $map_size->[1] * ($bbox->[3] - $bbox->[1]);
```

Basically, we divide the width of the marker icon (in pixels) by the width of the entire map (also in pixels), which gives us a proportion of the map that a single marker would cover, in the horizontal dimension. We multiply this fraction by the total span of the map in degrees longitude, to yield the number of degrees longitude that a marker would cover on a map of this size and span. We then perform the same calculation the marker height, map height, and map span in degrees latitude to get the marker height in degrees latitude. By making our grid cells at least this many degrees wide and high, we can guarantee that none of the markers we place on the map will visually overlap each other by much, if at all.

We then call the cluster() function, which takes the bounding box, the grid cell size, and the data points as arguments:

```
sub cluster {
    my ($bbox, $grid, $data) = @_;
    my %cluster;

    for my $point (@$data) {
        my $col = int( ($point->[0] - $bbox->[0]) / $grid->[0] );
        my $row = int( ($point->[1] - $bbox->[1]) / $grid->[1] );
        push @{$cluster{"$col,$row"}}, $point;
    }
```

These few lines of code actually do all the work of assigning each point to a cluster. We divide the difference between the point's longitude and the western edge of the map by the grid cell size, which, discarding the remainder, gives us the grid column that the point lies within. We follow a parallel calculation to determine the row of the point, counting from south to north. We then push the point on to a hash of arrays that lists the points within each cell. Since we plan to take each cell that contains one or more points as an initial cluster, this hash is simply called %cluster. We're already halfway finished.

The next bit of code is a bit tricker, as it concerns the neighbor analysis that we use to combine adjacent clusters into superclusters. As a heuristic, we assume that the points are already naturally clustered in some way and conclude that the densest of our initial clusters are most likely to be the "centers" of the combined superclusters. We implement this heuristic by sorting the list of clusters we've found, according to the number of points within each one, in descending order:

```
my @groups = sort { @{$cluster{$b}} <=> @{$cluster{$a}} } keys %cluster;
```

We then iterate over the list of clusters, looking at the eight cells immediately adjacent to each one. If any of the adjacent cells also contains a cluster, we add the points from that cluster to our new supercluster and remove the subsumed cluster from our list. Finally, when all is said and done, we return an array of arrays, containing our original points grouped into clusters.

```
for my $group (@groups) {
    next unless $cluster{$group};
    my ($col, $row) = split ",", $group;
    for my $dx (-1 .. 1) {
        for my $dy (-1 .. 1) {
            next unless $dx or $dy;
          $dx += $col; $dy += $row;
            if (exists $cluster{"$dx,$dy"}) {
                my $other = delete $cluster{"$dx,$dy"};
                push @{$cluster{$group}}, @$other;
            }
        }
    }
}

    return [values %cluster];
}
```

We won't bore you with the tedious details of generating XML from this data structure; once again, you can refer to the source code online, if you're particularly interested. However, in order to understand how the JavaScript frontend works, it's worth looking at an example output from this script:

```
<points>
  <cluster lat="40.76706" lon="-123.334565"
      points="187" width="1.85699" height="6.57074"  />
  <cluster lat="44.40734" lon="10.832265"
      points="70" width="3.33653" height="5.03806"  />
  <cluster lat="41.507245" lon="-72.426195"
      points="10" width="2.74580999" height="1.73063" />
  <cluster lat="39.27062" lon="-115.56396"
      points="239" width="13.66804" height="11.94808" />
  <point name="CAIRO" lat="30.05671" lon="31.23585" />
</points>
```

As you can see, this document contains enough information to draw each cluster, as well as to allow the UI to zoom directly in on the extents of any one cluster. Finally, any cluster with only one point isn't really a cluster: it's just a point and is treated as such. The JavaScript user interface therefore only needs to be able to pass the map center, span, and size into this script, and then be able to parse the cluster and point descriptions from the XML output.

The client-side JavaScript. Naturally, the JavaScript frontend to this cluster-ing experiment needs to do all the usual things to import the Google Maps API code and set up the map itself. These tasks are already well-covered else-where in this book, and, of course, you can always View Source on the demo page, if you're interested in the details. We'll go straight to the loadClusters() function, which calls our CGI script when the page is loaded:

```
function loadClusters () {
  var request = GXmlHttp.create();
  var center = map.getCenterLatLng();
  var span   = map.getSpanLatLng();
  var url = "http://mappinghacks.com/projects/gmaps/cluster-grid.cgi?"
    url += "ll="   + center.x   + "+" + center.y
         + "&spn=" + span.width + "+" + span.height
       + "&size=" + map.mapSize.width + "+" + map.mapSize.height;

  request.open("GET", url, true);
  request.onreadystatechange = function() {
      if (request.readyState == 4)
          showOverlays(request.responseXML);
  };
}
```

This code initiates a GXmlHttp request in the usual way, passing in the map center, span, and size. The map.mapSize property used here is undocu-mented in the Google Maps API, but you could almost certainly use the DOM API to find out the width and height styles of the map div element instead. When the HTTP request returns, the parsed XML document is passed to the showOverlays() function, which is shown below:

```
function showOverlays (xml) {
    map.clearOverlays();
    var cluster = xml.documentElement.getElementsByTagName("cluster");
    for (var i = 0; i < cluster.length; i++) {
        showCluster( cluster[i] );
    }
    var point = xml.documentElement.getElementsByTagName("point");
    for (var i = 0; i < point.length; i++) {
        showPoint( point[i] );
    }
}
```

The showOverlays() function clears the map of its existing overlays and then uses the getElementsByTagName() method from the Document Object Model API to extract each cluster and point element from the XML document, passing them one by one to the appropriate rendering function. The showPoint() function doesn't do anything more exciting than put a marker on the map in the appropriate place and bind an info window popup to the click event. Let's look at the showCluster() function, instead, because that's where most of the excitement really is:

```
function showCluster (elem) {
    var point = new GPoint(parseFloat(elem.getAttribute("lon")),
                           parseFloat(elem.getAttribute("lat")));
    var width  = parseFloat(elem.getAttribute("width")),
        height = parseFloat(elem.getAttribute("height")),
        count  = parseInt(elem.getAttribute("count"));

    var marker = new GMarker(point);
```

The showCluster() function parses the various attributes out of the cluster element and uses the latitude and longitude to create a new marker. So far, no surprises. The action that we bind to that marker's click event is much more interesting:

```
GEvent.addListener(marker, "click", function() {
    var span = new GSize(width * 1.1, height * 1.1);
    // undocumented: http://xrl.us/getLowestZoomLevel
    var zoom = map.spec.getLowestZoomLevel(point, span, map.
viewSize);

    loadClusters();
    map.centerAndZoom(point, zoom);
});
```

Instead of binding an info window to the click event on the marker, we bind an anonymous function that calculates the center point and span of the cluster, augmenting the span by 10% in each dimension, so that all of our points are well within the map view and not hiding out at the edges of the map. Next, we use the method described in "Find the Right Zoom Level" [Hack #58] to calculate the best zoom level for viewing the entire cluster. The anonymous function then calls loadClusters() to kick off a request for the new set of clusters and points for that map view, and then pans and zooms the map to that view.

The finale of the showCluster() function gives the cluster some visual clarity, by drawing a rectangular polyline around the extents of the cluster, so that the user can see which part of the map that the cluster covers:

```
var bbox = new GPolyline(
        [new GPoint(point.x - width/2, point.y - height/2),
         new GPoint(point.x - width/2, point.y + height/2),
         new GPoint(point.x + width/2, point.y + height/2),
         new GPoint(point.x + width/2, point.y - height/2),
         new GPoint(point.x - width/2, point.y - height/2)],
        'ff0000', 2, .80);

    map.addOverlay(marker);
    map.addOverlay(bbox);
}
```

The user can zoom into a cluster by clicking on it, but what if she wants to zoom back out? A single event handler takes care of refreshing the map display when the user zooms in or out [Hack #60].

```
GEvent.addListener(map, "zoom", loadClusters);
```

Conclusion

We've seen here that there can be viable solutions to the vexing problem of what to do when you have too many points to show on a map. We've also seen that some traditional clustering algorithms may be inadequate for certain tasks of practical digital cartography and that a more customized approach, using grid-based clustering, can yield pretty good results. There's no doubt that this method isn't perfect, though, and we'd really like to see it improved upon. If you do use this technique as an inspiration for your own projects, please let us know!

See Also

- Wikipedia on clustering algorithms: *http://en.wikipedia.org/wiki/Data_clustering*
- "Find the Right Zoom Level" [Hack #58]
- "Show Lots of Stuff—Quickly" [Hack #59]
- "Make Things Happen When the Map Moves" [Hack #60]

HACK #70   Will the Kids Barf? (and Other Cool Ways to Use Google Maps)

Google Maps Hacks are turning up everywhere; here are some things we just didn't have time to cover fully.

My kids get sick on curvy roads. It is just a fact of life. One measure of the curviness of a road is the *detour index*. This is the ratio of the shortest road distance and the straight-line distance. Some mathematicians also call this the "fractal dimension of the polyline."

```
Detour Index = road distance ÷ straight line distance × 100
```

We can get the road distance by calculating the driving directions and grabbing that distance. Figure 7-30 shows it is 68.1 miles from Cloverdale to Mendocino.

See "How Far Is That? Go Beyond Driving Directions" [Hack #12] for different ways to calculate the straight-line distance. I used our sample tool at *http://mappinghacks.com/projects/gmaps/lines.html*. Be careful to measure the same distance! I noted the start and stop points of the Google route and tried to match those in calculating the straight-line distance as shown in Figure 7-31.

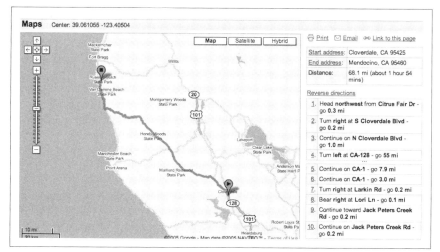

Figure 7-30. From Cloverdale to Mendocino is 68.1 miles on the road

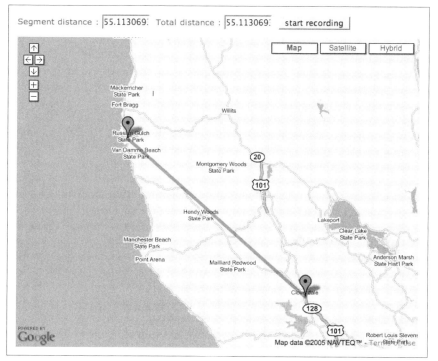

Figure 7-31. Straight-line distance from Cloverdale to Mendocino is 55.1 miles

The straight-line distance is 55.1 miles, so the detour index is 68.1÷55.1×
100=123.6.

Through careful analysis of four or five trips, as partially described in *Mapping Hacks*, I've determined that a detour index over about 120 is a recipe for carsick fun. If you are a motorcyclist looking for curves, you can use the number for your own ends. But remember, as the heartless half of this book's writing team says, "For some people, motion sickness is no laughing matter. For the rest of us, it is."

We really wanted to turn this into a Google Maps demo that you could experiment with yourself, but we just didn't have the time!

Other Cool Google Maps Hacks

One of the painful challenges in writing this book during the heady days of the release of the official API was that we just could not keep up with all of the cool work that was being done, much less contribute to it ourselves. We'd watch our email, and the Google Maps API mailing list, and Del.icio.us, and more cool "must include" hacks appeared than we could possibly ever write about. Here are a few of the coolest.

Google sightseeing. What could be better than standing on a sunlit peak overlooking the Grand Canyon at sunset with your loving family by your side? How about looking over it without the 10-hour car trip in an overheating station wagon with sticky seats, grumpy children, and a fed-up wife?

We have Google, so why bother seeing the world for real? The Google Sightseeing site at *http://www.googlesightseeing.com/* shows neat places on Google Maps. Consider it a map geeks blog: Alex, James, and Olly scour (imagery of) the Earth to bring you landscapes to amuse and amaze.

ZIP Code maps. Postal code boundaries are often a bit arbitrary. You can go to *http://maps.huge.info/*, enter a ZIP Code, and see the area it covers. Figure 7-32 shows 95472 on a map. ("Examine Patterns of Criminal Activity" **[Hack #18]** shows another example of rendering arbitrary GIS vector data on Google Maps.)

The site is careful to note its own limitations:

> ZIP Code data is derived from the Census 'ZCTAs (ZIP Code Tabulation Areas),' which may be different than the USPS defined ZIP Code delivery routes. A USPS ZIP Code is not a geographical area but a route which may not be definable as a polygon.

Google Planimeter. You can use Google Maps to measure areas at *http://www.acme.com/planimeter/*. Navigate to your selected area and then click on

Will the Kids Barf? (and Other Cool Ways to Use Google Maps)

HACK
#70

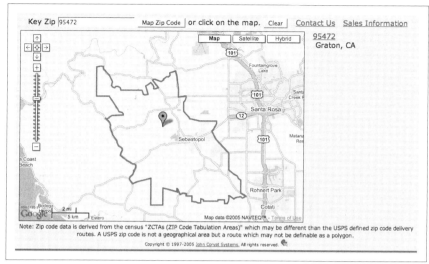

Figure 7-32. ZIP Code 95472 displayed on a map

at least three points, and it will calculate the area. Figure 7-33 shows that the Point Reyes National Seashore is roughly 137 square miles.

Play games on Google Maps. In Tripods, you "battle invading Google Maps Tripod markers that are invading Manhattan." This is a multiplayer game, so you can gang up with other players to fight the menace, as shown in Figure 7-34. You can play Tripods at *http://www.thomasscott.net/tripods/*.

Find the Landmark, at *http://landmark.mapsgame.com/*, gives you a landmark and times your attempts to find it. Figure 7-35 shows my "I give up" time at finding the Space Needle in Seattle.

Other games are discussed on the Games On Google Maps wiki page at *http://moloko.itc.it/trustmetricswiki/moin.cgi/GamesOnGoogleMaps*.

Map versus satellite. Overlay a small section of a map view over the satellite view, or vice versa, at *http://www.kokogiak.com/gmaps-transparencies.html*. This helps you to see discrepancies between the map and the imagery, as in Figure 7-36.

Edible plants in the public domain. The Garden of the Commons at *http://commonsgarden.org/* maps plants growing in public spaces that have food or medicinal value and offers users the chance to contribute their own finds.

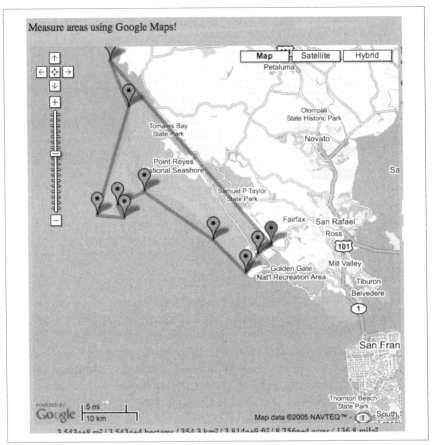

Figure 7-33. Measure the area of Point Reyes National Seashore

Animate a route. There is a bookmarklet at *http://www.ergul.com/maps/* that will animate your driving directions, even cross-country. Enter your end points and watch as the computer follows your route for you.

Track your credit card spending. Greg McCarroll has done work on mapping his credit card statement at *http://www.mccarroll.org.uk/~gem/creditcardtracker/*. Being able to see where you spend money might just help you manage your spending habits!

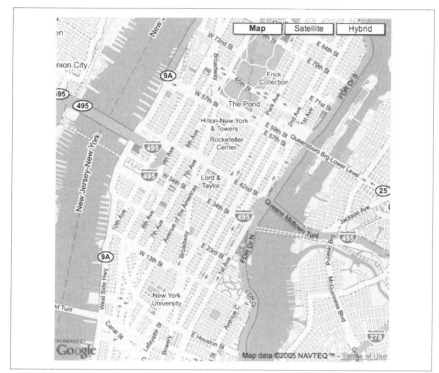

Figure 7-34. Fight the Tripods!

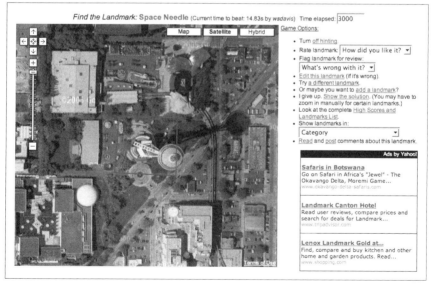

Figure 7-35. Find the Landmark—The Space Needle

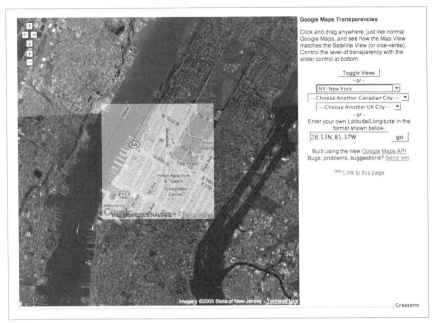

Figure 7-36. Compare the map with the satellite view

Where to from Here?

We can recommend a couple of web sites that track the Google Maps phenomenon in all its glory and bring you up-to-date on the latest developments. The first is Google Maps Mania, at *http://googlemapsmania.blogspot.com/*, a veritable cornucopia of Google Maps news and reviews. The other, of course, is our very own Mapping Hacks blog, at *http://mappinghacks.com/* where we hope to present a more vaired and in-depth view of the rapidly evolving world of digital cartography, including, of course, Google Maps.

So where to now? Google Maps has provided a brush or two, an easel, and a few pots of paint. Get out there and see what you can make!

Index

Symbols

- (minus) key, zooming with, 11
+ (plus) key, zooming with, 11
+ (plus) sign in URLs, 24
; (semicolon), separating queries in Google Weather Maps search box, 73

A

A9.com, 185
A9+Gmaps
   fragility of hack, 186
   loading A9 images on Google Maps interface, 185–187
ACLU (American Civil Liberties Union), police practices and, 176
ActivePerl, 164
advertisements on Google Maps, 41
aerial photography, 3
aggregator, polling Flickr for photographs, 196
ahding.com
   Internet Movie Database, querying, 115
   lowest gas prices, finding, 114
airport codes
   locating airports, 7
   obtaining driving directions, 17
AJAX, functionality afforded by, 12
algorithms, clustering, 305–308
   hierarchical clustering, 307
   k-means clustering, 306

naïve grid-based clustering (see naïve grid-based clustering algorithm)
Amazon, as platform, 67
American Civil Liberties Union (ACLU), police practices and, 176
anti-mega world weather site, 76
Apache web servers, 258
ApartmentRatings.com, 91
API (application programming interface), 33
Apple computer keyboards, panning/zooming controls, 11
application programming interface (API), 33
Area 51, aerial photographs of, 84
arrow keys, 3, 11
   horizontal/vertical panning, 9, 11
Art Director's Toolkit (Mac OS X), 62
Ask the Spider search engine, Geospatial Web, 283
Asynchronous JavaScript And XML (AJAX), 12
Atomic Archive site, 88

B

Backstage BBC, 69
   maps of traffic conditions, 121
BAHT (Bay Area Hiking Trails), 129
   copying to create local maps, 131
   Ning Playground, basis of, 131
Bay Area Hiking Trails (see BAHT)

We'd like to hear your suggestions for improving our indexes. Send email to *index@oreilly.com*.

D

dead spots, location searches for cell phone coverage, 128
Degree Confluence Project, 19
del.icio.us, 29–32
  bookmarklets, 30
  Community Walk integration with, 205
  tagging bookmarks, 31
detour index, 304, 314
developer's key (Google Maps API)
  application form, 36
  automatically using right one, 254–259
    JavaScript for, 257–258
    Perl script for, 255
  copying from code examples, ineffectiveness of, 38
  generating, 36
  sharing, using mod_rewrite for, 258
dew point, 74
display modes, 10, 12–16
  overlaying, 317
  possible additions to, 16
  switching among, 12
distances, 10
  calculating, 44–51
    from latitude/longitude coordinates, 50
    results displayed as kilometers or miles, 50
distortion of maps, 10
<div> tag (Google Maps API), 34
Dive into Greasemonkey, accessing text online, 106
Django, Python and, server code in, 72
.dmg files, 116
Document Object Model (see DOM)
documentation
  Google Maps, 7
  Google Maps API, 35
  GxMagnifier, 243
  XMaps, 276
DOM (Document Object Model), 226
drag panning, 3, 8
  alternative to, 8
  magnifier on Google Maps, 241

draw.pl script, 171
driving directions, 4, 16–20
  alternative search methods, 19
  animating, 318
  converting to other formats, 132–134
  emailing, 21
  mini-search box, 19
  to multiple locations, 134–137
  optimal routes, 44
  between points, obtaining, 53
  steps in obtaining, 18
  using "to" in Location Search box, 7, 17
Durius Java applet, 225

E

EasyGPS, 158
eBay, as platform, 67
edible plants in public domain, mapping, 317
elsewhere.org, converting driving directions to GPX, 134
emailing links, limitations of, 23
End key, panning with, 11
EPSG (European Petroleum Survey Group), 284
estimating time of routes, 48
European Petroleum Survey Group (EPSG), 284
EVDB (Events and Venues Database), 93
events
  mapping locations of, 92–93
  user-initiated, responding to, 249–253
    GEvent API, 252
Events and Venues Database (EVDB), 93
everything2 site, crontab, information about, 173
EVMapper, 92
Excel (see Microsoft Excel)
extents, 4, 243
  location searches and, 8

Webcams checkbox (Google Weather
Maps, Weatherbug-affiliated
stations), 74
webcams on weather maps, 74
weekend warriors (see hiking trails,
annotated maps of)
WFS (Web Feature Service), 33
WhatIsMyIPAddress.com, 98
Whereis service, 98
traceroute mapping service added
to, 100
widgets, running under
Konfabulator, 116
Wi-Fi, mapping wireless
signals, 148–155
tools for, 149
Wikipedia, List of Nuclear
Accidents, 88
Windows (see Microsoft Windows)
wireless devices, mapping signals
from, 148–155
tools for, 149
WiScan log, 150
WMS Cookbooks, 285
WMS interface, adding imagery
with, 276–285
WMS servers, finding/using, 282–285
WMS (Web Mapping Service), 33, 276
data and map imagery available
from, 41
World Wide Web Consortium
(W3C), 93
WSDL file, Geocoder.us SOAP
interface, 264

X

XMaps, 272
XMaps API, 274
XMaps Library, 273, 276
XML parser in Google Maps API, 35
XML proxy, browsing photographs on
Flickr, 192–194
XML-RPC
client libraries, 263
interface, accessing Geocoder.us data
within Perl, 261–263

XMLRPC::Lite module, 263
XML::Simple module, 264
XSLT processor in Google Maps
API, 35

Y

Yahoo! Maps, linking telephone
numbers to street
addresses, 126

Z

z parameter, Google Maps URLs, 26
ZIP Codes
boundaries delineated by, adding to
maps of crime data, 71
locating places by entering, 6
lowest gas prices in, finding, 115
maps of, 316
obtaining weather information by
entering, Google Weather
Maps, 73
patterns of criminal activity maps,
adding to, 71
in URLs, 24
Zoom Box button (Google Weather
Maps), 75
zoom control ruler, 9
zoom levels, 9, 66
approximate area of North America
in pixels for each, 65
determining scaling factor for, 62
displaying different levels in email
links, 23
finding right one, 243–246
length ratios from one to another, 64
setting span of maps, 25
zooming, 9
maps with GxMagnifier, 238–243
using plus and minus keys, 11

Colophon

The tool on the cover of *Google Maps Hacks* is an antique globe of the earth. Unlike maps, globes allow for undistorted geographical representations of the earth and other spherical celestial bodies. The earliest known globe, the Nurnberg Terrestrial Globe, was made during the years 1490–1492 by German navigator and mapmaker Martin Behaim.

The cover image is from the "CMCD Everyday Objects" CD. The cover font is Adobe ITC Garamond. The text font is Linotype Birka; the heading font is Adobe Helvetica Neue Condensed; and the code font is LucasFont's TheSans Mono Condensed.